Nature Smart

A Family Guide to Nature

by
Stan Tekiela
and
Karen Shanberg

Illustrated by
Julie Janke

Adventure Publications, Inc.
Cambridge, Minnesota

Dedication

My career as a naturalist began early with a passion for the outdoors. I want to thank a few special individuals who inspired and guided me along the way. I'd like to dedicate this book to them.

Many thanks to my mother and father, and to Kathy Heidel, Rod MacRae and Mark Webber, and of course to my wife Kathy for always being there.

Stan

I am thrilled and honored to be able to dedicate this book about nature to those who launched me in my career as an interpretive naturalist. It has been, and continues to be, a wonderful journey. To Siah, Leo, John, Don and Kent, my eternal gratitude.

Karen

Copyright 1995 by Stan Tekiela and Karen Shanberg

Published by Adventure Publications
P.O. Box 269
Cambridge, MN 55008
1-800-678-7006
All rights reserved

Printed in the United States of America
ISBN 1-885061-08-0
Library of Congress Catalog Card Number: 95-077077

Book designed by Paula Roth
Cloud Photos by Photogear: Image Club Graphics, Stan Tekiela, Frozen Images and Dr. Ronald E. Rinehart

Table of "Smart" Chapters

Acknowledgements

We are so lucky to have had the following people give us their time and expertise and support on this often overwhelming project. We want to especially acknowledge *Julie Janke*, who's natural history knowledge is only exceeded by her talent as an illustrator. Also:

Robert Bergad
Clara Bleak
Paul Dahlgren, a very special acknowledgment
Peter V. Erickson
Doug Franke
David Gammell
Rick Padrnos
Sujaya Udayagiri
And to our many close friends who have once again put up with our author antics.

And to our expert reviewers:

Sue Buettgen, Interpretive Naturalist
Deanne Endrizzi, Park Ranger/Interpretive Naturalist
Jim Grothe, Professor of Plant Pathology
Herb Harper, Ph.D. Entomology
Kathy Heidel, Interpretive Naturalist
R. Craig Hensley, Zoologist, Program Manager/Interpretive Naturalist
John D. Jackson, Ph.D. Botany
Paul R. Janke, Pan Terra, Inc.
John and B.J. Kohlstedt, Interpretive Naturalists
Mike Lynch, Meteorologist
Manfred Mielke and Peter Bedaer, USDA Forest Services
Steph Porter, Herpetologist
Siah St. Clair, Director/Interpretive Naturalist

About Nature Smart

Nature Smart is a book for families and individuals who love the outdoors and wish they had an interpretive naturalist with them when something
provokes their curiosity. For example, we see birds fly everyday but when a
child asks "just how do they fly?" we adults may need a little support in providing the answer. Nature Smart provides that support by sharing a wealth of
accurate and interesting information about nature in a simple and easy-to-use
format. We have also included interesting natural phenomenon—things about
the natural world that seem to intrigue both young and old.

As interpretive naturalists, we lead nature hikes for a living. It's our job
to connect people to their natural environment by teaching about plants, animals, insects and other natural phenomena. As interpreters we first locate,
identify and then describe different aspects of nature and discuss their role in
the natural world. Interpretation is also a process of environmental education,
which we hope will help people make informed decisions concerning our
environment. We think it is much easier to care for our environment when you
know something about it.

Our look into nature begins by discussing three general ecosystems and
their role in our natural world—wetlands, woodlands and prairies. These systems really don't exist separately but are connected to each other and the natural world as a whole. The birds, animals and insects go back and forth
between them for food, water and shelter. Less evident but of even greater significance is the way these places all influence the interdependent elements of
air, wind and rain.

The following chapters begin with a general overview of a particular area
of nature and how that area is important and relates to the others. This short
introduction in each chapter is followed with easy-access, question and answer
information. The questions are those that would arise when you are outside
and see something that makes you wonder—"how does that happen?" The
answers are short yet give a good basic understanding of what can be some
complex concepts. Fascinating factual information is presented about many

areas of nature. Technical terms are highlighted and defined right within the text so you needn't look them up in a glossary.

Following the question and answer section in each chapter is a species identification section. We introduce you to some birds, plants, stars, rocks, reptiles, amphibians, bugs, mushrooms, mammals and more that are commonly encountered in Eastern North America. We have selected only a representative sample of species and certainly not all you have in your area. We are providing a core of information that can be used as a stepping stone to learning more about nature. A description is provided with a detailed illustration to help you identify the species.

Sprinkled throughout Nature Smart are quotes and tidbits that communicate environmental ethics. We think it's important that preserving the environment become a part of everyone's value system. We hope these quotes will inspire you and your family to take action to protect our natural world no matter where you live.

The unique appendix includes some resources for further information. For example, you may wish to call birding hotlines to find out about migrating birds or join an environmental organization. These resources will guide you into further expanding your knowledge of nature.

The Nature Smart certificate at the back of the book is for when your family has gone through each chapter and you've been able to answer the majority of questions you have had. This certificate signifies that you are able to identify several birds, plants, rocks, etc. in your area and you know how they fit into the natural world. Have fun completing your certificate together and display it proudly knowing that you and your family are Nature Smart!

Nature Smart will make the outdoors come to life for you and your family and by using it, you'll have more fun on your next family outing. For parents, we hope it becomes a handy resource for learning about nature and sharing it with your children. By doing so, you'll equip the next generation with knowledge and inspire them to preserve a healthy world by instilling a sense of wonder and respect about the precious world in which we all live.

Enjoy the Wild,
Stan and Karen

Most of Nature Smart is applicable all over the U.S. and Canada. However, a few of the species included are found predominantly in the following regions, excluding Texas and the coastal areas.

Hike Smart

Hiking in the outdoors, whether for exercise or recreation is the ultimate silent sport. You move along under your own power, feel the breeze in your face, smell the fresh air and listen to birds. In our fast-paced world, we don't often explore new spaces using all our senses together. Hiking gives us the opportunity to sharpen our senses and get us closer to the land. It's a time to observe, explore and become tuned into nature.

The outdoors can be likened to an art museum in that it is the informed observer who has the expanded experience. The more you know about what to expect and where to expect it, the more that simple walk in the woods will turn into an adventurous discovery. Your experience on the trail will be much more engaging if you first read about an area of nature that appeals to you before your hike. Read some of the Nature Smart chapters and questions that interest you and familiarize yourself with some of listed species. Your heightened awareness will be the best preparation for discovering what has been before your eyes all along.

Getting Ready

Several items will go a long way toward making your hike more enjoyable and include a comfortable pair of hiking boots, insect repellent, hat, small container of water, comfortable clothing that can be layered, a pair of binoculars and a magnifying glass. A large net is good for capturing everything from frogs and snakes to insects and a margarine tub will scoop pond water to look for signs of life. Once an insect or animal is captured, a sketch pad is useful to record your findings. You don't have to be an artist to roughly sketch out the outline of a leaf, shape of a flower, the pattern on a snake skin or the shape of an insect's wing. You can use these sketches to help identify and read more about the plant or animal later. Include any thoughts, observations or even poems you might come up with at the time. Once equipped, you're ready to hike and observe.

On the Trail

The best times for finding the Bird Smart birds or the Critter Smart critters are at dawn and twilight—the hours just before and after full daylight. Although most people hike during the day, consider getting up especially early one day, so that you can spot some of the shyest birds and critters. Even if you are hiking during the day, there are still many things to see and explore—just turning over a log will send you deep into the world of insects.

Walk slowly and take in as much as you can. As naturalists, we are often teased that going for a walk with us means going only 30 feet in an hour. But in those 30 feet, we may encounter ten species of animals, a dozen interesting plants and numerous signs and tracks. It's important to take time to investigate the undersides of leaves or the cavities of trees. At a slow pace, you'll be amazed at how much there is to see and investigate.

Be alert to the many signs that will give you information about the area. For example, by following an animal trail, you may find a pond you didn't know existed. Owl pellets at the base of a large tree will certainly lead you to look up and explore what nests might be there. If you find holes in the ground, look for dirt around the openings and the size of the entrance—you may find enough clues to tell you who lives there. Look for groupings of different types of plants and ask what the variations in the soil moisture might be between these spots. Many clues about nature are very prevalent and they almost always lead to a logical explanation of why things are the way they are.

Once something has caught your eye, stop and take a closer look. If it's movement you've seen or heard, crouch down and stay quiet. Most animals either freeze or flee when they sense danger. You'll seem like less of a threat to these critters and you can watch them longer if you remain still. Many animals live out their lives in small geographic areas. Foxes patrol areas smaller than a few city blocks while most squirrels never leave an area the size of the average backyard. Insects and plants are restricted to even smaller areas and they don't move far! You don't have to be quiet when looking for bugs, either. Just find a fallen, rotting log, turn it over and take out your magnifying glass. Be sure to replace the log to its original position when you're done exploring; that log is probably providing shelter to many critters.

Questioning Nature

Some things in nature naturally prompt us to ask questions. When we hear a strange sound we ask where it came from and who made it. When we see a track, we automatically wonder what critter was there, how big it was and in what direction the animal was traveling. Besides these typical questions, prompt yourself to ask others that will help you become a better observer. For example, when you see a flower you're unfamiliar with, ask "What would likely be its insect visitor?" The shape and smell of the flower will probably tell you the answer. A flower with petals forming a long tubular opening invites hummingbirds to dinner. A flat-topped flower is a great "runway" for a butterfly. If a flower has a noticeable odor, it is trying to attract an insect that doesn't see so well but has a good sense of smell, such as moths.

Next ask "How do the seeds leave the mother plant and get scattered?"; in other words, what is the method of **seed dispersal**? A berry is a juicy morsel to entice a bird or animal to eat it and unknowingly carry the seed within to be deposited far from the mother plant. A winged or feathery seed drifts off on the wind and a sticker-like seed sticks to the fur or coat of a passerby to hitchhike its way to new growth spots. Each piece of information you gather will lead to more questions and more answers. More importantly, you'll continually recognize how all that you see on your hike is interrelated.

Using All Your Senses

Our everyday lives demand little from our senses. People who live in cities are numbed by the constant motion around them. We forget that our sight, hearing, touch, taste and smell can guide us in our pursuit of nature. Use them all on your hike. Stop often to smell the air or a flower. Listen for the rustling of leaves that may tell you a squirrel is close by. Many plants have scents when a leaf or stem is torn or crushed. Animals such as foxes and skunks can be detected without seeing them. Teach yourself to use **scanning vision**. Scanning vision is looking at an area in a slow, sweeping motion from side to side without fixing your sight on any specific object. Look for shapes and colors that are not consistent with the rest of the area. You may discover some interesting things such as a small group of mushrooms or that occasional rare wildflower.

> **"A land ethic changes the role of Homesapiens from conqueror of the land-community to plain member and citizen of it. It implies respect for his fellow members, and also respect for the community as such."**
>
> ALDO LEOPOLD
> SAND COUNTY ALMANAC

Picking Plants or Capturing Animals

Picking a flower is a natural tendency that is hard to resist. It seems that we want to enjoy nature by taking part of it home. Resist this urge to collect and be satisfied with discovery instead. Picking a single leaf now and then to detect its smell or texture is a good learning experience but stripping a plant or pulling it up by its roots is unacceptable. You can learn the most about animals by observing them in their natural habitat. You might capture some, like frogs and snakes, to get a better look but return them to where you found them. If you remove the animals from their established food and shelter, they might perish.

Don't taste anything you can't positively identify, including plants and mushrooms. If you want to know what is edible in the woods, take a class or buy a guide to wild edibles. Keep a close watch on young children. They are often fearless of things they know nothing about and will touch or put just about anything in their mouths.

Bring Along a Nature Smart Attitude

A Nature Smart attitude is a "stop and smell the roses" attitude. You are in charge of allowing the wonders of the natural world to affect you, to give you that sense that life is something marvelous and that you are a part of it. Our "civilized" lifestyles give us the illusion that we are somehow separate from the world that gives us life-sustaining air, soil and water. Getting in touch with the natural world requires more and more of a concerted effort to get out-doors and appreciate what's there. Take the time to daydream under a large oak tree or dangle your feet in the cooling water of a small stream. Lay in the grass of a field or prairie and watch the clouds change form. Get lost in the vastness of a starry night sky. All these experiences will go a long way to making you feel more connected to the earth. Besides being enjoyable and refreshing, the more we know about our natural world, the better care we'll take of it.

Prairie Smart

Prairies—Abundant Life

There is nothing like the vastness of the tall-grass prairie. Compared to a cool, inviting woodland or the intricacies of a wetland, the open spaces of the prairie may seem vacant and lifeless, but nothing could be further from the truth. Both native prairies and open fields are very special places with many unique plants and animals. The constant buzzing of insects, the splashes of color from prairie flowers and the flashes of fleeting birds will convince you how rich this habitat is. The native prairie is host to an amazing assortment of over 400 different plant species, 300 bird species and 80 mammal species living in harmony.

Prairie and Open Fields—What's the Difference?

For most people, the terms prairies, meadows and open fields are synonymous. They are both treeless, open spaces full of flowers, grasses, insects, mammals and birds. While on the surface they might seem similar, they are very different and in fact, naturalists see them as distinctively different ecosystems. Prairies, or native prairies as some call them, are unique because they have not been tilled or converted to farmland. Because the soil has been undisturbed, a natural cycle of growth has continued. This growth creates a sod so thick and compact that seeds of trees and invading, weedy plants such as bluegrass and sweet clover, are unable to get started. The nutrients trapped in the thick sod and the ability of the sod to retain moisture have made prairie soils some of most fertile on earth.

In contrast, the soil of the open field has been tilled, farmed or otherwise disturbed. While you may see many plants and grasses, the field may have grown crops the very season before. Open fields have less organic matter and the plants have shallower root systems. The types of plants and other life it supports are also different and less varied than that of the prairie.

Today nearly all the original prairie in North America has been lost to agriculture and urban sprawl. A tiny fraction, less than one percent, remains. While you may find remnants in tiny patches along highways and railways, in cemeteries or on hillsides too steep to farm, you'll have to purposefully look for the prairies to find them. Most nature centers and state or provincial parks in the eastern U.S. and Canada have a restored prairie or remnants of a native one. Although you are more likely to have an open field near you than a prairie, we'll discuss the prairie because prairies are great examples of how interdependent plants, animals, wind, water and other natural elements are on each other. It also exemplifies what an impact humans can have on entire ecosystems. Also, by learning about the prairie, you'll be more attuned to the very different characteristics of the open field near you.

Historic Aspects

The first non-natives to see the great prairies of North America were the French explorers who gained access to the interior of the country by following the St. Lawrence River to the Great Lakes. Near where present-day Chicago stands, these explorers saw a vast grassland. They had never seen so much land with towering grasses and no trees and they didn't know what to call it so they used the French word for meadow, prairie.

At its zenith about 200 years ago, the North American prairie stretched from southern Texas up into Canada. Native short and tall-grass prairies covered a full third of the continent—about a million square miles (259 million ha). The prairie was so large that it supported over 60 million grazing bison, along with several million whitetail deer and pronghorn antelope. Thousands of species of insects thrived among the prairie plants. Hundreds of small depressions that held spring melt water provided food and homes to millions of ducks and geese. The plants and animals flourished. Early in the 1800's, immigrants from Europe found a sea of grasses that stood six to ten feet (1 to 3 m) tall. The prairie was a vegetative, plant growing factory with extensive root systems that burrowed 15 feet (5 m) or more into the earth in search of scarce water. The sod was so thick, farmers often broke their plows trying to till the land for crops.

Characteristics of the Prairie and the Natural Elements That Shape It

Prairies are typically lands of extremes. Summers are hot and dry, while winters are cold and often snowy. The wind is a constant, sweeping force, shaping the prairie environment. The wind is created when the prairie, unshaded by trees, heats up in the summer sun. Since hot air rises, it creates updrafts which in turn creates wind. On the prairie, the wind becomes as much an experience as it is a life force.

Plants, animals and insects have evolved to use the wind to their advantage. Birds of prey, such as Red-tailed Hawks, use the updrafts from warming air to soar effortlessly while hunting for small creatures on the ground. Small falcons such as the American Kestrel will turn and fly into the wind to stall their flight, allowing them to hover in place while scanning the ground for grasshoppers and mice. Song birds like the Meadowlark sing from a tall perch letting the wind carry their songs to the far reaches of the prairie to the ears of a possible mate.

Insects have also adapted to the wind on the prairie. The female of some species, like the milkweed tussock moth, emit chemical odors into the prairie wind to attract a mate. From amazing distances, their male counterparts can catch this "scent" on small antennae that look like miniature fern fronds or leaves.

Over the millennia, the plants of the prairie have been shaped by the wind. Tall grasses and flowers have stems that are flexible, bending with the wind instead of breaking. To see this, just wave your outstretched arms through the grass. You'll see how they bend and spring back rather than break.

These grasses, like most plants, flower and produce seeds for reproduction. They use the wind to complete pollination. Plants produce male flowers that are small, yellow and banana-shaped. These are packed with pollen and are perched on even tinier stalks. The female flowers are even smaller than the male flowers and are made-up of a single stalk with a sticky knob on the end. They reach out to offer a sticky surface for the pollen to attach. Once this connection is made, a seed is produced. Because this match is so happenstance, grasses produce abundant pollen, much to the discomfort of the person who is allergic to it. If you visit the prairie in early summer, you'll see these tiny flowers which at first may appear unimpressive. Examine the tops of the tall grasses carefully. You could play Mother Nature by bringing the pollen together with the sticky female stigma within the same flower or with a neighboring flower, to complete the pollination. You will be helping the grasses make new seeds.

Unlike the small inconspicuous wind-pollinated flowers of the grasses, the large, showy flowers you'll see in the prairie likely depend on bees, butterflies and other insects for pollination. After visiting a flower, the insects catch the wind to the next one, thereby expending less energy and covering more plants. Grasshoppers spring into the wind to flee predators and to move to new feeding areas. During the day, monarch butterflies flit from flower to flower, sipping nectar and inadvertently spreading pollen. Try counting how many flowers a butterfly visits in five minutes and you'll be surprised at how busy these little critters are. During the night, the Isabella moths continue the work since some plants have evolved to bloom at night, reducing their competition for pollinators. These nighttime bloomers, such as yarrow and bindweed, are white and have exceptionally strong odors which increase their chance of being found in the dark. Besides evolving to bloom during different hours of the day, the large assortment of prairie plants flower at intervals from early spring through the summer and into late fall. This evenly distributed time of blooming reduces the competition for pollinators and results in greater reproductive success.

Once the process of pollination is completed, seeds are produced and even these are adapted to the wind. Most of them have an attachment which carries them on the wind to new homes where they won't compete with their parents for valuable sunlight, water and soil nutrients.

The wind also played a role in spreading legendary spring wildfires that swept across the prairie, blackening the earth like the historic steam engines. We may think of a wildfire as a natural disaster, but prairie fires were beneficial. Each year the plants of the prairie die and fall to the ground. While much of this dead vegetation will eventually break down, returning to the soil, it can take many years. Much of the decaying matter remains and builds up on the ground, shading newly emerging plants in spring. Periodic burning of this vegetation removes the screening effect, allowing full sunlight to reach the seedlings. Because the fires blacken the earth, the sun warms the ground more quickly. Warm season prairie plants emerge earlier in the rapidly warmed soil and faster-growing, healthier plants result. Also, carbon, nitrogen, and other valuable nutrients locked up in the old vegetation are returned to the earth in the form of nitrogen and phosphorus-rich ash. Today, native prairies are sometimes intentionally burned to recreate the natural cycle of the native prairie.

Like the wind, the sun also shapes the prairie plants. The sun is the source of energy for any plant, so the amount of sunlight available to it is extremely important. Prairie plants are bathed in sunlight and are also constantly exposed to heat and drying winds. They could easily lose too much water from their leaves if they weren't adapted to these conditions. The leaves of prairie grasses are narrow and long and they grow upright, at an angle to the sun, with as little surface as necessary exposed to direct sunlight, heat and wind. This makes them very efficient at conserving the little moisture they get. Conversely, the leaves of the trees in the forest are in constant competition for light. Tree leaves tend to be broad and turned horizontally to capture every bit of sunlight. Trees also protect each other from the wind, reducing evaporation.

The plants of the prairie provide the basis for its animal life. Hoards of insects eat tender young plant shoots and small mice and gophers utilize grasses for food and shelter. Small harvest mice harvest dead grasses and build a ball-like nest above ground to raise their young. You can easily find these nests which look like a round ball of grass, about the size of a baseball. Often the mice are at home and will scurry away as you investigate. These insects and small mammals become food for the larger prairie residents like foxes and birds of prey. Some insects have become so highly adapted they are plant specific. They spend their entire life cycle on a single plant. The milkweed beetle is an example of this, living only on a common prairie plant, the butterflyweed.

What to Look For

If you get a chance to walk through a prairie, take note of whether it is a tall-grass or short-grass prairie. These are the two distinct kinds of prairie and are easily discriminated by the height of the dominant grasses. A tall-grass prairie will have big bluestem grasses reaching six to eight feet (2 to 3 m) while short-grass prairies will have grasses like little bluestem only three to four feet (1 to 2 m) high. Is the prairie low and wet or high and dry? Are there some depressions where water collects and the sun and wind are not as intense? If so, you may see certain plants there that you won't see in other parts of the prairie. What kinds of plants are growing on other well-drained, sunny slopes where moisture is at a premium? Take note also of any rocky areas where vegetation is usually sparse. Often in these spots, animals like deer gather to roll in the dirt for a sort of dust bath. A coating of dust and dirt reduces the buildup of oils in an animal's fur and offers a layer of protection against the biting insects of summer. Any large boulders present are often gathering places for prairie chickens, songbirds and chipmunks, where they take advantage of a little height to watch for signs of danger. Try to imagine when herds of bison roamed the prairies years ago and used these prominent rocks to scratch their furry hides.

Loss and Preservation

The prairie was a dominant ecosystem for hundreds of thousands of years. The loss of this rich habitat with its unique life forms has been relatively rapid. Since the mid 1800's, farmers across the continent met the challenge of tilling the prairies and converting them to croplands. The incredibly fertile native-prairie soils grew progressively less rich. Without the natural cycle of the plants growing, dying and returning to the earth in the form of nutrients for other plants, the soil was less able to hold water and was being drained of nutrients. After the first 60 years of growing crops, the soil lost about one third of its organic matter. When the soil became depleted of the natural nutrients, farmers began to use chemicals to maintain crop growth. The use of these chemicals has contributed to the pollution of our lakes, streams and ground water. Besides the pollution, we have lost plants that depended on the rich soil and can only thrive there. Most of the endangered plants and animals in the U.S. and Canada today are ones that were once abundant on the prairie.

In the past 20 years, there's been renewed interest in returning abandoned fields and open spaces to undisturbed prairies. Local governments and private interest groups often lead the way by gathering seeds from native plants and spreading them on the bared soil of a selected site. Over time, with care and management, these infant prairies will replace the monocultures of cultivated fields with a variety of native plants. **Biodiversity**, or the existence of a variety of species in an ecosystem, is one of the most important reasons to restore or recreate prairies. Scientists have long suspected the importance of biodiversity and now studies show that the more species a habitat has, the more likely it will be able to accommodate disease and drought. While some species die under stress, others grow. With a variety of species, some success is more likely. So in a sense, biodiversity is nature's insurance policy against catastrophes.

Visiting the Open Fields

While it is not likely you have a native prairie in your backyard, it is very probable you are within driving distance of an open field. In contrast to prairies, open fields contain a smaller variety of mostly weedy, non-native, aggressive plants. Dandelion, curled dock, sweet clover, and leafy spurge are good examples of non-native plants with aggressive growth habits. Quick to take advantage of an open spot of soil, such plants establish themselves and multiply rapidly. They are usually strong plants with shallow roots that cannot survive long periods without rain. To ensure survival, these plants produce copious amounts of seeds which quickly spread. The hardiness and growing habits of some non-native plants are why they are often planted

> **During one year a family of four participating in a conservation program, can save an estimated $1200, 10 trees, 73,000 gallons of water, 104 cubic feet of landfill space, and 600 gallons of gasoline. They can prevent 3120 pounds of garbage, 140 pounds of acid rain pollutants, and 10 tons of CO_2 emissions.**

GLOBAL ACTION PLAN

along road sides after construction to quickly control erosion. This practice can present a competition problem when trying to restore native plantings. Many of these non-native plants actually poison the soil for other plants, thereby reducing competition from native and less aggressive plants.

Despite the small variety of more aggressive plants, the open fields have a beauty of their own. Smooth brome grass stands tall and contrasts with the chocolate-colored seedheads of the curled dock. Often a wide variety of common garden plants that have escaped from gardens find homes in open fields. Day lilies, daisies and phlox are flowers to watch for when exploring these neglected places. Thousands of insects, like the handsome viceroy butterfly and dragonflies, find these open fields great places to live. Many small animals are found in these areas too. Mice, voles and foxes are just some of the common animals that call these open fields home. They depend upon the plants and animals for food and shelter and most will live out their entire lives without leaving the boundaries of the field. Many birds like Field Sparrows, Tree Swallows and American Kestrels not only hunt for food in these fields but also build nests deep in the grasses or in nearby tree cavities.

Open fields offer an escape for an afternoon of exploration and discovery. Many times a neighborhood field needs a little tending or cleaning. Try organizing your neighborhood to band together and remove any trash and debris. City park departments are usually happy to provide a large dumpster to remove the collected trash. It only takes a little time and your initiative!

Once you've spent some time becoming familiar with a local open field, you'll have even greater appreciation of the uniqueness of our remaining prairies. Support their preservation and restoration because they represent the original richness, wealth and beauty of the North American heartland. Walking in a native prairie can catapult you back in time. Just like the early pioneers who stood atop a prairie ridge, you too can see a wild and untamed place. We need natural landscapes like the prairie to serve as standards from which we can measure the change brought on by humans.

Wetland Smart

Wetlands — A Rich Source of Life

Wandering along the edge of a freshwater marsh or pond at the height of a summer's day, you are surrounded by wonderful sensations. Red-winged Blackbirds trill, shorebirds poke around for a noon meal, and the odor of decaying matter mingles with the fragrance of pond lilies and arrowhead flowers. You have entered the most productive ecosystem in North America— the wetland.

Water defines our planet. Often called the blue planet, Earth takes that name from its abundance of water. Water is the ultimate setting for life; in fact, all life began in water. Fossils show that the first animals were aquatic, or water animals. Still today, pools of water surrounded by life-supporting vegetation offer a prime habitat for animal life. Water is critical not only to animals that live in wetlands, lakes, rivers and oceans, but also to animals of other habitats like the prairie and woodland.

What Is a Wetland?

This has become a very political issue now that wetlands have legal protection from being filled in unless another is "created". To the casual observer, a **wetland** is a shallow body of still water often known as a swamp, marsh, or bog which is surrounded by encroaching vegetation like cattails or trees. Plant growth can easily occur when the water is not moving or is not too deep. It is the variety of plant life both in and surrounding the water that creates the foundation for the abundant life found in this productive habitat. Its nooks and crannies offer shelter to nesting animals of all kinds.

Strictly speaking, rivers and lakes are completely different. A lake has its own set of plants, insects, amphibians and fish. The majority of life in a lake exists along its bottom, where it's not very accessible to human observers. Rivers are home to yet another set of plants and animals. The moving water of a river allows for less plant life and therefore it has less aquatic animal life. But in wetlands where the density of plants and animals thrive, you can witness life in abundance. As we learn over and over again in nature, all life is interconnected. In a wetland, we see its connections very clearly. The dragonfly that buzzes across the prairie in search of a meal of flying insects spent its

formative year as a wingless, hairy and much fatter nymph in a pond somewhere nearby. The toad hopping along the forest floor was once a fish-like tadpole hatching from a string of eggs in a nearby marsh. A wetland supports life for many miles around. The trees, shrubs and grasses around it provide nesting sites for ducks, geese and shorebirds, for songbirds and turtles and many more creatures. Plants also help to regulate temperature and humidity and provide food for mammals and insects alike.

As still bodies of water, wetlands act in three ways. First, like sponges, they absorb heavy rainfalls and thus reduce flooding. Second, they capture and neutralize surface pollutants, protecting the ground water which we depend upon for drinking. Third, they are the breeding ground for a wide variety of life, both plant and animal. Without wetlands, our landscape would become flooded, our ground water would suffer irreparable damage and we would lose valuable wildlife.

Natural Cycles and Destruction of Wetlands

To understand the value of wetlands, it's important to know that they go through a natural cycle called **succession**. To come upon a wetland is to see something that is likely to have already changed from a lake. Each year literally tons of plants, animals and insects grow and then die. Some of the decaying matter falls into small lakes so that over time, they fill in. Water-loving, shore-hugging plants literally grow into the water and speed the process. As the lake fills in, it becomes a wetland. This filling in continues and the wetland eventually becomes a meadow. The rich, thick black muck that was once at the bottom of a wetland becomes a perfect medium for the seeds and plants of the meadow. In this rich soil, a small forest begins and then becomes a substantial forest. The succession of ecosystems, from lake to wetland to meadow to woodland, is complete until another natural process like fire or floods change the landscape once again.

Had we understood the process of succession or if we had known the value of wetlands hundreds of years ago, millions of acres would likely have been saved from destruction. We used to refer to all wetlands as "swamps" and pictured them as bug-infested, useless parts of our planet just waiting to be improved by technology. We proceeded to drain and fill them in—a total of 65 million acres since the beginning of European settlement. Reduced duck populations are a good example of the result of this widespread destruction.

Today we understand the critical role wetlands play and we protect them against development, sometimes resulting in mile-high legal work. Even so, wetlands are still drained and rerouted as more and more people demand housing, roads and other buildings. Developers sometimes simply choose to drain the land and pay the large fines so they can proceed. The "replacement clause" in some legislation suggests that a wetland, with its soils that are laden with seeds and the eggs of insects, can easily be replaced by simply digging a hole in the ground elsewhere. It may look good on paper to dig a hole and call it a wetland but if diversity of life is the measuring stick, it is not an equal replacement.

Plants of the Wetland

Wetlands are a dynamic natural habitat. It is exciting to sit by a pond's edge and watch a muskrat dining on a cattail, a painted turtle basking or a whirligig beetle dancing on the water's surface. It takes more thought, perhaps, to appreciate the wetland's plants. They have an amazing ability to live under water. The plants in and around our homes would die if covered by water. Not so with plants such as bulrush, cattails and pond lilies.

One critical component of the wetland that is often misunderstood is algae. Algae are tiny, aquatic, plant-like organisms that float near the surface of most warm water ponds and lakes. Algae are often scorned by those who prefer clear water, but these primitive organisms are essential. They are at the bottom of the food chain on which the rest of life in the wetland depends. Plankton feed on algae which in turn is fed on by fish and other small animals which become food for larger animals. One type of algae, the blue-green algae, is most abundant in ponds containing a lot of organic matter such as decaying plants. When nearby housing and farms spread nitrogen and phosphorous-rich chemical fertilizers on lawns and fields, these chemicals eventually wash into wetlands and cause algae to grow at an abnormally high rate. Too much algae is therefore an indicator of pollution. When algae coats the entire surface of a pond it reduces the amount of sunlight penetrating the water. Plants growing on the bottom become shaded and die out. The great influx of algae reduces the oxygen in the water and can suffocate fish and other aquatic critters. Just like anything in nature, there is a delicate balance that exists. Humans often affect this balance causing something that in small quantities is healthy, to be destructive in large quantities.

While algae is common, the cattail is usually the dominant plant in many wetlands. The cattail spreads so effectively because it scatters countless seeds. It also spreads by sending its **rhizomes** (rye´zomz), or rootlike structures, under the thick muck. These send up many shoots allowing even more

> **"We abuse land because we regard it as a commodity belonging to us. When we see land as a community to which we belong, we may begin to use it with love and respect."**
>
> ALDO LEOPOLD

reproduction. They provide shelter for animals like ducks, food for muskrats and others, and camouflage for birds such as egrets and sandpipers.

Seek Out the Wetlands

The next time cattails advertise the location of a wetland, stop and treat yourself to the sights, smells and sounds of this magical place. Sit quietly by its shore and use a magnifying glass or a magnified "bug box" for a closer look. In the early spring, tug at a green cattail stalk and peel away the outer green layers. You'll see its white soft center which can be eaten raw or cooked like any other vegetable. Find out what it's like to eat the same food that muskrats eat. In late fall, it's fun to blow the seeds of a cattail head into the wind. You'll be helping ensure future generations of cattails. Examine each specialized plant and animal remembering that each is a small but significant part of a bigger picture called the wetland.

Woodland Smart

Forests — Deep, Dark and Scary?

Remember Little Red Riding Hood? She encountered a menacing wolf in the deep, dark forest. Or what about Dorothy in the *Wizard of Oz*? She was thinking about "lions and tigers and bears" when she walked through the woods. With its eery sounds, looming trees and absence of horizons, the woods have long been a setting for scary legends. Unknowing visitors can suddenly find themselves with their hearts in their throats at the mere hoot of an Owl or the rustle of leaves underfoot. Even visitors familiar with this habitat can be startled by sudden movements of branches overhead or by noises of unknown origin.

In the past, travelers took elaborate detours around forests that they believed held monsters and demons. The forest was feared because it was not understood. This lack of understanding bred stories like that of *Little Red Riding Hood*. Timber wolves, in particular, were thought to carry away young children and kill just for the pleasure. That reputation led to the wholesale killing of this mammal, even though the wolf has never made a documented attack on a human. In fact, this predator helps to preserve woodlands. Without wolves to keep the number of deer in check, deer overpopulate and strip the new growth of the forest floor.

To those who have come to love the woods, its dark mystery is part of its allure. Even the smallest patch of urban forest offers a welcoming buffer to the day-to-day stresses of life. Its fresh smells, splashes of seasonal color, coolness on a hot summer's day and snow-laden beauty in winter somehow connect us to nature in a way in which no other landscape can.

Importance of Forests

The forests of the world are extremely important to the health and well-being of all living animals on earth, including humans. From the paper this book is written on, to the wood that frames our homes, trees provide us with an endless list of products that are a critical part of our daily lives. Since long ago, wood has been a source of fuel, building materials and food. Thousands of years ago, maple trees were tapped for their syrup and our commercially grown apples and plums were derived from the wild species of those trees.

Forests also contribute to making rich soil as the leaves of the trees drop, decompose and add to the soil's nutrients. In fact, in the days of the pioneers, the forests were practically perceived as giant weeds that were in the way of farming the soils on which they stood. But the significance of forests goes far beyond the extraction of its trees. Forests produce oxygen and at the same time absorb carbon dioxide, making them a major defense against the polluting effects of our industrial activities.

Forests are extremely important to nature's water cycle. Raindrops are composed of distilled ocean water brought to you by the wind. After falling to the ground, they return to the ocean via the forests and **watersheds**, the area drained by a river system. In a forest, about 15 percent of all falling raindrops are intercepted by the leaves, vines, twigs and branches and never reach the forest floor. The remaining 85 percent is absorbed by the soil's rich humus layer, taken in by plant roots and later used by the plant or released into the air in a process called transpiration. On very dry days a large tree with broad leaves like an oak, can absorb two to three thousand gallons of what can be referred to as soil water. What water isn't absorbed by trees and plants, makes its way downward in the earth like a slow coffee percolator running into small cracks and spaces between pebbles. It eventually drains into a **water table** a place where the water can no longer flow downward. Water tables are the source of water for those cities that pump aquifer water. This process of the water filtering down through the earth is called **percolation**, and is nature's way of purifying the water. Trees, as well as other plants in the forest and other ecosystems, absorb the water from a rainfall acting as "waterkeepers" by sending the moisture into the water table rather than letting it run off into streams and eventually to the oceans. As the trees and other plants do this they are also preventing erosion, especially along streams and river banks. In addition, forests provide homes for an almost endless list of life forms, from the tiny centipede to the lumbering bear. Trees offer protection from wind and even shade the snow so that it melts slowly and finds its way into streams and rivers instead of causing flooding.

Understanding the importance of forests, it is disconcerting that they are being destroyed and fragmented at such a rapid rate. The escalating desire to

> **I went to the woods because I wished to live deliberately, to front only the essentials of life, and to see if I could not learn what it had to teach, and not, when I came to die, discover that I had not lived.**
>
> HENRY DAVID THOREAU

develop land into housing, the demand for wood and wood products, even the mining for minerals and over-grazing on public forest lands is threatening these special ecosystems. These threats are fueled by a human population growth of three million a year in the U.S. alone. We need to protect forests to preserve endangered species and make sure there is enough diversity of original plants and seeds.

Our concern for the loss of forests cannot stop at our borders. Many of our summer bird species certainly don't—they migrate back and forth from the tropical rainforests each year. According to the U.S. Office of Technology Assessment, we lose enough rainforest every two years to cover the state of California.

Forests of Our Past

All forests start out as open grasslands. In fact, woodland ecosystems are considered young in comparison to grasslands or wetlands. Trees evolved millions of years after grasses. Forests begin when small, aggressive shrubs and trees, such as sumac and aspen, get a toe-hold within the grassland. Larger and slow-growing trees like oaks follow, and the grassland becomes a thing of the past.

At one time people thought North America was an endless source of wood. It was said that a squirrel could travel from coast to coast without leaving the treetops. Maps of North America from about 1800 do show an impressive amount of forest (but not enough for that tree-traveling squirrel). Nearly all of the eastern half of North America was covered by woodlands that have since been cleared. Our current forests are **second growth forests**, which means they are not the original forest and have not reached a mature state. The tree species in second growth forests start with fast growing trees such as aspens that later give way to long lived trees like oaks. Few forests of true "old growth" exist today. That is one of the reasons why old growth forests are so highly valued.

When you are standing in the midst of a forest, you might wonder how long it took to get there. That all depends on what type of trees are in it and what the climate is like. The warmer the climate, the faster the trees grow, especially if they don't have to "shut down" for winter. The longer a forest has been there, the greater the chance of seeing trees with incredible girths. There are pictures of the loggers of the northern pine forests, before the turn of the century, laying down across the stump of a tree that was big enough to accommodate a full grown man. You can figure that if you are in a forest with tall shading trees, it took about 25 years to get there.

The Forest Ecosystem

Like prairies and wetlands, the forest is a community of interactive plants, animals, soil, water and air. The forest is a giant living and breathing system which produces food and recycles its own waste in a constant, dynamic way. New plants grow and old ones die. They decompose, recycling their nutrients into food for new plants. For example, a tree produces oxygen, provides food for caterpillars, squirrels and songbirds, and enriches the soils around it by dropping its leaves. For quite sometime after it dies, its hollow core provides homes for animals like skunks. In the meantime, decomposers ranging from bacteria to mushrooms to worms, work on converting its wood into soil. The enriched soil is then ready to start a new growth cycle when a seed is buried by a squirrel or blown in by the wind. These cycles are ongoing in a forest, all occurring at different stages, making it a much more complex system than one would think at first glance.

Moist, humid forests, as in the tropical regions of the world, have so many decomposers from ants to bacteria, that they end up recycling their nutrients so quickly their soils never get too rich. Without an annual dropping of leaves, the soils are handicapped with this lack of nutrient supply. Dryer, temperate forests, made up mostly of trees that lose their leaves, build up a rich soil called **humus**, which when cleared and farmed, can produce crops for decades. This explains why in the tropics, when forests are cut down to grow crops, the soil cannot support more than a few years of farming.

The soil of the forest is another component of the forest community. If you take a shovel and plunge it into the ground, you will find only about 12 inches (30 cm) of black, loamy soil, unlike the several feet of black soil in the prairie. Forest soils also have more moisture than those of the prairie. The root systems of the forest tend to reside in these upper loamy soils where the moisture is concentrated. The roots of prairie plants dwell deep within the earth searching for scarce moisture. Fallen leaves, twigs and branches are continually broken down by the forest decomposers. The nutrients are quickly picked up by the surviving trees, creating a delicate balance between nutrient supply and demand.

The forest ecosystem is home to a vast array of animal life. Because it is rich with shelter and food, it is also rich with wildlife. Some, like centipedes and other small critters of the forest floor, exist totally within the confines of the forest. Others, like the raccoon, live there but seek out their food supply from other ecosystems. Still others live there only seasonally like the Oriole and other migrating songbirds. Animals, like the Red-tailed Hawk, which nests high in trees, but hunts for rabbits and mice in open fields, demonstrate that forest ecosystems are intimately connected to other ecosystems. Some, such as the red squirrel, are more at home in a coniferous forest and others, like the gray squirrel, are more at home in a deciduous forest. Animals of a forest exist in each of its levels and nooks and crannies, some so specialized that they never see the other parts of the forest. Songbirds, such as the Cedar Waxwings, live their lives at the tops of the trees in the canopy, while skunks which are not equipped to climb trees, remain on the forest floor. Enter the forest and the noises of its often hidden creatures will let you know that you have entered a well-inhabited place.

Types of Forests

The world is divided into ten major vegetation zones, depending on the plants that can grow in the given climatic conditions. These are arctic tundra, northern coniferous forest, temperate forest, temperate grassland, tropical rain forest, mountains, Mediterranean vegetation chaparral, tropical seasonal forest, tropical savanna grassland and scrub, and desert. The earth is also divided into climate zones which are (from top to bottom) polar, temperate, tropical, temperate and polar. Only certain types of plants and the animals that depend on them are adapted to live in these zones. The eastern U.S. and southern Canada are in the northern temperate zone which is composed of three vegetation zones— temperate forest, temperate grassland and northern coniferous forest. A zone together with all of its plants is called a **biome**.

This very general category of temperate forest can be further subdivided into the types of forests called coniferous, deciduous and mixed. These terms indicate the main types of trees growing in a forest. **Coniferous** trees retain their leaves, which are typically needle-shaped, remaining green all winter long. Pines, firs and spruces are examples of coniferous trees. **Deciduous** trees shed their leaves each fall, sometimes after a brilliant show of color. Trees such as maples, oaks and aspen are examples of deciduous trees. A **mixed forest** has both types of trees. The types of forests can be even further divided into the specific kinds of forests such as maple/basswood, where one or two types of trees predominate.

Each type of forest thrives in the climate that is most favorable to it. The needle trees of coniferous forests flourish for the most part in climates too cool for most of the broad leaved deciduous trees. The needles of the conifers are adapted for harsher climates in several ways. They have a smaller surface area and so do not lose as much moisture to the air. They also have a waxy covering which helps to reduce water loss, allowing them to stay on the tree and provide shelter for over-wintering birds. The acid in the conifer's tough needled leaves and the resin in their timber slow down the rate at which they can rot. This means that the tiny life forms in the soil cannot as easily break down the needles and wood of pines, spruces, firs, etc., into the nutrients that help other plants to grow. Specialized fungi and lichens help in the process to recycle the nutrients, but the forest floor in a coniferous forest is almost barren compared to a deciduous one where nutrients are more available. Where deciduous forests flourish, the annual leaf drop makes for much richer soils, because the nutrients of the leaves are decomposed by millions of microscopic and larger organisms called decomposers. In the process of obtaining a meal for themselves, they leave the soil rich and ready to produce more life forms.

The mixed forests thrive in the transition zones between the climates and offer a more diverse habitat to animals. However, contrary to what you might think, the number of bird species in a given forest is more dependent on the height and density of the trees than it is on the tree type. The more dense a forest is and the more layers it has, the more species will inhabit each specialized area, called a **niche**.

There are exceptions to these general characteristics of tree categories. For example, there are deciduous conifers such as the tamarack, which is a tree that seasonally looses its needles. Also, in tropical regions there are many types of deciduous trees with broad leaves that do not need to lose their leaves because the climate is warm year round.

Levels of the Forest

The forest is sometimes best understood if it is likened to the floors of a hotel. The penthouse is the **canopy**, it is made up of the crown of trees and is home to only those who can "afford" to climb or fly there. It's a bit greedy in that it gets the most light and the most rain of any of the floors. It also has the highest temperatures. The middle floors are the **understory**, made up of smaller trees and bushes just waiting for the chance to overtake a bigger tree's position in the canopy. The winning tree of this competition needs to be in the right place and the right time, should one tree fall and leave enough space and light for it to start growing at a faster rate. The lobby or **forest floor** is the busiest place. Like the hotel lobby, most of the restaurants are located on this level and whether or not you live on the upper floors, you most likely will have to come downstairs to eat. Each layer has its own unique environment that it provides to the animals and plants that live there. Light, moisture, temperature and wind are all different depending what floor you are on. In a mature oak forest, only 6 percent of the total midday sunlight reaches the forest floor. Some canopies are so thick that nothing can develop under them, especially in the summer months which is when the forest floors are so dark that photographers must use a flash for successful pictures. Most pine forests, because of the density and color of the needles, are so dark that nothing much can grow on the forest floor. Their floors are also covered with shed pine needles, making the soil quite acidic. The acid soil in combination with low light, results in poor growing conditions for other plants. If you get the chance to walk in a pine plantation, you will see how bare the forest floor is. It is therefore not well populated by varieties of animals.

Micro-habitats Within the Levels

Each layer is filled with even smaller **micro-habitats**, or small places, where the conditions are right for certain types of life forms. An example would be how a fallen, rotting tree in the forest creates a habitat for fungi, moss and the small animals like land snails that live under it. The south side of a tree is often warmer than the rest of the tree, making it more suitable for some insects than others.

> **To live beautifully and successfully on the land, we must live with it. We must be part not only of the human community, but of the whole community.**
>
> JOSEPH WOOD KNUTCH

Since the amount of humidity varies at each level of the forest, it also has an effect on the micro-habitats. The forest environment is a sheltered one. Wind velocities are reduced by 90 percent in the heart of a forest so the wind does not dry the air as it does on the prairie. Moisture becomes trapped and is added to by the leaves that give off water. The highest humidity is on the forest floor, and the lowest humidity is just above the canopy. Water is certainly a great stimulator for growth and the most diverse forests are those that are the most humid. The protected, humid environment of the forest gives seeds and more delicate plants a chance to be successful no matter what floor they are on.

Some animals spend all or the majority of their lives in one level, others frequent them all. Birds are the most free to visit them all, but some birds are quite picky as to exactly which floor they prefer to reside. For example the Blackburnian Warblers and the Scarlet Tanagers behave like Hollywood stars and enjoy the penthouse suites of the upper canopy where they are not easy to see. Ovenbirds, Hooded Warblers and Ruffed Grouse live almost exclusively on the forest floor. Most bird species will occupy the canopy where there is more room for them. Surprisingly enough, some millipedes and spiders move up and down the floors of the forest hotel in order to reach the right level of humidity.

Explore the Forest

When you take your first step into the understory, you may feel insignificant as the trees tower above you. Here you are like a mouse in a maze trying

WOODLAND SMART

to find your way in a habitat that is vastly different from a prairie or a wetland. In the woods you can see only a small part of the whole forest at a time, whereas the prairie can be taken in at a glance. The wind that is so evident on a prairie or even a wetland is tamed by the trees of the forest, which buffer all but the fiercest of winds. If there is any wind at all when you are in the woods, stand quietly and listen. You will hear the rustling of the leaves high in the canopy instead of feeling it on your face. Kneel down and sift the fallen leaves through your fingers. Note their various stages of decay as their nutrients are recycled into the soil by tiny decomposers. Each season in the forest is captivating. In spring, sunlight dapples the understory and bright spots of early wildflowers make winter seem eons away. These flowers must hurry to bloom and set seed before the thick canopy of leaves darkens the forest, making it difficult for them to capture sunlight. Sumac and poison ivy are the first plants to let us know that autumn is on the way, for their pointy green leaves are the first to blaze with brilliant shades of orange and red. For those areas that experience the four seasons, winter arrives all too soon for some, but its muffled quiet and fluffy whiteness create a wonderland of beauty.

But we don't have to wait for the change of seasons to experience a change in the forest. Each time the sun sets and points of starlight pop out into the night sky, the forest is transformed. Try visiting the forest at night when the excitement of the woods is even greater. Under the cover of darkness, many animals take the opportunity to hunt for food. Since we are not adapted for darkness, it seems miraculous that anything could negotiate the fallen branches and tree stumps without getting bruised in the process. But what appears dark to us, is much lighter to nocturnal mammals who have a multitude of rod receptors in the retinas of their eyes. Take advantage of a moonlit night when the forest will hardly seem a dark place.

Bring along a flashlight for safety when you ramble at night, and as a precaution, travel on a known path. Try being still with your flashlight off for at least 15 minutes. In that time, the irises of your eyes will open up and adapt to the darkness. At night the forest floor becomes alive with sound as mice scurry in the leaves and Owls hoot. If you have children with you, prepare them for the unusual sounds they will hear. All sounds have an explanation so make a game of trying to determine the source. Have them help you count the sounds you hear or the flashes of fireflies you see.

As part of any daytime woodland excursion, bring a small plant press, notebook and binoculars with you. Leaves can be collected and preserved in your press and you can make sketches of any insects or birds you might see. Binoculars make identifying birds much easier. Kids might want to try to walk without making a sound like the fox or try hopping around on their hands and knees looking for nuts and seeds like a squirrel. It's a great idea to keep a magnifying glass handy so you can give insects a closer look. Do this in any season, for even on a winter's day, the insulation provided by the decaying tree can be enough to protect some hardy decomposers. Mosquitoes like the coolness of the forest too, so get all decked out in a hat, long sleeves and long pants if you want a pleasant forest jaunt on a summer's day.

Bird Smart

A small flash of yellow and black alights on the willow branch in front of you. For a moment, you glimpse a bird's cocked head and bright eyes, then it's gone. You stop in your tracks and marvel that something could be that beautiful. Many of us see something grand stored in the body of a bird. A bird's fascinating behaviors, melodic songs and majestic colors add beauty and mystery to our lives. We marvel at birds' ability to fly, the way they travel from south to north and back again to precise locations and the way they build their intricate nests with just their bills.

Bird watching has a magic like no other type of nature observation. It brings many to the woods, wetlands and prairies to see a new or rare species and to reconnect with the land. In fact, bird watching is a billion-dollar industry in this country. It is a wonderfully simple yet rewarding hobby that is a great family activity. The only expense involved is a pair of binoculars and whatever traveling you wish to do. You needn't go far. It is not uncommon for a bird watcher to see as many as 50 kinds of birds in their backyard.

Birds are a distinct group of animals that have feathers covering their bodies, scales covering their legs, reproduce by laying eggs and have bills. Even though all birds share these characteristics, there is tremendous variety in their size, shape and color. They range from the tiny, iridescent Hummingbird, weighing one-tenth of an ounce (3 gr), to the largest bird, the Ostrich, often weighing up to 300 pounds (137 kg). Worldwide, there are nearly 9,000 kinds of birds. Of those, about 1,800 species live in North America.

The first birds appeared in the middle of the Jurassic Period of the dinosaurs approximately 150 million years ago (humans have been around only two million years). They have adapted to every imaginable habitat. We find some birds soaring over the oceans and some living exclusively in the highest branches of a rainforest. They each have body parts that allow them to take advantage of the food available in their habitat. The long necks of geese and swans enable them to feed on plants deep in the water. The dagger-like bills of Herons are adapted for catching fish. And the broad, flat wings of Hawks permit their soaring flights in search of mice and snakes.

There is wide variety in the diets of different species of birds. Some are seed eaters, others eat insects and still others eat mammals or even other birds. As seed and berry eaters, they inadvertently act as important dispersers of seeds. In fact, some seeds such as the sumac won't germinate unless the outer seed coat is softened by going through a bird's digestive system first—a process called **scarification**. Insect eating birds provide natural controls for abundant insects such as grasshoppers. Birds of prey such as Hawks and Owls help to keep populations of rodents in check. Each bird species plays an important role in the food chain.

There are also interesting differences in how birds mate and raise their young. For most species, parenting is a job for both parents such as the Great Horned Owl or the Canada Goose. For others, such as the Mallard Duck, it is strictly a female task. For others, such as some Sandpipers, only the male care for the young. Some species, such as the Cliff Swallow, breed in social units of as many as two dozen birds in a colony. There is even a bird, the Brown-headed Cowbird, that has other birds hatch and rear its young. Many birds in North America do share a common reproduction cycle. They breed in northern regions, then migrate south to winter in warmer climates.

People that study birds professionally are called **ornithologist** (or-ne-thol'e-jest), but many amateur bird watchers are so into their hobby that their knowledge could earn them honorary college degrees. In fact, ornithology is one of the few scientific fields in which amateurs contribute greatly to our knowledge. Some have become involved in bird banding, which is a specialized skill of catching birds and placing tiny metal rings, marked with a number, around their legs. The bird is released and if it is captured by someone else, the location and habitat is recorded. This information helps in learning about their flight patterns and habits. If you happen upon a dead bird with a band, you can mail the band to a central information clearing house that will send a certificate displaying the age of the bird and the location where it was originally caught and banded. Send the band to Bird Banding Lab, 12100 Beech Forest Road, Migratory Bird Management, Laurel, MD 20708.

Like so many other creatures, birds are under pressure from humans. The population of some species has fallen sharply. The coveted eggs, feathers and meat of birds have contributed to the demise of some. In the 1890's, thousands of birds were killed so their feathers could adorn hats. Today the Migratory Bird Act offers protection for many bird species. The threat to them is no longer unsustainable hunting, at least in our part of the world. Rather it is the destruction of habitat as natural places give way to human development, fueled by the huge population growth of humans. For example, the U.S. population increases by three million people each year, and worldwide increases are 95 million per year. Each person demands resources, for example housing, that competes with land that birds and other species need.

The filling in of wetlands for expanding cities and agriculture has created a downward slide in duck populations. Other threats include the pollution of waterways and the increased populations of raccoons, skunks, housecats and other suburban predators of bird eggs and young.

Many options are available to us to preserve bird populations. Planting berry-producing trees and shrubs will help to provide much needed nesting and food for birds. While backyard bird feeding will not directly affect the preservation of birds, it is a way to learn more about the birds in your area. The more informed you are, the more you'll want to learn of their need for habitat. Supporting organizations that preserve land and joining your local Audubon Society will contribute to reversing the trend of dwindling habitat.

How many feathers do birds have and why do they have them?

Small birds, such as the Hummingbirds, have about 1,000 feathers while large birds can have as many as 25,000. Feathers are essential for all birds and they are what makes them so unique in the animal kingdom. As birds have evolved from dinosaurs, their feathers have evolved from the scales that covered those reptiles. Today, birds still have some of those reptilian scales—their legs and feet are covered with scales. Birds alone have feathers as a body covering. Their feathers provide warmth and protection from water and extreme weather. Some modifications help with hearing, swimming, sound production, cleanliness and camouflage. Brilliantly colored feathers are used as a means of communication between birds. For instance, bright red and yellow patches on the wings of the Red-winged Blackbird are held up and forward in an expression of aggression between competing males. And, of course, feathers are the key for flight.

Why do birds stroke their feathers?

Feathers are composed of keratin, very similar to the composition of our fingernails. Feathers are actually thousands of small, thread-like strands with microscopic hooks all along each strand. Each strand is hooked to an opposing strand, much like the hooks of a zipper, to make up the complete feather. If the feather is disrupted by a twig or the wind, the feather can be repaired simply by zipping the affected area back together with the stroke of the bird's bill. This stroking is called **preening** and

❝The air is precious to the red man, for all things share the same breath: the beast, the tree, the man...the air shares a spirit with all the life it supports.❞

CHIEF SEATTLE

fills much of any bird's day. Because of the extreme importance of feathers, much time is dedicated to the care and grooming of each feather.

Why do I sometimes find feathers on the ground?

Just in the same way we are constantly losing and replacing the skin on our bodies, the birds are replacing their feathers. A typical feather will wear out in about a year's time and is replaced in about three weeks, once dropped. Feathers are typically shed and replaced each year during seasonal molts. A molt is when a bird slowly, over time, loses old feathers and replaces them with new ones. Some birds will lose only one or two flight feathers at a time, which doesn't affect their ability to fly. Others will lose 10 or 20 flight feathers, rendering them flightless until the new feathers grow back. For example, Canada Geese molt shortly after their goslings hatch, grounding the entire flock at one time.

What helps birds to fly?

Birds don't just fly. They are avian acrobats, twisting and diving, soaring and gliding. Birds are like fluid motion in the air. Some birds, such as the American Kestrel, can hover in place; some, such as the Hummingbird, can even fly backwards. Others, for example the Penguins, can "fly" underwater.

No one thing enables birds to fly. It is a combination of highly evolved body parts, such as different types of feathers, strong muscles and specialized bones that allow a bird to jump into flight at a moment's notice. Weight is extremely important to any bird—too much weight and the bird is grounded like the rest of the animals on earth. Weight-saving measures, such as a strong but light-weight bill that replaces heavy teeth and jaws, are critical. The legs are thin but strong and very light-weight compared to the heavy, thick-muscled legs of most animals. Even more critical to this ability to fly are the bird's bones. Unlike our bones, the bones of our bird friends are hollow, making them light yet incredibly strong. The wishbone is also an essential element for flight. This specialized bone prevents compression of the chest during strong downward flapping. If the chest would compress with each downward stroke, the movements of the lungs would be restricted and interfere with flight. The wishbone is also the place of attachment for the strong pectoral (chest) flight muscle.

Large and very flexible joints allow the wings of birds to fold neatly against their body during rest, but are strong enough to endure the stress of flight with its powerful wing beats. Special muscles enable bursts of activity for those quick take-offs needed to escape predators. Still other types of muscles are used to sustain long, steady flight, such as during migration. If you eat birds such as chickens and ducks, you may have a preference for light or dark meat. The color of this meat is actually correlated to flight. The light meat, which is predominant in Ruffed Grouse and Ring-necked Pheasant, is the muscle used for rapid and powerful contractions during flight; these fatigue quickly. The dark meat is the muscle used in sustained, long-term flight. Without any one of the important flight elements of bones, feathers, joints and muscles, a bird would be a ground-dwelling reptile.

How do birds fly?

Bones, feathers and muscles are the elements used in flight; the actual mechanics of flight are something that scientists have been studying for years. The simple act of flapping only moves the bird forward. This alone is not enough to fly, or in the case of humans, each time we sped off in our car we would be airborne. It is the shape of the wing that enables flight. The front of the wing is thick and rounded, the back of the wing is thin and sharp. Wind, created by flapping, rushes over the wing unequally, creating low pressure above and high

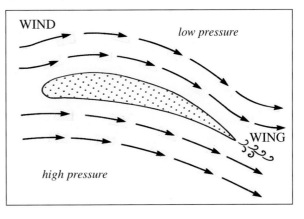

pressure below. The wind under the wing which creates a pocket of still air, produces lift. While wings are necessary for flight, the bird also needs a steering system. The tail feathers act as a rudder. The bird folds the tail feathers to make them more streamlined for speed. When the tail feathers are spread, they create drag and are used to slow or stop the bird. Turning is achieved by tilting the tail to one side or the other. Take a moment to watch a few birds in flight to see them use their wings for flight and tails for brakes and rudders.

What's unusual about a bird's heart?

Birds have very powerful heart beats which rapidly replenish oxygen to their flight muscles and help them stay warm in cold weather. Like humans, the heart of a bird has four chambers to pump blood. Unlike humans, birds have very fast heart rates. Our normal resting heart rate is about 70 beats per minute while an average-sized bird has a resting heart rate between 150 to 350 beats per minute, averaging about 220. That's more than three times our heart rate! The smaller the bird, the faster the body metabolism and heart rate. Hummingbirds have heart rates at an incredible 1200 beats per minute. That's an unbelievable 20 beats every second.

The size of a bird's heart is also larger in proportion to its body than our heart is to our body. On average, a bird's heart is 50 to 100 percent larger and more powerful, having more muscle than those of mammals. For example, the heart of a hummingbird accounts for two to four percent of the total body weight.

All of this high-performance heart beating comes at a cost. Birds have chronically high blood pressure (300 to 400 mm of mercury compared to a normal human's of 150 mm) which leads to ruptured heart vessels or heart failure when a bird is frightened or otherwise stressed. That explains why some birds die when captured by humans or cats without any apparent damage to the bird.

Why do birds have different wing shapes?

House Finch wing-actual size 4½"

Feathers are one of the keys to flight but the wings are what make the feathers work. All flying birds have wings that are in proportion to their body size and weight and, even more importantly, to the type of flying. The shape of the wing determines if the bird flies fast and with precision or slowly and clumsily. Birds such as House Finches, that flit around a thick tangle of branches, have short rounded wings. Birds that soar on warm updrafts in open fields, such as Turkey Vultures, have wings that are long and broad.

Barn Swallows have short, pointed wings that slice though the air, propelling a swift and accurate flight. The next time you see a bird in flight, compare their flight pattern with the shape of their wings.

Turkey Vulture wing-actual size 2′

Why do birds fly in "V" formation?

Barn Swallow wing-actual size 6"

Each autumn the gray skies are filled with birds flying south in "V" formation. The actual reasons are not clear, but two theories have emerged over the years. The older theory, and the one most nature enthusiasts are aware of, is the wind resistance theory. It is thought that one bird following another will gain some extra lift from the turbulence created by the bird in the lead. This extra lift makes it easier for the following bird to fly. However, from the study of aerodynamics we know that for this to be correct, each bird should remain within one-forth of a wingspan from each other. From your own observations, you probably have noticed that when you see birds flying in the "V" formation, they are much farther than one-fourth of a wing span apart.

The new theory is much simpler and most agree is probably correct. Birds in flight need to keep in contact with each other. Since birds' eyes are located on the sides of their head, not in the front, they have no vision directly in front of them. Flying just off to the side and slightly in front allows for continuous visual contact. The birds can stay within close contact and yet avoid crashing into one another. The next time you see a flock of ducks or geese in the "V" formation, stop and take notice of the distance between each bird and decide for yourself.

How do birds know when and how to migrate?

One of the most amazing things about many birds is their ability to **migrate**, or fly from northern breeding grounds to southern wintering grounds. It is truly amazing that a young bird that has never migrated before can fly thousands of miles to a winter home it has never seen. Think of yourself driving to find a far-off place you've never heard of without the aid of a map, compass or directions. Their pre-programmed instructions for migration, as well as eating and flight, are attributable not only to instinct but also learned behavior. We know it's somewhat learned since birds become better migrators over time. Instinct doesn't guarantee successful migration for each bird, however. Some birds are hit by cars or planes during migration and occasionally some are even caught up in storms and end up in areas in which they have never been seen before. Thousands more are shot during annual hunting seasons.

We used to think that birds knew when to migrate because the amount of daylight decreased with approaching winter. Now tests have shown that birds placed in cages that have artificial light for a consistent 12 hours each day still showed **migratory restlessness**. This is the term used for the behavior birds exhibit when they are preparing to fly south. These birds would perch on the south side of the cage and become more active at night which is the usual time to migrate. This suggests that birds have some internal, year-long clock.

How do birds know how far to fly during migration?

It seems that birds are not programmed to arrive at a particular destination, but instead migrate as long as they continue to sense the feeling of migratory restlessness. In several experiments, birds were captured along their migratory routes and trucked down to where they would normally spend the winter. The birds were released but instead of staying where they normally would, they continued to migrate further south, beyond their typical destination. They traveled the same distance they were trucked by the scientist. It seems that as long as the birds feel the migratory restlessness they continue to fly south, regardless of where they are. As the sense of restlessness stops, so does the bird. Typically this will land the bird in its winter home.

How far do birds migrate?

Birds don't always travel great distances during migration nor do they always migrate south. Some birds such as the Dark-eyed Junco, migrate from their summer home in northern Canada to the northern U.S., even though they still find mountains of snow and cold weather. Other birds migrate west to east or visa versa. Some birds such as the Tundra Swans travel from northern Canada to the coast of Maryland and the Chesapeake Bay. Some birds, such as the Goldfinch, may only travel as far as they need to find food. This is an example of what is known as a **partial migrator**. Some birds travel enormous miles to get away from winter. The champion of migrating birds is the Arctic Tern, which flies 22,000 miles (35,405 km) a year to reach its summer and winter homes. If only it got frequent flier miles!

Why don't all birds migrate?

The majority of bird species migrate each year; only about two dozen different kinds of birds, such as the Chickadees, Nuthatches and Cardinals remain in the northern U.S. and Canada to tough out the winters. Birds that don't migrate are able to stay behind because they are good at finding enough food to survive. They search out seeds and berries produced by plants and insect eggs in the cracks and crevices of trees. Without such foraging abilities, all birds would leave us for warmer weather. Not all birds visit bird feeders, but of those that do, only about 25 percent of the winter diet of these seed and grain eaters is provided by the feeder. Some birds, such as the Cedar Waxwing, depend totally upon berries. It seems difficult to believe, but even a small number of worm eating Robins overwinter in the northern states and Canada and seem to do just fine. They eat berries and stay in low, swampy areas where they can turn over leaves in search of small, hibernating insects.

Why are there so many different shapes of bills?

Because birds are descendants of dinosaurs, their mouths are similar to reptiles, such as turtles. Both are beak-like and have no teeth. The wide variety of bill sizes and shapes found in different birds have evolved according to what that species eats. Birds who eat seeds or grains, such as the Cardinal, have large strong bills for cracking the coats of hard seeds.

Birds of prey, such as the Red-tailed Hawk, which hunt and eat small animals, would starve to death with such a bill. Instead they use their sharp, curved bills to cut and tear their food. Birds with long pointed bills, such as the Hummingbird, feed on nectar from flowers.

Why do birds peck at the ground?

Have you ever noticed birds pecking at the ground along the roadside? They are picking up small pebbles, not food. Birds that eat seeds and grain swallow their food whole. After the seeds have been swallowed, they are passed into a strong stomach called a **gizzard**. Pebbles are also swallowed and passed into the gizzard. These pebbles stay in the gizzard and help pulverize or grind up the food so it can be digested. Since a bird does not have teeth to chew its food, the gizzard serves a very important function.

Are all birds born helpless?

In the spring you may have found a featherless, baby bird lying on the ground with its eyes closed. Once away from the nest and out of the care of its parents, such a baby is destined to die, having no resources of its own for survival. Although some birds, like all of the songbirds, are born totally dependent on their parents, not all birds are born helpless at birth. Those that are born helpless are called **altricial** (al-trish´el) birds. These include Hummingbirds, Pigeons, Robins and Bluebirds and many others. Other birds are born with the ability to walk, run and even find their own food. These are called **precocial** (pri-ko´shel) birds. A duckling or gosling can follow its mother and swim as soon as it is hatched. Most shorebirds and birds, such as Pheasants, are also precocial. Some birds, for example the Ring-billed Gull, are born with some ability to care for themselves but still need their parents. They are **semi-precocial**, which means they are mobile but remain in the nest and are still fed by their parents. **Semi-altricial** birds, such as the Great Blue Heron, are born immobile but with downy feathers and open eyes and are fed by their parents.

These different strategies have the same goal—survival. Altricial birds have smaller eggs, with less yoke to nourish the developing young. Altricial mothers don't have to sit on their eggs as long as precocial mothers. In this way, altricial mothers spend less energy to produce and hatch eggs, but more energy to feed and raise their young.

Precocial birds have large eggs with yokes that are 15 to 20 percent bigger than those of altricial birds. Precocial mothers sit on their eggs longer. They spend more energy producing these large eggs and hatching them. But by doing so, their young can develop more fully before they are hatched and need less care after hatching. Either way, the expense of reproduction is high and has been influenced to a great extent by millions of years of evolution.

What if I find a baby bird on the ground?

Very young birds that fall or are pushed from their nest usually don't have a promising future, but slightly older birds that have some feathers stand a much better chance. If you should find one of these hapless birds and you are able to locate the nest, simply return the bird to the nest. Don't worry about the old story that the mother will reject the young because of human scent on the baby. This is completely untrue since birds have little, if any, ability to smell. Remember it is illegal to possess any bird without special permits, so if you find an injured bird, call your local Humane Society or nature center. If they don't take in wild animals they will usually know who does. Birds that are fully feathered and running on the ground have left the nest on their own. Their parents usually follow them around and continue to feed and care for them. These birds should be left alone.

❝The choice, after all, is ours to make... we should no longer accept the counsel of those who tell us that we must fill our world with poisonous chemicals; we should look about and see what other course is open to us.❞

RACHEL CARSON

How many kinds of bird nests are there?

All originating from the dinosaur's nest of a basic depression in the ground, there are many distinct types of nests in the bird world and they all serve many purposes. They protect the occupants from predators, provide a place for incubation, hold the young birds after hatching and provide a place for adults to sit for long periods of time while they attend their eggs or young. There are many different types of nests in the bird world: ground, platform, burrow, cavity, cup, pendulous and no nest. The **ground nest** is usually a simple nest of either stones or gravel and is typically used by shore birds or gulls. **Platform nests**, like those of the Great Blue Heron are nests built by large birds and consist of an accumulation of twigs and sticks arranged in a flat assembly balanced in the top of a tree. **Cavity nests** in trees, such as those of the Downy Woodpecker, or **burrowing nests** in river banks, for example those of the Belted Kingfisher, are more complicated. Site selection is extremely important for these birds, but the actual nest inside the tree is usually nothing more than a few wood chips for the Downy or fish bones for the Kingfisher. A nest hole small enough and facing the right direction eliminates any weather threat. It also deters many predators, both flying and climbing.

Cup nests are an adaptation of the platform nest and are probably the most common nest type. The American Robin builds a classic cup nest using grass and mud, while other birds, such as the House Finch and Sparrow, weave the grasses together instead of pasting them with mud. **Pendulous nests** are some of the most complicated nest types and probably the safest for the young. Suspended far out on a tiny twig and away from predators, the Northern Oriole constructs a pouch-like nest of woven plant fibers, bark, yarn and hair, if available. The final product is a soft hanging bag with an entrance hole on the side that is lined with dried grasses. Lastly, there are several birds that make no nest at all. The Great Horned Owl lays its eggs directly in a depression of a stump or on top of an old squirrel's nest, constructing no nest at all. Or they may take over an old nest of a Crow, Hawk or Heron.

Who selects the site for a nest?

No matter what type of nest is built, it begins with site selection. The location of the nest is very important as it must be safe from predators, such as house cats, skunks and raccoons. Depending upon the species, the female, male or both will select the nest site. Once the site has been selected, often the female will construct the nest, as is the case with most backyard birds. Robins prefer flat areas to build their nests, such as the tops of porch lights, where the females will construct her mud and grass nest. Male Bluebirds will select a site and attract females with songs and displays, but it is the female who builds the nest. Some nest sites, like those for Bald Eagles, are built by both the male and female and are added to every year for many generations.

How long does it take for a bird to lay an egg?

After fertilization, an egg takes about 24 hours to develop. The egg starts out as two cells that come together, one from each parent. Moving though the mother's oviduct, layers or linings are added to form the egg. From the inside working out, the shell and the pigment or coloring is the last layer to be added. The number of eggs produced is determined partially by innate body function and also the health of the mother. Producing eggs and caring for young is very strenuous, costing the parents much physical energy.

Does the mother bird lay all her eggs at the same time?

For backyard birds, like Bluebirds and Cardinals, the mother deposits one egg per day. Egg laying is usually done in the early morning hours, taking only a few minutes to complete. The mother leaves the nest and returns the following morning to lay another egg. The coming and going of the mother is done discretely so as not to advertise the location of the nest to predators. After all the eggs are laid the mother will settle down and incubate them all together. By doing this, all the chicks will hatch at the same time in a process called **synchronous hatching** (sing´kre-nes). Most large birds, such as Owls and Hawks, will start incubating the first egg immediately, causing the first egg to be laid to be hatched first; this is called **asynchronous hatching** (a´sing-kre-nes). This is important for these birds since they often nest very early in the year when the temperatures are still cold; without immediate warmth, their eggs may freeze. Also, their young take longer to hatch and mature so they need an early start.

Why are all eggs shaped the same?

While eggs are not all the same size they are all the same familiar shape. The ellipsoidal shape of eggs are a blend of many aspects. The egg shape maximizes shell strength which is necessary since the egg must be strong enough to resist breaking while the mother sits on them yet fragile enough for the young to breakout. The efficient shape, being no larger than it needs to be, also conserves heat, reduces the cost of calcium to the mother and helps it pass through the mother's body. The shape also allows for the pointed ends to be grouped in the center of a circle of eggs, maximizing the number of eggs a mother can sit on. If an egg does roll away, the shape keeps them rolling in a tight arc, keeping the eggs close to the nest.

How do birds keep their eggs warm?

A bird's entire body is covered with a dense layer of feathers designed to keep the bird insulated and reduce heat loss. To solve the problem of retaining heat, yet warming their eggs, they have developed a **brood patch**. This highly specialized area is located on the belly (or breast) of the bird. The brood patch automatically sheds its feathers (comes off or is plucked off) when it's time for incubation and contains a set of vessels that bring hot blood close to the surface of the bird's skin. When a bird nestles down on its eggs, the brood patch comes in contact with the eggs. Longer feathers cover this patch when the parent is off the eggs. Once brooding is over, the missing feathers on the brood patch are regrown. Some birds, such as Ducks and Geese, don't automatically lose their feathers but instead they pluck the feathers from their brood patch and use the feathers to line the nest for added insulation. For those species that have males and females incubating the eggs, both will have a brood patch.

How long do birds sit on their eggs?

For an egg to develop normally it has to be exposed to temperatures just under the normal temperature of a bird, which is 104° F (40° C). Birds do this by transferring their body heat through their brood patch (see above). Eggs are more sensitive to heat than to cold. Even though eggs cool when incubation is interrupted, this is usually not harmful. Birds will vary the amount of time they sit on the nest, depending on the outside temperature. They have receptors in their brood patches and they regulate the time they spend on their eggs more accurately this way. This also helps them to know when to turn the eggs. Small birds turn their eggs many times during an hour and larger birds do so hourly.

How long a bird sits on eggs varies with each species. Some birds, such as Wrens, sit on eggs for less than 10 days while other birds sit on them for up to three weeks. Birds that have only one parent incubating the eggs will spend about ⅔ to ¾ of the available daylight sitting on the eggs and the rest feeding. The average backyard bird hatches in about eleven days. You don't have to worry if you happen to scare off a bird sitting on eggs. All eggs can withstand temporary cooling. As soon as you leave, the mother will return to the nest to warm the eggs back to incubating temperatures.

How much and for how long are young birds fed?

Only parents of altricial or helpless birds directly feed their young. The amount of food is amazing. Experiments in feeding young Crows proved that they need at least half of their own body weight in food each day just to remain alive and could eat up to their full weight in food. Nestlings do not eat much at a time but they digest their food so rapidly that they must be fed almost continuously. They do not require as much food when they are newly hatched as when they are ready to leave their nest. Although the rate varies depending on the species, four to twelve meals a day are fed to the average small bird. With four to six birds in each nest, the parents make many trips! Adult songbirds feed their young mostly in the early morning when they are hungriest. They usually feed the one with the highest raised opened mouth first. When the young leave the nest (usually at their parents coercion by withholding food from them), but still cannot fly, they are called **fledglings**. Their parents will continue to feed them while they are hopping around on the ground or perched in bushes for days or even weeks, depending on the species. Few young birds ever come back to the nest once they leave, except in the case of certain Woodpeckers, Wrens and Swallows, which return to their nests to sleep.

B I R D   S M A R T

How can birds that are so little sing so loudly?

Animals communicate in a variety of ways: by sight, touch, smell and sound. Birds have mastered two of these—sight and sound. They have a tremendous range of sounds from the short clicks and clucks of Blue Jays to the sharp, crisp whistle of the Cardinal. Not all birds have the ability to sing; the Turkey Vulture is a bird with no vocalization. Bird songs have much in common with human music and speech because they share similar tones and sounds. The source of these beautiful bird melodies is the syrinx, an organ unlike the human vocal box. The **syrinx** (sir´ingks) is a whistle-like organ with two thin membranes, not cords as in humans, that vibrate as air passes through. It is located deep within the lungs, unlike the human vocal box which is perched at the top of the passageway to the lungs. Bird calls are very loud compared to the size of the bird because nearly 100 percent of all the air in the bird's lungs passes through the syrinx, compared to only two percent in human sound production. It amplifies its call with a small air sack that is located next to the syrinx, which produces additional pressure sufficient for louder calls.

Why do birds sing?

Birds have a variety of vocalizations, depending upon the species, that can be categorized into two groups: **calls** and **songs**. Bird calls are short, simple sounds used to warn of danger, distress, flight (given just before flight) or feeding (tells others in the flock of food). For example, Blue Jays will call with short sharp warning calls when a house cat is in the woods. Bird songs are specific repeated patterns, often very pleasing, and are sung to attract mates or claim territories. A male Cardinal will perch on top of the tallest tree and loudly proclaim his territory.

Most birds have more than one simple call or song. Chickadees will sing what are commonly called "seasonal songs" announcing warm weather in spring. Others will sing "morning songs" that are not heard at any other time of the day. Birds such as the Blue Jay and European Starling have a whole repertoire of songs and can even imitate other bird's calls and songs. There are "flock calls" given by birds, such as Nuthatches, to maintain contact within the flock when moving around the forest. These calls are low, soft calls usually not heard by the casual observer. Babies call to their parents when hungry and birds can call to each other and identify individuals within their family.

Not all bird calls are produced by the syrinx. In addition to their standard calls, birds such as the Woodpeckers use dead branches to drum out their territorial "song." Listen for Downy Woodpeckers drumming on hollow branches or logs. Woodpeckers have been known to drum against metal gutters, stovepipes and even metal trash cans to amplify these mating calls. Other birds such as the Ruffed Grouse beat their wings so quickly that the rushing air off their wings sounds like the beating of a drum. This is the mating call the male Grouse makes to attract a female.

How can the Woodpecker pound its head so hard and fast?

Most of us would get a severe headache from using our heads like the Woodpecker does! These birds have developed some unique adaptations in their tongue, neck, feet and tail that allow them to do what they're so famous for. One of these adaptations is that their tongue is so long it wraps around the inside of their skull. Inside, the tongue is anchored at the base of the upper bill. It extends through a narrow space between the outer membrane of the brain and the brain itself, wrapping around the brain and exiting out the mouth. This odd positioning, along with strong neck muscles, serve to cushion the Woodpecker's brain from each blow of the bill against a tree. Not only is the tongue long within its body, but outside, a Woodpecker's tongue can reach out three times the length of its bill, making it easy to snare insects deep within a tree. A series of barbs line the end of the tongue which helps to grab insects.

The shape of the Woodpecker's bill helps with its chisel-like action. Its bill is long and pointed like the chisel of a carpenter. Powerful neck muscles stiffen to hold the head rigid, hammering home each blow. Another interesting adaptation is the Woodpecker's feet. Most birds have three toes pointing forward and only one back, but Woodpeckers have two toes forward and two back, giving them a vice-like grip when clinging to the side of a tree. One of the most noticeable adaptations is the Woodpecker's stiff tail. The stiff tail braces against a tree, anchoring the Woodpecker like the third leg on a tripod as it pounds against the hard wood. The next time you see a Woodpecker, stop and take a close look at this bird that is amazingly adapted to chipping out holes where no other bird can.

How long does it take for a Woodpecker to excavate a home?

Most Woodpeckers chip out a new home each season to raise their young. The old abandoned holes are quickly taken over by other birds and animals making them a very important commodity. They provide safe, warm homes to these second time users without having to expend any energy. Depending on how dense or rotten the trunk of the tree is, most Woodpeckers are able to drill out a home in seven to ten days. Often they will chisel off several shavings and fly off with them in their bills to drop at a remote location. This may be a strategy to reduce the quantity of fresh chips at the base of the tree, thus making their home site less obvious. The urge to build these complicated nests is triggered by hormones within the bird, but hormones do not totally account for their ability as builders. Since the constructing of the cavity nest improves for a particular bird each season, we know the bird is benefiting from previous experience.

Piles of woodchips at the base of a tree usually indicates the Woodpecker has been feeding, not nest building. For example the Pileated Woodpecker excavates huge oval shaped holes up to several feet long and six to twelve inches deep. Large piles of wood chips usually accompany these feeding stations.

What are Owl pellets and how can I find them?

Owls swallow their food whole or tear off chunks which they then must process into usable energy and waste. The acids in their digestive system are so strong that everything but the prey's bones, fur or feathers is liquified and utilized by the bird as food. The remaining, undigested portions are ejected from the bird's mouth, approximately one pellet for every animal it eats. The pellet is so compacted that the skull of the prey is full of compressed fur and hair. The size of the pellet is determined by the size of the Owl; the larger the Owl, the larger the pellet.

Owls cough up their pellets from a familiar perch high in a tree near its nest, so to find one Owl pellet at the base of a tree is usually to find several. If you find these pellets, which are dry and not at all disgusting to handle, examine them to see how many bones you can find and try to identify what the bird has eaten. Notice how bleached the bones are by the acid in the bird's stomach. The process of sending the pellet up through the crop or throat of the bird helps to remove harmful bacteria. Injured Owls that have been taken in by well meaning caretakers and fed a diet of hamburger soon die because there is nothing to regurgitate.

Hawks also eject pellets. Because they have an even stronger acid at work in their digestive systems, their pellets are moister, contain less hair and have fewer bones in them. Also, Hawks tear the flesh off their prey and do not swallow the heads. Other birds that eject pellets include Kingfishers, Flycatchers and Herons.

Are some birds extinct?

Unfortunately, yes! Throughout history, humans have hunted birds and their eggs for food and for ornamentation. Birds such as the Tundra Swan and the Snowy Egret were hunted for their feathers, which were used for dusters and as decorations on hats. When North America was settled by Europeans, bird populations seemed limitless. The thought of extinction of any bird species probably seemed impossible. This ill-thought perspective resulted in the extinction of several species in just the first 150 years of settlement. More recently, in the early 1800's, birds such as the Passenger Pigeon were hunted extensively for their delicate taste. This bird was at one time the single most numerous bird species in the entire world. Estimates of a typical flock were in the hundreds of millions with a total population estimated at two billion birds. That was twice as many birds as humans at that time. Unfortunately, their great numbers did not protect them and they were still hunted into extinction. The last known Passenger Pigeon, a female named Martha, died at the Cincinnati Zoo in 1914. Conservation ethics now limit the hunting of some species and forbid the hunting of others. This practice has revived the dwindling populations of some birds such as the Great Blue Heron.

How can I get birds to come closer so I can get a closer look?

Some bird watchers will go so far as to bring a tape recorder along and play a noisy call of a Screech Owl. You would think that this would send songbirds away since this is a predator, but it brings them in, perhaps out of curiosity. We strongly discourage this lure because it can be very disruptive and might even cause some birds to abandon a nest site or even worse, abandon eggs or nestlings. An easier way to have birds check you out is to make a noise by loudly kissing the back of your hand. This simulates a distress call of an animal and will bring the birds in who can hear it. Also try imitating the calls that you hear. The Cardinal has a call that is fairly easy to imitate. In the spring try to mimic it—it's a thrill when you can get them to "talk" to you. The best way to see birds is to use a pair of binoculars and patiently wait for the birds to come to you.

How do I attract birds to my backyard?

Attracting birds to your backyard is as simple as providing some food and shelter. Plant shrubs and trees that produce fruit or berries for the birds to eat. These same plants will provide nesting habitat. Birds also will use these trees to roost at night and they are a good place for a bird to fly to when danger approaches. There are many different kinds of bird feeders on the market. Spend a little extra to get a well-constructed tube feeder. These feeders will have openings that are lined with metal to stop squirrels from chewing. The favorite food of just about any backyard bird is black sunflowers. You will attract a greater variety of birds to your yard when you offer this seed. Consider feeding birds at several stations. Some birds are most comfortable on the ground. Cracked corn is a good food to use in ground feeders for birds such as Juncos. The corn is cheaper and you can put out a lot at one time. Place several other styles of feeders like platform or hopper feeders around the yard.

Situate some feeders near trees and shrubs for the birds to fly to in case of danger. Water is usually a very popular amenity in many backyards. Not only will the birds drink from it, but they will bathe at these stations. In winter you can offer beef suet. Hang these bags from tree branches or the eaves of your house and wait for birds such as Woodpeckers and Nuthatches.

If I stop feeding the birds, will they die?

Bird feeding should be seen as something we do for ourselves. Birds survived before we began to offer them seeds and they will continue if we don't. Many people believe that if you start feeding birds and you stop, the birds will starve. Experts estimate that the birds that visit your feeders will get only 25 percent of the food they need from the food that is provided. They spend most of their time searching out their natural foods. If you stop feeding, they will return to their natural diet or fly to another backyard feeder.

Feeding birds has become one of the fastest growing hobbies in North America. About 65 million Americans feed millions of tons of bird feed to their backyard birds each year. This love affair with feeding birds is only a recent one. It came about after World War II, when Americans had extra money and time for leisure activities. Before then, most backyard bird feeding was done by only a few rich and privileged people.

How have environmental concerns affected birds?

Birds have been around for millions of years but they are now facing far greater threats than an empty bird feeder. Deforestation, the clear cutting of an entire forest, has destroyed habitat vital to birds. Birds known as **neotropical migrants**, ones that fly back and forth to the tropics each year, are particularly hurt. Each year they return to ancestral wintering grounds to find more and more trees have been cut down and burned for development and to create pastures for grazing cattle. In North America, trees are cut down to build more and more homes. Each spring, birds return to nesting grounds where they find fewer trees and more buildings.

Chemicals in the environment are another cause of concern. A classic example of this is the pesticide DDT, a lethal persistent chemical that was sprayed to control insects. Small birds and animals eat large numbers of insects. As they ate many of the infected insects and worms, large amounts of DDT were ingested, often reaching lethal levels. Birds of prey were particularly hit hard. If the chemical did not kill the bird, it had other effects. It caused the eggs to develop an unusually thin shell, resulting in failed reproduction each year. It only took a few years for birds such as the Bald Eagle to nearly become extinct. Fortunately, with the awareness raised initially by Rachel Carson's book *Silent Spring*, the chemical DDT was banned in our country and birds of prey, particularly eagles, have enjoyed a great comeback. However, it is still sold in Mexico by American companies and trace amounts can be found in the fatty tissue of birds and animals years after being banned in the U.S.

How can I get started bird watching?

You will be able to identify most birds at a glance but some birds will require a closer look which means you'll find a pair of binoculars very useful. They are essential for identifying birds and just about anything else at a distance. Naturalists rarely go for a nature walk without a pair. A good time to start learning to identify birds is in the winter. Only a few species of birds do not migrate to the south so you'll have fewer to discriminate. You can start by first putting out a simple bird feeder and identifying the birds that are attracted. When the winter vacationers return, you will already be familiar with several species and you can concentrate on the newcomers.

How can I use the Bird Smart species section?

To help you begin identifying species, we've arranged birds into three large categories—backyard birds, birds around water and birds of prey. Backyard birds are those small birds that sing and visit your feeder. You see them perching on trees and shrubs or flitting from shrub to shrub. They include Cardinals, Robins, Bluebirds and the like. Birds around water include ducks, geese, shorebirds and wading birds. Birds of prey, such as Hawks and Owls, are those birds perched at tops of light posts and trees. These birds, at the top of the food chain, are the ones you'll see soaring over open fields in search of other birds, mammals or insects.

After identifying the bird's habitat, notice the size and shape of the bill. Bills are unique to different species of birds because of the types of food they eat. Take note of the color of the bird and any distinctive markings, especially on the wings. Also note the size and shape of the tail and the style in which the bird is flying. Another helpful observation is how the bird is positioned when resting. Does the bird stand upright with its head directly above its tail? This is a good sign it is a bird of prey. Birds that lean forward, almost horizontally, are backyard birds. Birds such as Crows are somewhere between.

No matter how skilled you are at attaching a name to a particular bird, you will still be able to admire and appreciate their many attributes. Bird watching, seen in your own backyard or while traveling to a special place to see migrating water birds or birds of prey, is a hobby that can be enjoyed by everyone for a lifetime.

BACKYARD BIRDS

American Crow — *Corvus brachyrhynchos 19" (48 cm)*

All over the U.S. and Canada all year long, one can readily recognize this diverse eater that noisily "caws" in the woods and open fields. In flight you can tell them from Hawks by their constant wing flapping. Crows are smaller than their look-alike cousin, the Raven and have a higher pitched call. A partial migrator in North America, Crows make large stick nests high up in trees and feed their young everything from corn to **carrion** (a nice way to say dead animals). They are important recyclers in this way and demonstrate their cleverness by seldom getting hit by cars as they pick away at road kills. They are also great Owl detectors, as they will mob an Owl, raising quite a ruckus. In fall they gather in large groups and noisily move from one field to another looking for food. In captivity, they can easily mimic sounds of people, much like Parrots do. They often collect shiny objects and place them in their nests.

American Goldfinch — *Carduelis tristis 5" (13 cm)*

This brightly colored seed eater, sometimes called a wild canary, is with us all year long. Look for its roller-coaster-like flight and listen for its cheerful call which makes this songbird of the fields and roadsides easy to identify without binoculars. In winter, the male, who is bright yellow with black wings and a black cap during summer, molts (changes) to an olive green, closely matching the color of the female, leaving many to think that it has migrated. Goldfinches stay in flocks of both males and females well into summer when all other birds have paired up for mating. They are late nesters because they depend upon the thistle plant, which goes to seed in summer, for food and special soft nesting material to line their nest. They construct small cup nests in the forks of small saplings or shrubs in which they lay 4 – 6 pale blue eggs. You can attract flocks of Goldfinches to your backyard with a thistle feeder.

American Robin — *Turdus migratorius 7" (18 cm)*

Robins, members of the Thrush family, are generalists when it comes to where they live and can be found nesting in forests, fields, gardens and backyards. Juvenile Robins have spotted breasts and all Robins eat worms, insects and fruits. Robins become territorial during nesting season and they will try for hours to jump at the reflection of themselves in a window, thinking it is another Robin out to squelch their territory. Robins will migrate as a rule but some stragglers will stay in sheltered areas where fruit bearing trees provide a food source. It will raise two and sometimes three broods of 3 – 7 young each year in cup nests on flat surfaces like lamp posts. Once hunted for food, this bird was also threatened by the pesticide DDT which earthworms absorbed; once into the Robin's system it caused reproductive failure. You may see Robins cocking their heads as if they are listening for worms but experiments have shown that these songbirds find worms by sight, not by sound. With their eyes placed on the sides of their heads, the cocking enables them to see the worms better.

Barn Swallow — *Hirundo rustica 7" (18 cm)*

There are several kinds of swallows and they all have a common characteristic—forked tails. In flight they swoop like tiny airplanes over water and ground in order to catch insects "on the wing". Since they eat only insects, they migrate to places where insects are abundant and not dormant, going as far as Argentina each winter and covering up to 600 miles a day. Swallows are much beloved around the world and herald the signs of summer. Many ancient societies considered the Swallows to be lucky. The Barn Swallow is the only Swallow with an orange breast. Before the abundance of buildings, they built their characteristic, inverted cup nests of mud, lined with feathers, on rocky ledges or on tree trunks. They now utilize structures like barns, bridges and garages which gives them their common name. They make their amazing nests in less than 2 weeks after migrating back north in May and lay 4 – 5 eggs. They tend to take over areas with their colonial behavior and return each year to the same colonies, often with the same mate.

BIRD SMART

Black-capped Chickadee — *Parus atricapillus 5" (13 cm)*

One of the sounds this bird makes resembles its name, chick-a-dee-dee-dee. These common, year-round visitors of bird feeders are seen as cheerful birds that even come out in snow storms. The reality is these tiny birds have a limited fat reserve and must consistently forage for food or die. This little bird can eat both insects and spiders as well as seeds and berries. The Black-capped Chickadee has some rather interesting adaptations to sticking around in winter. Although in the summer you'll likely see it in pairs, in the winter look for it in flocks of other Chickadees, Nuthatches and Goldfinches. In a larger group, it is more likely one of them will spot a food source and it is less likely any particular one will be eaten by a predator. It nests in tree cavities which it lines with moss, feathers, soft plant fibers, hair and even insect cocoons and will lay about six eggs. It will also use birdhouses. The male and female are monogamous and keep their young with them for three weeks before they disperse. The male will feed the female while she sits on the eggs. If disturbed while she is on the nest, she will make a snake-like hissing sound.

Blue Jay — *Cyanocitta cristata 11" (28 cm)*

Although an intelligent bird, this member of the Crow family has a bad reputation earned from stealing eggs, nestlings and even shiny objects from camps. The common name "jay" comes from the Latin *gaius* meaning gay or merry. Blue Jays are omnivorous, meaning they eat everything from insects to carrion, but mostly they eat nuts and seeds which is why you will find these birds at your feeder. This beautiful and much maligned bird can imitate the cry of several Hawks so well that smaller birds flee for cover, sometimes leaving their food. They don't migrate and come spring the cries of the Jay fall silent. During this quiet time they build a cup nest consisting of sticks, usually in an evergreen tree and raise 4 – 5 young. Just as squirrels do, Jays will bury or hide hundreds of acorns and seeds in the ground or branches of trees. Not all are recovered, which adds to the future of the forest.

48

Cardinal
Cardinalis cardinalis 8" (20 cm)

This beautiful, unmistakable red bird treats us with its presence in every season. Although it isn't necessarily found in church yards, its name certainly came from a religious reference. The inspiration for both the common and Latin name of this brilliantly red bird comes from the Cardinals of the Catholic Church and the red robes they wear. Both males and females sing from the tops of trees and poles throughout the year but the male is more conspicuous. Cardinals are a type of Finch and their heavy bill is typical of finches that use their bills to crack open hard seeds. Once established, they rarely leave their territory of about one-quarter to one mile (1.6 km). In winter, Cardinals gather together in groups of 10 – 15 to visit backyard bird feeders. You won't see them in groups in the spring however, as they break into pairs to mate. Watch for males gently feeding cracked seeds to the females, proving they are good providers. Cardinals build a cup-shaped nest lined with grasses, often in evergreen trees or thick shrubbery. The female lays 3 – 4 eggs but once they are hatched, the male takes care of the young while the female lays a new batch of eggs. They have a particular love for black oil sunflower seeds which bird watchers use to attract them to feeders. Cardinals may be new to your area if you live in the far northeast or upper midwest and Canada. These birds have extended their range north in just the past 20 years.

Common Grackle
Quiscalus quiscula 12" (30 cm)

Any animal with an ability to take advantage of so many food sources is usually successful in maintaining large populations and the Grackle is no exception. They eat a wide variety of food from eggs and nestlings to grain, grass, insects, fish and fruit. The Grackle earned a bad reputation by stealing eggs and nestlings from other birds such as Robins. In flocks, they can devastate crops such as wheat. Grackles are migratory and usually nest colonially in groups of a few pairs to over 100 each spring. They make their cup-like nests in open woodlands, near human dwellings laying 4 – 5 eggs. Look for the male Grackle to fly holding its tail vertically, at a right angle to its body, allowing you to tell the difference between males and females during flight.

49

Cowbird
Molothrus ater 7" (18 cm)

This bird gets its name from its habit of following cows around and eating the insects it kicks up. It's important to be acquainted with this **partial migrator** (a bird that migrates only as far as it needs to survive winter) because of its very unusual and destructive nesting behavior. It could easily be called the "day-care-center bird", for it always lays its eggs in the nests of other birds, never building a nest or raising its own young. The female produces over a dozen eggs each year and searches for the nests of other birds such as Warblers. There she will lay a single egg in each nest she finds. These young Cowbirds are often twice the size of the foster parent and four times the size of the other babies. They grow faster than the young of the host and demand the food, often leading to the death of their nest mates. Occasionally the host bird will identify the egg as not being its own and will abandon the nest or build one right on top of the original. Most often however, in the process of caring for its own young, the host bird brings food which is quickly devoured by the largest baby there. Because it inhabits forest edges and grasslands, its numbers and accompanying negative impacts on other native birds, have spread with housing development and the subsequent fragmentation of our forests. Over 200 species of birds serve as hosts for Cowbirds. The increase in the number of Cowbirds has particularly hurt many songbirds such as the Kirtland's Warbler, which is an endangered species living in only six counties in Michigan.

Dark-eyed Junco
Junco hyemalis 6" (15 cm)

In many parts of the country the arrival of the Juncos announce the coming of winter. They are commonly called "snowbirds", related to their Latin name *hyemalis*, which means "wintery." This migrating bird is easy to identify by two white markings on either side of its tail as it flies away from you. Juncos were formerly thought to be many different species but now the Slate-colored, White-winged and the rest are all considered to be one Dark-eyed species. Juncos nest on or near the ground in a well made, cup-like nest of grass and moss in the evergreen forests of Canada where they lay 3 – 5 eggs. Here, insects are plentiful and they feed their nestlings partially regurgitated bugs. The Junco then migrates southward but to areas that still experience a fairly harsh winter. Also being seed eaters, they are one of the most common birds at feeders in winter. Find it traveling with flocks of Chickadees and Nuthatches in the spring and fall. Junco's are a good reason to set up a winter feeding station on the ground.

Downy Woodpecker — *Picoides pubescens 6" (15 cm)*

Downys, as they are lovingly called, can be enjoyed year round all over the U.S. and Canada. Listen for their characteristic pecking as they look for insects in trees, excavate holes or drum (a loud riveting noise) to attract mates. They get their name from soft downy tufts near the base of their bill. Look for them in woodlands, parks and orchards where each year they make a new hole in a tree. It is easy to tell Woodpeckers from other birds by the way they land, clinging upright on the side of a tree and by the way they fly in a flap/flap/glide pattern. Males are easily distinguished from females by the red markings on the back of their head. Their short, stout bills and their smaller size distinguish them from the larger Hairy Woodpecker whose bills are longer and more slender. The bills of Woodpeckers make it easy for them to chisel out holes in trees or pry spider eggs from hard-to-reach places. They don't build nests but they lay 3 – 6 eggs in the holes they've made; the female selects the site but the male does most of the excavation and both sit on the eggs. Put out suet to attract these and other species of Woodpeckers. The habit of all types of Woodpeckers of making holes in trees, provides homes for a wide variety of birds and mammals. Some types of small Owls, squirrels and Wood Ducks all take advantage of former Woodpecker homes.

Eastern Bluebird — *Sialia sialis 7" (18 cm)*

This cheery sounding native bird is a favorite of birders and conservationists who have worked so hard to help it make a comeback. Their habit of nesting in tree cavities made by Woodpeckers has made Bluebirds susceptible to local extinction when many trees have been felled in one area. Fortunately, their use of cavities for nesting has also made them adaptable to using human-made nesting boxes. Bluebird trails, which are several man-made birdhouses set along a route to facilitate maintenance, are placed in open lands where the birds can easily find grasshoppers, berries, spiders and caterpillars. They will perch on a post or small tree and fly down to capture dinner. Two common competitors for nest boxes are the House Sparrow and European Starling, which will kill baby Bluebirds. House Wrens and Tree Swallows will also compete for these nest boxes. They will often build their own nest directly over a Bluebird nest. These blue beauties make a nest of fine grass and lay 4 – 5 light blue eggs. Often they will have two clutches per year in warmer climates. They are true migrators with the males returning weeks ahead of the females to establish territories. They winter mostly in the warmer parts of the U.S. Try putting up a nest box in your yard to see if you can attract these cheerful birds of open places. Use an approved Bluebird style box which has restricted openings. Check with your local nature center, library or a local Audubon Chapter for specific patterns.

Eastern Meadowlark   *Sturnella magna 9" (23 cm)*

The call of an Eastern Meadowlark is the call of open fields and pastures. Its loud, clear whistle-like call welcomes you to the vastness of its home. Find it calling from a conspicuous perch on a fence row. They eat insects and seeds but rarely visit backyard feeders. The bright yellow markings of the male's neck and breast are displayed to the female in its courtship display. Nesting is done on the ground in a partially domed, grass nest, laying 3 – 5 eggs with several females nesting with a single male. Meadowlarks don't fully migrate, moving only far enough to survive winter (a partial migrator). The practice of mowing fields for hay is very detrimental to this grassland bird. It is a common Cowbird host because they share the same habitat.

European Starling   *Sturnus vulgaris 8" (20 cm)*

The Starling is one of the most, if not the most, abundant bird in the world. It is a habitat generalist, living in a variety of areas from suburbia to woodlands. This iridescent bird has a bill which is yellow in summer and black in winter. Its plumage also turns speckled white in winter. It eats fruits, seeds and insects but in a most unusual way. Its beak is built so that it has its strength not in clamping shut but in prying apart. It will stick its beak into plants, cavities and even the ground to search out bugs that other birds would miss. Watch for this behavior when Starlings are walking around on your lawn. It was introduced into New York City's Central Park in 1890 and has been the source of aggravation of bird lovers since its rapid spread across the U.S. and Canada. Like the House Sparrow, it has disrupted the nesting and feeding habitats of many native birds, especially the Bluebird and Woodpeckers. Females even occasionally lay their eggs in the nests of other species just as the Cowbird does exclusively. The male Starling starts building a nest in a cavity and the female completes it, laying 4 – 6 eggs. He helps with incubation but for only a small part of the day.

House Finch   *Carpodacus mexicanus 5" (13 cm)*

This delightful little seed eater is increasing its range beyond the eastern U.S. and parts of Canada, moving farther westward. If you have an old bird book, it will show that the House Finch resided only in states and provinces to the west of the Rockies until a few were released near New York City in the 1940's. By the 60's and 70's they had established themselves in urban areas up and down the Atlantic coast and since then, they have been spreading west. It could be called the recycling bird, for it uses materials like twigs, grasses and hair that it scavenges from other birds' nests to build its own cup nest. The female lays 4 – 5 eggs and may have up to three broods in a season, making a new nest for each new family. The male will do a courtship dance for the female by fluttering its wings and hopping about the female with a raised tail and head feathers and dropped wings. The House Finch faces competition for food and nest sites from the non-native House Sparrow. It is also a host to Cowbirds.

House Sparrow   *Passer domesticus 6" (15 cm)*

The House Sparrow may be more adaptable than other birds when it comes to living among human activity. This adaptation is reflected in its Latin name, *domesticus*. These birds are actually not sparrows but a type of Finch, a Weaver Finch, and are not related to our native sparrows. Look up at the sign of the gas station while you are pumping gas—if you see a little brown bird, it is undoubtedly a House Sparrow. This bird is very common due to its aggressive nature, its ability to nest in any nook and cranny, and its varied diet of anything from human food, such as bread, to seeds and spiders. Introduced to North America in Central Park in New York in 1850, this seemingly innocent little creature has been reeking havoc throughout the native songbird world, especially among Bluebirds and Swallows. The Sparrows aggressively take over the songbirds' nests and destroy their eggs and nestlings. You can tell the difference between their own nests and other nests because Sparrows' nests contain scraps of paper and plastic. They usually lay 4 – 6 eggs. It doesn't migrate and is often the most common bird seen at feeders in urban areas. You can discourage this bird from your feeder by only offering black oil safflower seeds.

Mourning Dove   *Zenaida macroura 12" (30 cm)*

The familiar cooing of a dove gives this bird its name and it is a rather mournful sound. Notice these birds in groups perching on wires and on the ground feeding on seeds like its cousins, the pigeons. These birds are common in almost all habitats and are easily attracted to backyard bird feeders that offer safflower seeds. It makes a rather makeshift, platform nest from flimsy crossings of sticks and twigs, lined with finer materials and usually lays two eggs. The female dove builds the nest but the male brings her the materials. Young doves are fed a regurgitated, partially digested food known as pigeon milk. Not all Mourning Doves migrate, but the ones that do, winter south to Central Panama. They are actually expanding their range northward due to the cutting of forests in North America.

Northern (Baltimore) Oriole   *Icterus galbula 8" (20 cm)*

This brilliantly-colored orange and black male and beautifully-colored female come to nest in our backyards from their winter homes in the tropical rain forests of Central and South America. When you see one with duller colors, you may think you are seeing a female but the young males take two years to get the full orange and black coloring. These year old birds are referred to as **immature**. Males return about a week before females and set up a nesting territory. Watch for the male who has claimed your backyard as his territory, chasing away other male Orioles who enter. When the female arrives, she and the male together construct a very unique, hanging nest, called a pendulous nest. This distinctive, gray colored nest droops from the end of a twig like a hanging sack and contains 3 – 6 eggs. The nest is woven from plant fibers, down, hair and grasses. Orioles feed on insects and nectar. Try attracting Orioles to your yard by slicing an orange in half and attaching it to a pole or feeder with a nail. You can also offer several foot-long lengths of yarn that they will use for nesting material.

Ring-necked Pheasant — *Phasianus colchicus 33" (84 cm)*

The white band of feathers around the male's neck gives this bird its common name. Few birds can claim an organization just for them but Pheasants Forever is a conservation based organization with a mission to help keep this game birds' numbers up. They are threatened by loss of habitat, especially by the mowing of roadsides where it feeds and nests. They will eat insects and fruit as well as grain so they can be attracted to your backyard. Like the House Sparrow and the Starling, it too is not originally from North America. Introduced from China, it is much more welcomed than its previously mentioned counter parts of the songbird world. Its short wings and heavy body make it a poor long distance traveler and therefore it doesn't migrate. Each spring the males will "crow" every 3 – 5 minutes for an hour or so to attract a mate, then it will rest. Females have one brood of about 6 – 12 each year so if the weather is bad or the nest is disturbed, the population is greatly affected. The young are able to leave the nest following their mother, as soon as they have dried off after hatching.

Ruby Throated Hummingbird — *Archilochus colubris 3" (8 cm)*

The Hummingbird looks and sounds like a large insect as it hovers over a trumpet-shaped flower. Known for their love of nectar from red tubular

flowers, they also take tree sap from holes drilled in the bark of trees by special Woodpeckers, called Sapsuckers, and they'll eat spiders. One of most amazing things about the Hummingbird is its rapid wing beats. To see a Hummingbird is not to see its wings. When hovering, its flaps 55 times per second, 61 times per second when moving backward and 75 times per second when moving forward. The rapid flapping creates a humming noise which lends the common name. All of this flapping makes this one of the few birds that can truly fly backwards. This North American bird is the smallest of all birds and flies all the way to Central America under its own wing power, although myths still abound about it hitching a ride on the backs of Canada Geese. Males and females migrate separately, the males arrive and depart first. Hummers nest in extremely small (1"x1") cup-shaped nests. The nests, about 10 – 20' (3 – 6 m) off the ground, are not in a fork of a tree but glued on top of a branch with a mix of spider webs and green moss. They use the same nest several seasons, refurbishing it yearly. They lay two eggs, each about ½" (13 mm) long. You can attract this bird to your yard with a Hummingbird feeder filled with sugar water.

White-breasted Nuthatch   *Sitta carolinensis 6" (15 cm)*

The antics of this "nutty" bird can be enjoyed year round. Watch how it searches for insects by clinging to tree trunks head-down, picking out insects and spiders that other birds missed when they go upright. Acorns are also a favorite food; watch as they carry an acorn into a tree and wedge it into a crack and hammer it open to eat the inside. It can be found with flocks of Chickadees and Downy Woodpeckers in winter. The male is particularly romantic and will court the female by bowing, singing and carrying food to her. Nuthatches will nest in an old Woodpecker hole, lining it with soft strips of bark and feathers and laying 5 – 6 eggs. Mated pairs will remain together all year long but still feed in mixed flocks in winter. Put out some suet in winter to attract this common woodland bird.

BIRDS AROUND WATER

American Coot — *Fulica americana 15" (38 cm)*

These are the only all black duck-like bird with a white bill found in North America. They are most closely related to rails—tall, thin, secretive birds of the marsh. Their common name comes from the Latin *fuligo* or soot indicating its color. The Coots have **lobed feet**, not webbed so each toe looks like a club with no webbing between, which enables them to be good walkers and swimmers. These special feet also conduct heat out of their bodies more easily, helping them to adjust to hot weather. The American Coot eats mostly aquatic plants and fish, tadpoles, snails, worms, and insects eggs. They are known to be pirates as they quickly swoop up vegetation brought to the surface by diving ducks. They have 14 different displays for communication with each other. They lay 8 – 12 eggs on the ground in tall vegetation in nests built by the male. They breed across Canada and throughout the U.S. and winter in the southern U.S., Mexico, Central America, the West Indies and northern South America.

Belted Kingfisher — *Megaceryle alcyon 13" (33 cm)*

This bird does just as its name suggests—it fishes for food in a most fascinating way. Often it is seen on a favorite perch over water, watching for small fish. Or, like the terns, they'll fly over the water looking for signs of fish, then stall in flight to pinpoint a fish's location and suddenly dive head first into the water. It quickly recovers and flies away with its catch. The term "belted" comes from the white belt of feathers around its neck. Its loud rattling call will let you know it's nearby. Generally these are solitary birds but mates recognize each other by their distinctive calls. Look for them along rivers and lakes. Their nest is a horizontal burrow in the side of a hill or riverbank and takes anywhere from two to ten days to excavate. 5 – 10 eggs are laid in a nest chamber filled with fish bones, scales and ejected pellets. Although they catch and eat fish and other animals found in water, they feed their young regurgitated food. Kingfishers are great parents. They teach their young to fish by dropping dead meals into the water for retrieval practice.

BIRD SMART

Canada Goose — *Branta canadensis 40" (101 cm)*

These large birds are unmistakable in the autumn skies as they migrate south as far as Mexico, flying in "V" formation and honking loudly. Not all will migrate, leaving some in open patches of water, if available. They are so common now around city marshes, lakes, fields and golf courses in some parts of the U.S. and Canada that they are sometimes perceived to be a nuisance and are transported by truck or plane to less inhabited areas. They have adapted to so many places because they eat shoots, roots, grass seeds and grain. They will also eat insects and snails. Their long necks allow them to reach the bottoms of deeper water where ducks can't reach. Geese nest in marshy areas on the ground or often on the top of muskrat dens in the water. They make long-term pair bonds and raise their young together. They are very protective parents of their 1–15 goslings that are able to follow their parents as soon as they are hatched. The parents molt their primary flight feathers as soon as the goslings hatch and don't fly for several weeks while their young are small and flightless.

Great Blue Heron — *Ardea herodias 52" (132 cm)*

With a wingspan of 7' (2 m), the Great Blue Heron stands about 4' (1 m) tall and is our largest and most widespread Heron. It is often incorrectly called a crane. In summer, it can be found everywhere from southern Canada to Mexico, except the Rocky Mountains. In winter, it migrates to the warmer part of its range. It flies with its neck held in an "S" shape and its legs stretched out behind like a rudder. A white variation of this graceful bird is found only on ocean coastlines and used to be thought of as a separate species. It feeds on a diet of small fish, snails, frogs and other aquatic animals. It nests with other Herons in secluded areas in colonies called **rookeries** or **heronries**, building platform nests of sticks in the tops of trees. Like all Herons, the Great Blue has no oil glands to waterproof its feathers. Instead it has **powder down** produced from soft feathers on the breast. The powder is spread around to insulate and waterproof this water bird. From a canoe or riverboat you'll see this bird motionless, stalking its prey with its long bill.

Great Egret *Casmerodius albus 38" (97 cm)*

This lovely and graceful white wading bird inhabits both fresh and saltwater where it stalks small fish, frogs, snakes and crayfish. It is one of the most common and widespread of its family, the Herons, migrating from fresh water lakes in the north during summer to saltwater marshes in winter. It feeds alone, traveling up to 20 miles from its colony home in search of food. The Great Egret seldom stretches out its neck, preferring to carry it in an "S" shape, even when flying. Dozens will nest together high in trees well away from human disturbances in places called rookeries or heronries. Here they build platform nests loosely made of sticks and twigs and lay up to three eggs. Several species of Herons and Egrets can be found in these crowded and wonderfully noisy places which are often on islands or in woodlands near water. The Great Egret and its cousin, the Snowy Egret, were once subjected to massive hunting pressure for their elegant white feathers. Now, with protection they are making a comeback.

Herring Gull *Larus argentatus 25" (63 cm)*

Gulls can be seen almost anywhere, even away from water, and are very comfortable around humans. Herring Gulls migrate south each year just far enough to avoid the cold and find food. They eat everything, including scavenging from garbage dumps. Some follow coastal ships waiting for handouts of garbage or remains from fishing boats, a practice which has actually increased their numbers. The common name "herring" comes from the birds' ability to catch small fish such as herring. They are colonial birds that nest on the ground near water, building a nest of seaweed and rocks. Only one brood of 3 – 4 a year is raised. Gull chicks hatch with their eyes open and are able to walk right away (semi-precocial), but they remain with their nest for two to three weeks while their parents feed them regurgitated food. The young beg for food by bowing to any adult and touching the adult's bill, but its parents recognize their own young and will not feed others. Experiments show that the parents' habit of mobbing around approaching predators actually teaches the young to be wary of such animals as foxes and weasels.

Mallard
Anas platyrhynchos 25" (63 cm)

The brilliantly colored green head of the drake (male) is unmistakable on this common relatively large **dabbling duck**. Dabbling ducks dunk their heads in the shallow water with their tails in the air, to get vegetation, insects and other invertebrates off the bottom. You can tell them from **diving ducks** even at a distance because divers disappear from the surface to feed. The term "duck" comes from a Latin word meaning "to dive" so technically speaking, it doesn't apply very well to all duck species. Their feathers are kept waterproof by glands that secrete a special oil. A thick layer of down feathers keep these birds insulated from cold water. Mallards have been raised in captivity for years by individuals and game farms. This has resulted in them being very tame and accustomed to backyards and parking lots. Although the female is comfortable around people, it can be a problem when she tries to lead her newly hatched brood across a parking lot or a busy street to get to water. If you find a mallard hen on a nest, note the date. You'll probably be treated to the chirping of ducklings in 28 days.

Red-winged Blackbird
Agelaius phoeniceus 8" (20 cm)

The Red-winged Blackbird does much to make our summers more comfortable because they consume trillions of insects each year. Each year, the males return north from its winter range in Costa Rica, Mexico and the southern U.S., two weeks earlier than the females. He seeks out a marshy territory of cattails and sings his phone-ringing imitation song to attract his mate. He flies from tall stalk to tall stalk, proclaiming his territory and chasing out any intruding birds. After the females arrive, a cup nest is woven between the tall blades of cattails and 3 – 5 spotted blue eggs are laid. One male can have several females nesting within his territory and each female can have several broods each year. Sometimes these birds are seen feeding at backyard bird feeders where they are easily scared off by the regular visitors to the feeder. They are hosts to Cowbirds.

Wood Duck
Aix sponsa 18" (46 cm)

The male or **drake** of this species is often considered to be the most beautiful duck in the U.S. and Canada. It was nearly driven to extinction from hunting and habitat loss before laws were passed to limit hunting. All Wood Ducks nest and roost high in trees but they are not the only duck to do so. It has also been helped by replacing felled, Woodpecker-hollowed trees with nesting boxes. Since they eat larva of mosquitoes and other aquatic insects, there is also evidence that they suffer because of chemical treatment in mosquito controlled districts. Wood Ducks also eat grain, acorns, berries, snails and crayfish. After the 6 – 15 young are born, the female calls to its newly hatched young from the ground or water beneath the nest. One by one the young use their sharp claws to climb out and drop to the ground, anywhere from 10 – 30' (3 – 9 m) below, cushioned by their downy feathers. They then waddle off with their mother to feed on small insects and plants. They make a high-pitched whistle noise in flight when disturbed.

BIRDS OF PREY

American Kestrel
Falco sparverius 12" (30 cm)

Commonly seen resting on wires and fence poles, Kestrels are fun to watch as they hover like a helicopter before swooping in on their prey. Also known as a Sparrow Hawk, this smallest of North American falcons can be found in all sorts of habitats including deserts, marshes, grasslands, farmlands, suburbs and big cities. The Kestrel eats mostly grasshoppers and other insects as well as small mammals such as mice and birds. Their hunting is made easier by their incredible eyesight which is eight times that of our own; it can spot a grasshopper from over 100' (30.5 m) away. This bird hunts from perches, flies off to find its prey and hovers briefly while it locates it. Note that it will characteristically pump its tail up and down when perched, especially after it has landed. They lay 4 – 5 eggs in cavities such as Woodpecker holes, not really building a nest, and will readily use a nest box. Some of the Kestrels will migrate as far south as Panama while others stay if an adequate source of food is available. Some states such as Iowa have Kestrel conservation programs and install nest boxes on the backs of highway signs. Males are distinguished from females by their bluish wings.

Bald Eagle   *Haliaeetus leucocephalus 40" (102 cm)*

The Bald Eagle gets its beautiful, white head and tail plumage only after five years of age when it has a wing span of about 7' (2 m). In this earlier stage you'll see a large, nearly black bird with white specks on its head and tail. Look for the Bald Eagle near water since it eats mainly fish that are live or dead, but it will also eat small mammals, birds and carrion when available. It makes bathtub-sized, platform nests near water, usually at the top of the highest tree, and raises only one brood of one or two young each season. If you are very lucky, you may witness their amazing courtship display when both males and females lock talons (claws) in flight and descend in a series of somersaults. They mate for life and return to the same nest every year. At the end of each season, Bald Eagles will migrate to areas with open water in search of fish. The national symbol conspicuously found on U.S. coins and currency, the Bald Eagle was not so conspicuous in the days following World War II when the widespread use of the chemical DDT wiped out nearly all of them. This persistent chemical, now known to cause cancer in humans, made its way through the food chain and caused the birds to lay soft eggs which could not survive. The population of Bald Eagles took a long time to recover, but recover they have. Minnesota has sufficient Eagles, to ship some to areas where they have been wiped out.

Great Horned Owl   *Bubo virginianus 25" (63 cm)*

These Owls are commonly called "tigers of the sky" because of their cat-like appearance and ferocious behavior. They are the most common Owl and are always a treat to see in suburban forests where they hunt skunks, rabbits, pheasants, mice and just about anything they can catch. They are one of the only predators of skunks because of their lack of a sense of smell. They are well known for their ability to turn their heads, almost completely around. They have many calls, some very eerie sounding but most are familiar with the "who-whoo---who-whoooo" which is their mating call. Owls such as the Great Horned hunt from perches in the dark using their hearing even more than their eyesight. The function of the "horns" on the Great Horned is a bit of a mystery as they are not ears as many think they are. Their ears are located on the front of their face near the eyes, one higher than the other to help it pinpoint its prey even under a foot of snow. Great Horns don't migrate and are the first animal to reproduce each year; they start to breed in January and sit on eggs in February, even in the far north. They don't build their own nest so they either take over a Crow's nest or they'll simply lay up to 2 eggs in the nook of a tree. The young learn to hunt by staying with their parents all summer and are on their own by the following January when breeding starts again. They mate for life and return to the same nesting territory each winter.

Red-tailed Hawk   *Buteo jamaicensis 25" (63 cm)*

This predator is readily seen from the car as it prefers open country with scattered trees and woodlands. Red-tails soar the skies displaying their orangish-red, wide tail making them easy to identify. It is by far our most widespread **buteo** or wide-winged and wide-bodied Hawk of open areas. Listen for its high-pitched screaming as it circles above fields looking for prey. It has a habit of perching on light poles and fence posts while it is looking for rabbits and other small mammals, reptiles, birds and insects to eat. The eyesight of these Hawks is five times that of our own. Red-tails make or remake large platform nests high in the crotch of tree branches out of twigs, branches and leaves, lined with bark strips. Only once a year Red-tails raise 2 or 3 young. The young are fed a diet of mice and small birds which the parents tear into tiny bits. Just like the adults, after the meal is digested, they cough up a pellet consisting of the undigestible bones and fur or feathers. Some of these birds migrate as far as south as Central America but some don't so you may see them all winter.

Turkey Vulture
Cathartes aura 30" (76 cm)

Turkey Vultures perform a great service to the natural world; like Crows they eat carrion and therefore help to recycle dead animals. They will eat any dead animal found. They are thought to be the only bird with a developed sense of smell and they use this to scavenge in fields and along roadsides. The common name "vulture" comes from the Latin "to pluck or tear" referring to the way it feeds. They have no feathers on their heads which reduces the chance of picking up parasites when feeding. They are twice the size of Crows and in flight their wing tips have finger-like projections, unlike the Crow. In profile they fly with their wings forming a "V" as opposed to the other less common type of vulture, the Black Vulture, which fly with their wings out flat. Turkey Vultures can be seen drying themselves off after rainstorms by sitting at the top of a tree with its wings outstretched. They lay their eggs in a shallow depression on a rocky ledge, in a cave or in the hollow of a tree stump, not really building any nest at all. A Turkey Vulture will not re-nest if its nest is destroyed. They migrate each year to places like the Bahamas.

Bug Smart
(and other creepy-crawlies!)

A field brimming with yellow, purple and gold blooms is made only more beautiful by the sporadic visits of fanciful butterflies. We marvel at their delicate magnificence and yet these tiny creatures are capable of feats that defy human abilities. They travel thousands of miles without plane tickets and attract mates from miles away without subscribing to a dating service. Some of the little "buggers" (excuse the pun) are natural-born chemists. For example, the green-yellow glow of a firefly, which fascinates young and old alike, is a chemical reaction between a chemical in the firefly's abdomen and oxygen (see fireflies in the species section). The life stories of many amazing insects would make a great movie. A few of the movies would need a PG (Parental Guidance) rating, such as one about the immature dragonfly. In the process of changing from a water insect to an adult dragonfly, it splits open its back to reveal a completely different critter.

No matter where one goes in the world, one can find insects—lots of them in every continent on earth. While you might like the idea of escaping from insects, it's a good thing we can't. Butterflies and other, less popular (but no less fascinating) insects are some of the most important creatures on the planet. Because we have found insects in fossilized tree sap, known as **amber**, we know they have been around since before the time of dinosaurs, about 425 million years. In addition to having an ancient history, their sheer numbers make quite a statement. To date we have identified millions of different species of insects and within many of those species, there are probably billions of individuals.

Insects play a very important role in our lives, both positive and negative. Since they are small and numerous, they serve as food for many animals and their importance to the food chain cannot be overstated. Some toads and frogs eat nothing but bugs, worms and slugs. Surprisingly though, larger animals such as skunks, which eat grasshoppers and other ground-dwelling insects, rely on them too. Bears feast on ants, termites, beehives and others. Bats and birds devour insects by the thousands. Also, some insects eat other insects. Even humans in some cultures eat insects regularly—they fry them just as we would eggs.

Another important role that insects play is in pollinating the plants that produce the food we eat; plants such as apple trees, cucumbers, strawberries, tomatoes and many others. For example, while honeybees poke into a flower for a sweet treat of nectar, they inadvertently pick up pollen, which adheres to the hairs on their bodies. When they move to another flower of the same kind, they transport the pollen enabling that flower to produce a fruit and/or seed. Without pollination, the plants would not reproduce.

The impact that insects have had on human health has been extraordinary. Malaria, a disease transmitted by certain types of mosquitoes, has killed more people than both World Wars put together. The impact that insects have had on crops has also been significant. Although less than one percent of the total number of species of insects cause crop damage, even one species can devastate a particular crop. That's especially true in modern day farming, when rows and rows of the same plant are grown together, called a **monoculture**. Insects usually specialize in one type of plant and in such large, uniform fields, they find no "stop sign." Combine one kind of grasshopper and field upon field of its specialty, corn, and you have lost the entire corn crop.

> **"Teach your children what we have taught our children that the Earth is our mother. Whatever befalls Earth befalls the sons of Earth. Man did not weave the web of life, he is merely a strand of it. Whatever he does to the web, he does to himself."**
>
> CHIEF SEATTLE

People have found several ways to control insects in crops. One is planting different kinds of crop plants together. Another is biological control which is introducing beneficial insects to eat pesky insects. A common solution to damage from insects has been the use of ever-higher concentrations of pesticides or poisons to kill them. Pesticides can control insect damage, but they have had an extremely detrimental effect on the environment. Pesticides are not selective and kill not only pesky, but also helpful insects. In addition they poison wells, sterilize soil and collect in the fatty tissue of animals. This happens when fields are sprayed with pesticides and small animals such as mice eat the insects. When larger animals, such as Hawks and foxes, eat the rodents, they are also absorbing the pesticides which are stored in the fatty tissue of these animals. For animals like Hawks, which eat large numbers of rodents, the amount of poison can accrue to dangerous and sometimes fatal amounts. This is known as **bio-accumulation**.

Sometimes poisons persist in the environment for many years. For example, DDT is still found in the environment even though it was banned in 1978. Pesticides can have a deadly effect on humans, too. Certain types of cancer have been directly linked to the thousands of different petro-chemicals that have been poured on wheat, corn and other vegetable crops. Pesticides haven't had overall success in curbing insect damage because insects quickly mutate into varieties that are tolerant to the chemicals. Breakthroughs in using other insects to control insect pests will help to alleviate this critical environmental and health problem.

The title of this chapter is Bug Smart, but we've used that term very loosely to describe critters that are "creepy-crawly" in nature. We've included earthworms, spiders, slugs and others, even though these are not really bugs at all—in fact, they're not even insects. We lovingly refer to them as squirms. Everything we do talk about in this chapter is an **invertebrate** (in-vur´te-brit), meaning it is an animal without a backbone. Only some of these invertebrates we discuss are insects. Insects are animals with three body parts: head, thorax and abdomen. They also have six jointed legs. They are covered by a hard outer coating called an **exoskeleton** (ek-so-skel´i-tin). Animals with an "exo" skeleton don't have any bones inside their bodies. An insect's hard shell serves as its bones. Beetles, mosquitoes and grasshoppers are all insects.

Technically, bugs are one specific type of insect. The only true bug we've included in our species section are the water boatmen and the spittlebug. Bugs have all the characteristics of insects, but in addition, bugs have two pairs of wings for a total of four wings. They live on land or water, have piercing and sucking mouth parts and go through incomplete metamorphosis. This means they change from egg to **nymph** (nimf) (a general term to describe a stage between the egg and adult) to adult. See the question on metamorphosis for a more complete definition. The following chart shows that all "bugs" are insects, but not all insects are bugs. It also shows that while all the critters we talk about in this chapter are invertebrates, others such as slugs, spiders and earthworms are not insects at all. Having explained these important differences, we will follow convention and continue to use the terms insects and bugs loosely.

While our chapter is called "Bug Smart", the following chart shows that everything we include in this chapter is technically not a bug. In fact, bugs are a subset of insects which are a subset of several other "layers" of classifications. The diagram is not exhaustive and includes only some of the classifications. This may help with the sometimes confusing questions such as: Are all insects bugs? Are worms insects? What's the difference between an insect and a bug?

VERTEBRATES & INVERTEBRATES

GROUP & DESCRIPTION	EXAMPLES
VERTEBRATES (animals with backbones).	*humans & other mammals fish, birds, etc.*
INVERTEBRATES (animals without backbones)	*all those below*
ANNELIDS (soft, segmented bodies)	*earthworms leeches*
MOLLUSKS (soft bodies, some have shells, some don't)	*snails, slugs oysters*
ARTHROPODS (jointed legs, shell covered body)	*all those below*
Diplopoda (round body, many segments, each having two pair legs)	*millipede*
Chilopoda (flat body, many segments, each having 1 pair of legs)	*centipede*
Crustaceans (many jointed legs, shell covered body)	*crabs, lobsters crayfish*
Arachnids (four pairs of legs, no feelers or wings)	*common spiders wood ticks*
INSECTS (3 body parts, six jointed legs, hard body covering)	*all those below*
true bugs (two pairs of wings, sucking/piercing mouths; wing that is half hard and half soft)	*water boatmen spittle bug*
butterflies, moths (4 wings, powdery scales on wings)	*monarch butterfly isabella moth*
true flies (2 wings, halteres)	*bluebottle fly mosquito*
beetles (4 wings, 2 hard & often shiny)	*ladybird beetle firefly*
dragonflies, damselflies (4 wings, large eyes, long abdomen)	*green darner dragonfly black-winged damselfly*
grasshoppers, crickets (large hind legs, 4 wings, antennae)	*american grasshopper field cricket*
ants, bees (jointed antennae, thin waist)	*little black ant honeybee*

BUG SMART

How many "bugs" are there?

Because they are so small and the trees and soils they live on so vast, especially in the tropical rainforests, it is difficult to make an accurate guess. When you hear that we are losing hundreds of plant and animal species each day due to deforestation, they usually mean insects and their kin, some of which we haven't even identified yet. We do know that the largest group of animals are the insects. About 1.7 million species of insects and about 35,000 species of spiders have been *named* since 1753 when Carolus Linnaeus, the Swedish botanist, started the **binomial** (bi-no´me-el) naming system (the scientific way of using two names to identify creatures). In 1982 scientists from the National Museum of Natural History developed a new way of collecting insects from the **canopy** (tree tops) of trees in the rain forest and calculated a new estimate of 30 million species of insects. All of this goes to show that even now we can't be sure we know the exact number. What we do know is that more species of insects are becoming extinct now than at any other time in the past, which is unraveling many of the incredibly intricate and delicate food chains.

How long do adult insects live?

The answer to this varies from several days, as in the case of the adult cecropia moth; to several weeks, as in the worker honeybees; to seventeen years, as in the life cycle of one species of cicada. In general, adult insects live just long enough to reproduce, then they die. The cecropia moth emerges from its cocoon to find a mate and lay eggs. It does not have any mouth parts and therefore does not even feed in this stage, so it dies shortly thereafter. Soon after a cicada egg hatches, the nymph burrows into the earth. In cold climates, it may live underground, feeding and growing, for as long as 17 years before it emerges as a noisy adult. In the south, this insect emerges in only 13 years, probably because its feeding pattern is not interrupted by winter and it can grow in a more continuous fashion.

The majority of insects are eaten before they have had a chance to reproduce, which explains why insects lay so many eggs. If all insects lived long enough to reproduce, we would be overrun with them.

What makes an insect a true bug?

Only one group of insects can be called "true bugs." Like most insects, true bugs have four wings—two hind wings that fold up against the back and two fore wings that fold over the top of the hind wing and serve as a covering. Also like most insects, the hind wings of true bugs are thin and membranous. What distinguishes true bugs from all other insects is the make-up of the outer or fore wing. Over half of the fore wing is hard and leathery while the tip is thin like clear plastic wrap. This half-hard, half-soft wing, called **hemelytra** (he-mel-i´tra), is easy to see in this group of insects. The water boatmen is only one of about 4,500 species of true bugs in North America.

Do insects shed their skins like snakes?

Yes, just as snakes need a new, larger skin in which to grow, so do insects! In fact, perhaps the most remarkable story in the world of these minia-ture wonders is how they mature from egg to adult and how they deal with their outer hard body coverings when it's time to grow. All insects have an outer covering made out of a hard substance called **chitin** (kite´n) which is somewhat similar to fingernails. This skin is called the **cuticula** (ku-tik´u-la) and needs to be shed and replaced by a new one underneath it in order for the insect to grow. This process is called **molting**. Just before discarding the old skin, the insect forms a special kind of new skin underneath it. The skin is formed from a liquid secreted by glands called **hypodermal** glands. This new skin is pliable, allowing the insect to grow. And the insect does grow—just as soon as it splits open its old skin and crawls out of it—definitely a Hollywood movie in the making! Over time, the new skin hardens and yet another molt is necessary for more growth. The insect will go through this process several times, how many times depends on the species. You can often see the old, brittle, brown casings of dragonflies, cicadas and other insects left on rocks or leaves. The stage between each molt is called an **instar**. This process ends when the insect reaches adulthood.

How does a caterpillar change into a butterfly without magic?

When a caterpillar forms a chrysalis and emerges as a butterfly, it has gone through a complete restructuring and make-up of its cells in a process called **metamorphosis** (met-e-mor´fe-sis). There are three types of meta-morphosis, one more complicated than the next. **Gradual metamor-phosis** is the oldest from an evolutionary perspective. It is also the type of metamorphosis that is most like the way we grow. An example is when a tiny grasshopper hatches from its egg. It just keeps molting until it is full size. It never changes its overall appearance or basic function. That's why you find only small ones in the spring and larger ones through summer.

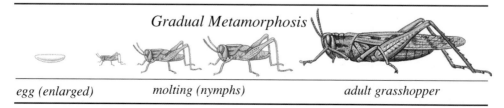

Gradual Metamorphosis

egg (enlarged)   *molting (nymphs)*   *adult grasshopper*

The next process to evolve was **incomplete metamorphosis**, also known as three-stage metamorphosis. Dragonflies fall into this category. The dragonfly lays its eggs in water and the eggs hatch underwater as wingless, bug-eating **nymphs**. They resemble a smaller version of their parents without wings but with a larger abdomen. Some may stay in the nymph stage as long as three years before crawling out of the water, splitting open their skin and emerging as delicate-winged, mosquito-eating adults.

Incomplete Metamorphosis

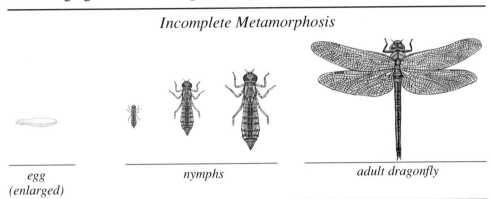

egg
(enlarged)   *nymphs*   *adult dragonfly*

The most advanced and recent growth process is **complete metamorphosis**, otherwise known as four-stage metamorphosis. This is the complete structural change from one stage to another. In other words, it begins its life looking like one thing and ends its life looking like something completely different. The familiar life cycle of butterflies is a great example of this spectacular occurrence. The stages proceed from 1.) egg to 2.) larva, (caterpillar in the case of a butterfly) to 3.) pupa, its outwardly stationary phase, (chrysalis, in the case of the butterfly, cocoon in the case of the moth) to 4.) adult. This all happens often within a few short weeks.

Complete Metamorphosis

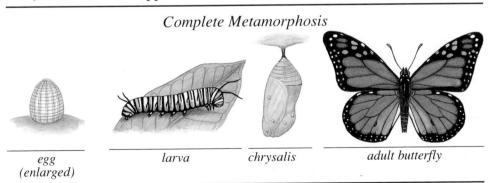

egg
(enlarged)   *larva*   *chrysalis*   *adult butterfly*

You can observe these stages in the life of a butterfly or moth by looking for their eggs under the leaves of plants. As a larvae, you may see the caterpillars eating leaves or crawling on twigs. As a chrysalis, in the case of a butterfly, look for a dry, metallic-colored, oblong-shaped structure with many points and projections, attached at one or more points to a twig. As a cocoon, in the case of a moth, look for a dry, brown, papery, egg-shaped structure, wrapped in a leaf or attached to a twig along the length of the cocoon.

How do insects breathe without lungs?

Having no lungs like humans do, insects breathe through holes in their bodies called **spiracles** (spi´ra-klz). Use a magnifying glass to see a row of these tiny holes on the side of a grasshopper, dragonfly or butterfly, right along

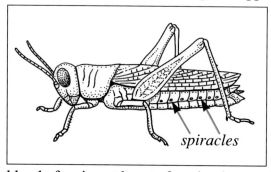

spiracles

the side of the abdomen. Usually along the side of the body, these holes are connected to an internal tube system called the **tracheae** (tra´key-a). Tiny channels connect with even smaller ones until they reach the muscles or organs where oxygen is transferred to the hungry muscle. The blood of an insect has no function in carrying oxygen as ours does. Spiracles have flaps to seal off the opening which helps to reduce water loss when it is excessively dry or to keep out moisture in water-dwelling insects. To move air throughout the tracheae system, tiny air sacs connected to the tube system expand and collapse and, just like a bellows, move a large volume of air throughout the tracheae system providing the insect's body with much needed oxygen. Take a moment to discover the breathing movements of a grasshopper.

Being so small, can insects defend themselves?

Yes, but most insects use passive defense systems, that is, they try hard to avoid danger. Hiding is a successful technique they have evolved over time. They use camouflage very effectively to look like their habitats, often to incredible degrees, in order to escape becoming lunch for a predator. The pressures of being coveted as a meal for so many different species have produced these evolutionary adaptations. The colors green and brown are common insect colors because they are the colors of the insects' surroundings and serve to hide them. Some insects are even shaped like the objects in their surroundings. To resemble a twig or a leaf, as the walking stick bug does, is an effective way to hide from even the best of predators.

The sting of bees and wasps is a very aggressive defense system, although most species prefer to go about their business and attack only when provoked. The chemical formula for these stings is not unlike the venom in some snakes. Anyone who has had the misfortune of stepping on, or otherwise disturbing these critters, knows how painful their sting can be. The real concern comes when a person is allergic to the sting. Otherwise, no permanent damage or life-threatening condition occurs from a bee or insect sting.

Still other insects, such as the mosquito, survive by using a great escape plan—flight! Also, their sheer numbers protect them. It's easy to hide in a crowd and therefore less likely that a particular insect will be eaten.

You may have thought that mosquito bites were a defensive action. Actually, only the female mosquito bites and it is not a defense technique. It is just a way for the mosquito to obtain protein from the blood in order for her eggs to develop.

How and why do insects "talk" to each other?

Insects talk to each other to communicate danger, locate sources of food and to attract mates but they don't use voices like people or birds. While our voice boxes use the air from our lungs, insects breathe through holes on their abdomens. So. without lungs, there are no cords to vibrate. Because they don't use voices to "talk," there is no reason to hear either, so most insects are deaf. Insects communicate in other ways; some use sight, others use sound made by various body parts and still others use touch for communication.

The most common way insects communicate is through smell. They don't have noses, but they do have scent receptors on various parts of their bodies, such as their antennae, feet and wings. These insects use body chemicals which they obtain from plants that they eat during their larval stage. The chemicals are called **pheromones** (fer'e-monz) and produce chemical odors. Pheromones can be described as a sort of chemical language. They convey messages that they are looking for a mate or where food has been found or that danger is present. Pheromones are released by specialized glands located on various parts of an insect's body. Moths are an example of a species that can locate each other by releasing pheromones. Female moths release the chemicals and males, equipped with antennae that look like a small pair of feathers, can pick up their scent up to three miles away! In some species, the chemicals on the insect's body are not released into the air. Instead, they are communicated when the insects touch each other, as in the case of ants.

Other species of these ever-fascinating creatures use sound to communicate. Sound can travel both through the air and through vibrating surfaces. When in danger, some termite species bang their heads rapidly on the roof of their nest. The resulting vibrations are received much the way we would feel a sonic boom nearby, or the way we would feel a neighbor knocking on the wall to say the TV is too loud. These sound waves are picked up by the receiving insect with sensing organs, much the way we hear with our ears. In the termite, the sound is received through the receptors on its legs.

Some insects use movement and sight to communicate. For example, when honeybees move about in circles, figure eights and other configurations, they are communicating the location of a great spot for gathering nectar. The other bees, by watching and sometimes touching the bee doing the dancing, know which direction to go to find the food.

Do all insects live in colonies?

No, most are solitary. They only need to find others of their kind in order to mate. But many insects do live in colonies, or groups. Species that live in colonies, often called social insects, have several common characteristics. They have definite divisions of labor for feeding the young, mating and finding food. This hierarchy of labor is set up in much the same style as the royalty of ancient (and not so ancient) Europe. The bulk of the individuals are the workers and only a select few reproduce. Social insects rely on each other to perform the greater communal tasks of nest building, food gathering and reproduction.

How many insects live in a colony?

The communities of some tropical species reach populations in the millions. In the more temperate regions, numbers never get quite that high. For instance, the paper wasp, has a colony of about 50 wasps. A bumblebee colony will have upwards of 30 to 40 members. The colonies of the bald-faced hornet and the honeybee are much larger. A hive of honeybees can have up to 80,000 members! All ants live in colonies, with the colonies of some species numbering only a dozen to some numbering over a million members!

How can tiny bugs and other small things avoid freezing during the northern winters?

Each species has a different way of coping with winter. Some crawl into the ground or hibernate in a crevice of a tree. Most die but lay eggs that survive the winter to hatch in the spring and some stay above the ground using various chemicals that act as anti-freeze to prevent them from freezing. Insects that overwinter as adults "migrate" away from winter underground instead of going southward like birds. Only a few, such as the monarch butterfly, fly to the warmer climates of central Mexico. Some of these move below the frost line. The soil freezes only so deep and varies from inches to several feet with the harshness of the climate.

No matter what stage the insect is in over the winter, there are many **micro-climates** in nature. Even though weather forecasters might say that the temperature is 10° F (–12° C), they are measuring the overall air temperature. Under a log, inside a hollow tree, or under deep layers of snow, the temperature is likely to be warmer. These micro-climates have been warmed enough by the sun to provide a habitable winter home for many overwintering insects.

Each year earthworms tunnel down to between five and seven feet (1.5 to 2 m) below the surface when the ground is not frozen. They dig out areas where they spend the winter sleeping intertwined in a ball with half-dozen other worms. The larva of some beetles move below the frost line to hibernate. Woolly bear caterpillars overwinter in their fuzzy caterpillar state using leaf debris as an insulator. These insects that seemingly freeze solid and yet come back to life in the spring use several complex body functions to survive, probably one of which is the use of natural anti-freeze, called **glycerol** (glis´er-ol).

It's not a sign of bad housekeeping to find a fly in your house in the middle of the winter. It just means that in the fall an adult housefly found a tiny crevice in your house in which to hibernate. On a warm winter's day, the heat of the sun awakens the tiny hibernator and suddenly you have houseflies buzzing in your home.

Most bald-faced hornets do not hibernate, but die when the weather turns cold. Just one of them, a fertilized queen is able to hibernate and does so under the soil or tree bark. In the spring she awakens and flies off to start another colony by herself.

Other insects survive the harshness of winter as eggs. Female grasshoppers stick their **ovipositor** (a projection off the tip of the abdomen) into the soil or into plants and lay their eggs there, before dying each autumn. The eggs are dormant over winter, hatching in spring when the soil warms up. In the fall, female mosquitoes lay their eggs in tall grasses surrounding ponds. When the snow melts in the spring, the run-off carries the eggs to a pond where the mosquito will go through its life cycle. In dry years, the eggs will not mature because they need to reach water to do so. They can remain viable for years waiting for the right conditions. Some species of mosquitoes will lay their eggs directly into pools of water. The adult mosquitoes die off at the first sign of frost and leave their legacy behind in the hundreds of eggs that they lay.

Some insects overwinter as adults. In northern climates honeybees stay alive in protected hives (those provided by humans or natural structures like trees) by moving continuously, which keeps most of the colony warm. They live off the 50 to 60 pounds of honey they made during the warmer months.

How do insects make things like honey, wax and hives with their bodies?

To make honey, honeybees collect nectar from flowers, and stored it in a special stomach while flying back to the hive. They then combine it with glandular secretions from their bodies, regurgitate it and place it in the combs for storage. They also fan it with their wings to evaporate some of the water, making it the right consistency. The taste of the honey we eat is affected by which flowers the bees visit and the nectar they collect. Even secretions from aphids on leaves can be collected by some bees and results in the delicacy known as leaf honey. Honeybees also produce wax for their honeycombs. The wax used in forming the hives comes from the four pairs of wax glands located on segments of the bee's abdomen. Each gland is a disc-like area covered by a smooth cuticle called a **wax plate**. The wax is exuded though these plates and accumulates, forming little scales that are used in making the honeycomb. The plates are stacked up one at a time to make the combs. Other insects, such as wasps, mix chewed-up plant materials with saliva to produce rapidly drying materials with which they build their papery houses.

Is a spider an insect?

Spiders are another of those "buggy" critters that are not insects. They are one of the largest groups of non-insects in the class of **arthropoda** (ar´thre-pod-a) (invertebrates with jointed legs) and are called **arachnids** (a-rak´nidz). There are more than 3,000 kinds of spiders in North America. They can be found living just about anywhere from open fields and woods to your own home. Spiders are different from insects in many ways. They don't have wings, or antennae and have eight rather than six legs. All spiders have large jaw-like fangs called **chelicerae** (ka-lis´er-ree). They are located in the front of the mouth and are used to crush their prey or to inject venom to paralyze the victim before eating. Also, spiders only have two body parts unlike the insect which has three. The head and thorax in the spiders are combined to form a **cephalothorax** (sef-a-la-thor´aks). The other body part is the abdomen.

Most spiders have eight eyes and the way they are arranged on the spider's head identifies each species. For instance, the orb weavers have eight eyes arranged in two rows of four eyes each. Another interesting fact about spiders is that if a spider loses part of a leg, it is able to regenerate another. These new legs don't suddenly appear but are regenerated during the next molt.

Spiders are unique in that they are one of only a few creatures that can spin silk. Although not all spiders spin webs, their ability to produce silk and spin webs is their most intriguing feature. A female spider deposits eggs into a silken ball that she spins herself. The sacs are attached to the web or nearby on a twig. She will guard the sac until autumn when she dies with the cold weather. When the young hatch in spring, they emerge and disperse in all directions. The young release long silken threads which they use like parachutes to ride on the wind to new locations. This is called **ballooning**.

Is there a reason to be afraid of spiders?

There is nothing to fear from most spiders. Some species do have toxic and even harmfully poisonous bites, but of the approximately 35,000 species of spiders, only 20 (one of which is the black widow spider) are fatally poisonous to humans. The bite of a spider is meant to paralyze its insect victim. Since spiders are so much smaller than people, their bites are usually harmless to humans. People's fearful reaction to spiders is not based on the knowledge that spiders actually help to control exploding populations of insects and are an important part of nature. Instead, it is a learned behavior passed on from one generation to the next that tells us we should dislike things that creep and crawl. Childhood stories often affect our perceptions of life and some exaggerated childhood stories may contribute to our spider phobias. Even the innocent rhyme we learned as toddlers, Little Miss Muffet, may have tainted our view of this generally beneficial creature.

Do all spiders spin webs?

No. Some spiders capture their prey by waiting at the water's edge to catch insects or even small fish that swim past. Some, for example the crab spider, are well camouflaged and hide so they can pounce on their prey from the top of a flower. Some use trap doors in the ground to hide under, then dash out to grab insects as they pass by. Other spiders spin webs but in different shapes, depending on the species. Some build funnel-shaped webs, others build webs resembling a tube and others use a strand of silk like a miniature lasso. The most familiar type of web is the orb weaver's web. The word "orb" meaning circular, it is the web with many circular threads and other strands radiating straight out from the center point.

> **While we are born with curiosity and wonder and our early years full of the adventure they bring, I know such inherent joys are often lost. I also know that, being deep within us, their latent glow can be fanned to flame again by awareness and an open mind.**
>
> SYDNEY SMITH

Why and how do spiders spin webs?

Spiders are carnivorous and spin webs for several reasons—to catch their prey, protect their eggs and to provide shelter. Spiders of the same species all spin identical webs making them easy to identify once you become familiar with the different shapes and patterns. Chances are you won't see a great number of spiders on your next nature walk, but spider webs are as common as the dew on the grass. Webs may seem simple at first glance, but stop and take a closer look. They are marvels of nature. Have you ever wondered how the spider gets from one blade of grass or twig to another to start the web? Have you ever seen a spider spinning a web? How long does it take to make these suspended traps? Why doesn't a spider become entangled in its own web? Let's take a closer look.

If you want to see a spider spinning its web, you may have to venture out into the fields and woods in the dark. Most spiders make their webs under the cover of darkness, usually just before dawn or just after sunset. One complete web takes about one hour to spin. Most spiders make new webs each day after eating the old web. Their old webs supplement their high protein diet of insects. It is the female that spins the large orb web. Males spin a small secondary web off to the side of the female web. Not all kinds of spiders spin webs but of those that do, all start by producing a liquid in the abdomen which is secreted by a special organ called **spinnerets** (spin´e-rets). Six of these organs are located beneath the abdomen and can produce thin or thick webs as needed. When the liquid is excreted from the spinnerets, it solidifies into a silk strand upon contact with the air. First the spider releases a web into the breeze. When the single strand catches on a nearby twig or blade of grass, it is pulled tight and the spider crosses to make the upper cross-bridge. Additional bridges are laid and reinforcing lines are secured. The spider finds the center of the top cross-bridge and lowers herself to a safe landing. This new drop-line is pulled taut forming the three main lines of the web in a "Y" shape. The spider climbs back up to the fork and begins to spin the rest of the radial lines, each resembling a spoke in a wheel. Once all the radials or spokes are in place, she returns to the center and lays temporary spiraling circles, working from the inside out. She measures the distance between each strand by probing with her legs to feel for the correct distance. So far all of these threads are not sticky and won't catch an insect. The sticky threads come next.

Now that the basic outline is complete, the spider returns to the center and lays down the sticky spirals, eats some of the dry, non-sticky threads and the airborne trap is set. The spider usually moves to the side or stretches out in the center of the web to wait for breakfast, "herring" not to touch the sticky strands. Its sensitive feet are positioned to feel any disturbances in the web, called **web vibrations**. Once an insect is trapped in the web, the spider races out, being careful not to step on the sticky strands and grabs its prey. Spiders are very beneficial because they help to control the population of some harmful insects, such as grasshoppers.

Can you distinguish female spiders from male spiders?

This is where a bug box, a plastic box with one side magnified, will really be useful. Put your spider in the box, close the lid and look for some of the following features. You can usually tell the difference between male and female spiders in a number of ways. Female spiders tend to be larger, they position themselves at the center of a web and have particularly large abdomens. The large abdomen holds the organs to produce eggs and spin webs. Male spiders not only are smaller, but sometimes they have a different shape and color than the female. These differences are called **dimorphic** (di-mor´fik). Both male and female spiders have appendages near their mouths called **pedipalps** (ped´e-palps), sometimes referred to as just palps. The palps of the males are larger, somewhat bulb-shaped, and are used as sensory organs. These are waved about to attract females during courtship. Female pedipalps are small and look like miniature straight pins.

What makes an ant an ant?

Ants are a part of the largest order of insects called Hymenoptera and are cousins to bees and wasps. Most ants are black, brown or red and are less than one inch (2.5 cm) long. You can tell ants, bees and wasps from other insects by their slender "waists," called **pedicels** (ped´i-slz), located between the abdomen and thorax. They also have jointed antennae that look like elbows, unlike other insects. Ants, like most all insects, have large **compound eyes**, which means they have many tiny, hexagonal eyes clustered together to make up one compound eye. All ants have two sets of jaws. The larger outer jaws are used for digging and carrying food or larvae, while the inner jaws are for chewing food. Most ants live in large, underground social communities headed by a fertile female. The rest of the colony is made up of sterile, female, worker ants. Some colonies live in galleries hollowed out of dead wood. Now and then a winged male and female emerge from the colony and fly off in a courtship flight to start a new colony. Once the mating is completed, the male dies and the female drops her wings. She burrows into the ground and starts a new colony. Most ants are predators of other insects but a few will eat seeds or raise fungus for food.

How many ants and ant types are there?

For every single person on earth, there are one million ants! In fact, if you weighed all the people in the world and then weighed all the ants in the world, they would weigh about the same. There are over 10,000 species of ants and all live in colonies. Because they live in cooperative communities in which they share food and the task of raising their young, they are very successful. The majority of the diet of ants is insects and because there are so many ants, they are the greatest insect killers on earth. Besides eating insects, ants actually plant seeds. It is estimated that about one-half of all woodland flowers are planted by ants. This happens when they carry seeds back to their nest, and eat the outer covering. They discard the seed into a waste chamber in their home, where the seed germinates. Many violets, trilliums and spring beauties are planted this way.

What's inside an ant hill?

Large ant hills can measure up to several feet tall and inside, up to half a million ants can reside. Large mounds represent many years of construction and are as deep underground as they are tall. Each grain of soil is carried to the surface by worker ants. On warm sunny days, these mounds capture the sun's energy and are several degrees warmer than the ground around it. The ants within use the heat to brood the pupae in the nursery chambers. Typically all the vegetation near the mound is cleared by the ants by climbing to the top of each plant and chewing it down to the ground. Blades of grass and other vegetation are laid across the mound to help reduce heat loss and shed rain.

Tunnels traverse the interior, leading to chambers that accommodate seed storage, waste storage, brood raising and even burying the dead. Most tunnels are angled to allow good drainage. Chambers are located to the side of these near-vertical tunnels to keep out any water. Tunnels are sealed each night to conserve heat and reopened the following morning, circulating the mound air. Try a little experiment to see how fastidious ants are about these routines. After they have sealed up the mound for the night, rearrange the collection of plant debris and add several foreign objects to the mound. Check the next day and you'll see the ants have returned it to its original state by removing the new objects and rearranging the old. Be sure the ants have closed up shop for the night, though. You don't want to disturb the colony because most ants will attack if disturbed, delivering painful bites to anyone nearby.

There always seems to be a lot of activity around these miniature cities. While the queens are laying eggs, workers nurse the brood. Others are capturing food or repairing tunnels. They bring up the soil from their excavations to add to the overall size of the mound each year. Some types of ants, such as leaf cutter ants, gather leaves to feed a fungus garden underground. Each day long lines of ants leave the mound and march in single file to the chosen tree or shrub. Small portions of green leaves are chewed off and hauled back to the mound. Once inside, the leaves are carried to the garden chamber where the ants tend a special fungus. The ants adjust the temperature and humidity of this chamber by opening or closing tunnels that lead to the surface. This maximizes the growth of the fungus. The ants are rewarded by eating the rapidly growing fungus. A good way to get a look at the inside of a ant hill is to start your own ant colony. These clear sided plastic containers give a great view of the inner workings of an ant hill.

Do all ants make mounds?

There are several kinds of ants that build underground homes without building a mound. You'll see thousands of these ants scurry about when you disturb them by turning over a log or a large flat rock. Often you will see hundreds of white eggs and larvae laying right at the surface. When you turn over the rock, the worker ants grab a larvae or egg and head underground. Eggs and larvae are normally kept in brooding chambers but on warm sunny days the workers bring them to the surface to incubate in the added warmth. Some ants, such as the little black ant, build underground nests creating small mounds usually seen in the cracks of sidewalks. These are the common ants you might find in your house. They also have a multitude of chambers for the rearing of young, and waste and food storage.

How do ants talk to each other?

Ants are social insects, which means they live together in large cooperative communities, much like people. They communicate through a language of ten to twelve chemical signals and touch. When any danger is encountered by some members of the colony, they release formic acid into the air. Other members of the ant community pick up the warning signal and become alarmed, giving off more formic acid. In a cooperative effort some ants will take cover to protect the young, while others swarm, attacking anything near the nest. Formic acid not only warns the colony of incoming danger, it's what puts the sting into ant bites. Directly after biting you they inject formic acid, which causes burning and itching. While a tiny bite alone would not cause you pain, the formic acid does. The next time you turn over a rock and find an ant colony or disturb an ant hill, try to observe this warning process taking place. Always return logs and rocks to their original positions.

How do ants get around in the dark tunnels of their nest?

In the dark of the nest, getting around can be quite a challenge. Ants meet this challenge quite well by using several well-developed senses such as vision, smell and a keen sense of gravity. Ants can feel a rise or fall in the grade of the tunnel, so they know if a tunnel leads up to the exit or down to a chamber. This helps to guide them in the blackness. They also use a chemical scent that is produced in the Pauan's gland, located in the abdomen. As they walk along they touch the ground with the abdomen, producing scent markers. Used over and over by many ants, the tunnels become well marked. These tunnels can be followed by an ant simply by smelling as it goes along. This same kind of marking is used outside to help ants find their way around in the vastness of the outside world. You can see this by placing a drop of sugar water or small piece of lunch meat near their nest. Once an ant finds it, she rushes back laying down a chemical trail. Notifying others of her find, they simply follow her chemical trail back to the food. Called **recruitment trails**, the finder of the food recruits others to follow and in doing so, they reinforce the trail markers. These trails, however, evaporate within a few minutes.

How do earthworms see?

Earthworms don't have eyes or ears like you and I do. These slimy critters spend most of their time below ground so they really have no need for typical eyes. They do sense light right through their skins, though, and this limited sight helps guide the worm in its travels above and below ground. Earthworms also hear with their skin. They feel vibrations, such as footsteps on the ground. This works to detect the earthworm's worst enemy, the Robin. Watch a Robin run gently across the ground, then stop, look and wait. This pausing tricks the worm into thinking it's safe to move, thus revealing its hiding spot.

Why are earthworms slimy?

Wet and wiggly, earthworms are constantly moist to help them squeeze though tiny holes in the earth and more importantly to breath and reproduce. A special gland located in that large band near the front of the worm, called a **clitellum** (kli-tel´lum), produces a mucus to keep the body moist, which facilitates its breathing done through the skin. The clitellum also produces a jellylike ring that serves as a cocoon for earthworm eggs. When two worms join their clitella, mating is complete. After separating, a mucus band slides along the length of the body collecting eggs and sperm from the mating process. Final fertilization occurs when the band slips off the end of the worm and seals into a cocoon, trapping the eggs and sperm inside. This tiny packet called a cocoon is deposited into the soil and five months later up to twenty young earthworms hatch, starting the life cycle over again.

82

Why are there tiny piles at the entrances of earthworm holes?

Earthworms are tiny eating machines. They consume millions of leaves, depositing small piles of droppings called **castings** wherever they go. You can see castings by looking at the entrance holes of worms or along worm trails. It is estimated that up to 40 tons of castings per acre are produced by earthworms over a year's time. These piles increase the phosphorus, nitrogen and potassium of the soil and thus foster the growth of plants. This is why gardeners like to have a healthy population of earthworms in their favorite flower beds and have compost beds to invite earthworms to stay. If everyone fed earthworms their vegetable scraps, we would need fewer garbage dumps.

Can earthworms regrow a lost tail or head?

It was once thought that if an earthworm was cut in half, both ends would grow back into a new worm. This is not true. Earthworms do have the ability to regenerate a new tail if too much isn't lost but once the front or head of the worm is destroyed, it will die. Earthworms are helpful creatures so, hopefully, you won't have a chance to witness this.

How do bees find flowers?

Finding flowers is what bees do best. They use their senses of sight to not only locate flowers but to find their way home again. They then communicate to the other bees in the hive where the best flowers are located. Bees have large compound eyes (many eyes grouped together) but don't see the world as we do. In addition to seeing all the colors we see, their eyes are sensitive to short wavelength ultraviolet light. Because of this, bees foraging for food see the flowers quite differently than we do. Flowers have evolved visual characteristics to attract the ultraviolet-seeing bees. The petals of the flower reflect the ultra-violet light, much like a black-light poster. The colors of the petals appear brighter and bolder than they do under the normal spectrum of light. Besides these brighter and bolder colors, the petals are often adorned with special lines that point to the center of the flower where the nectar is located. These lines, which appear black and are in contrast to the rest of the flower, are called **nectar guides**. Unseen by our eyes, they are easily seen when one of these flowers, such as a foxglove or geranium, is held under an ultraviolet light source. Some nectar guides can be seen without any special aid as many flowers will have lines on their petals showing the way to the nectar. These will also appear bright and bold when seen under ultraviolet light. The next time you are out in a field of flowers try to imagine how things would be if you could see like a bee.

How do bees carry the pollen back to the hive?

Bees do more than sip nectar each time they visit a flower. They collect pollen and carry it back to the hive to feed the young. Each time a bee leaves the hive to collect pollen, it takes along a bit of honey in its honey stomach. Landing on a flower, the bee scrapes the pollen loose with its legs and mouth. Simultaneously it moistens the pollen with the honey it brought from the hive, making it sticky. Often there is so much pollen the bee becomes dusted with pollen. When the bee flies to the next flower, its legs which are equipped with comb-like hairs, sweep or comb the pollen out of its coat of hair. The accumulated pollen is collected and transferred to a "basket", called the **corbiculum** (kor-bik´u-lum), on the outside of the rear legs. Bit by bit, pollen is collected until these saddle bags are full. They are easy to see. Sit down next to some flowers in your garden or favorite field and wait for a bee to come along. Look for large bright yellow bumps that look like a pair of saddle bags stuck to the bee's hind legs.

How does a bee tell the other bees where the nectar is?

Flying to and from the hive, bees use physical landmarks, their sight and an awareness of the sun to guide them on their journey. It seems that the bees can sense the polarization of the sun's rays, which helps guide them in their navigations. This polarization is evident on sunny and cloudy days and the bees can interpret it even though the sun moves across the sky. They also have a sense of time that not only helps them find their way around but allows them to correctly time when certain flowers will produce the most nectar.

After discovering a patch of flowers, the bee returns to the hive to tell the others. She will dance around turning circles and figure eights while she wiggles her tail. Other bees follow behind, sometimes touching the bee, trying to follow all the twists and turns. Lasting up to 30 seconds the dance takes different forms depending on the location of the food. The dance begins with tight circles, alternating left and right. If the bee makes turns going straight up the comb, the nectar is in the direction of the sun. If it makes turns going straight down, the nectar is away from the sun. If the turns are at a 45 degree angle, that is also where the nectar is in relation to the sun. Besides direction, their dance tells the others just how far away the nectar is. If the food is over about 100 meters (109 yds.) away, they do waggle dances making about nine to ten turns in 15 seconds. If the food is about 500 meters (550 yds.) away, they turn only about six times; 1000 meters (.6 mi.), they turn four or five times; and over 5000 meters (3 mi.), only twice. The greater the distance of the nectar, the more sedate the dance. Keep in mind that all of this takes place in the darkness of the hive. And you thought you had difficulty understanding directions!

How many males, females and queens are in a hive?

Typical colonies will have between 40,000 and 70,000 worker bees (females), about 200 drones (males), and only one queen presiding. This queen may lay up to 2,000 eggs a day when she and the hive are mature. In her lifetime of one to five years, the queen can produce two million eggs! When the hive becomes a certain size, some workers will build a few queen cells and feed and care for new, young queens, one of which will either take over the old hive or fly off with many of the workers to start her own hive.

How is it determined which bees will become the queens, the workers and the drones?

It is all decided at the egg and larvae stages of development. The eggs that are fertilized become female worker bees. The eggs that are not fertilized become drones. The eggs hatch into larvae and the queen is determined by which larvae are fed a special food, called **royal jelly**. Those that are selected to receive the royal jelly are also put in special chambers to develop. In the early summer, just before the new queens hatch, the old one flies away, taking many of the bees with her. The new queen then hatches, mates with several drones and returns to the hive. There it will sting to death any rival queens. In late summer the drones also meet with a similar fate. The workers drive them out, bite them and sting them and let them starve.

In the hive, how is it determined which bees do what work?

This is really determined by sex and age. A worker recently hatched will spend her first days keeping things neat and tidy, cleaning the combs. Later, after the pharyngeal gland in the head develops, the bee begins to feed the larvae with the secretions of this gland and later with pollen and honey. When about ten days old, it will fly out of the hive for the first time. The pharyngeal gland shrinks in size and the wax glands on the abdomen begin to function. The worker bee then becomes a construction worker, building the combs and carrying away refuse. When about 20 days old, it begins guard duty at the entrance of the hive. A worker then spends much of its time gathering pollen and nectar. After laboring for a month and a few days, the bee dies.

How do grasshoppers jump?

If you have ever tried to catch a grasshopper, you know how far these little "bugs" can jump. Insects have evolved many different ways to obtain food and to avoid becoming food. The adaptation of the grasshoppers has been to combine flying with the incredible ability to jump. Like all insects, grasshoppers have six legs. The front two pairs are small and used mainly for walking.

The hind pair of legs is nearly three times longer. These legs are the jumping legs. Several aspects of these super legs allow grasshoppers to jump. Starting with the bottom of the leg, it is lined with sharp spurs that dig in for traction when jumping. Working up, the knee joint is backwards compared to our own. Strong muscles are attached at this joint along with a special protective device to prevent the joint from overextending during maximum exertion. The upper leg, called a femur, is up to four times as large as the femur in the front two pairs of legs. These thicker legs are filled with strong extensor muscles and provide the power to jump. Combine all of these special features and you have the powerful legs of the jumping grasshopper.

How and why do crickets chirp?

Male crickets are usually responsible for the night-time music they produce by rubbing together special a special section at the base of each fore wing called a **stridulating** (strij´e-lat-ing) **organ**. A rough file is drawn across an associated scraper to produce its chirping. The song is amplified by a portion of the wing that is stretched like a drum called a **tympanate** (tim´puh-nate). Crickets also have a resonating cavity that can be enlarged during chirping to sound louder or quieter. The song produced is so specialized that many species are identified by their characteristic pitches and chirp speeds. Their music serves many functions—establishing territory, attracting a mate or warning an enemy. Cricket songs are much higher pitched than those of grasshoppers, which tend to be more machine or mechanical sounding. Some songs are so high pitched that they are beyond the range of human hearing, but the crickets can hear them. Crickets have large, flat, round hearing organs called a **tympana** (tim´pan-a), located in the middle of the front legs. Not only do crickets hear with their legs, they have powerful hind legs that are nearly as strong as those of the grasshopper. Crickets are fun to track down by sound. Approach slowly until the wary cricket stops chirping. Sit still and try to imitate the song of the cricket with your own high pitched whistle. This should get the cricket to sing again and then you can move in for a closer look.

Why do fireflies glow?

The firefly's glow is produced when a substance called luciferin is oxidized by the enzyme luciferase. This takes place in the firefly's abdomen when the firefly breathes in oxygen through its abdominal trachea. Light is the by-product of this chemical reaction. The duration of the flashes depends on how long the luciferin takes to oxidize. The "fire" which we notice, is really a cool fire because it has none of the infrared wavelengths in it. These beautiful insects use the light to attract a mate. They are one of the few insects that attract their mates using sight rather than smell. The firefly is neither a true bug nor a fly but a beetle.

How do we know so much about the details of insect behavior?

The research that it takes to discover these insect behavior is fascinating if not a bit tedious. For example, very patient research scientists record the sounds that insects make and play the recording back to them. They conclude from their lack of an agitated reaction that the insects cannot hear in the usual sense. Those who make a career out of the study of insects are called **entomologists** (en-ta-mal´o-jist)—a name that may make some wonder! Studying "bugs" may sound fun and easy, but it's truly a complex and vital science. It is complex because there are so many insects to study and many have very complicated life cycles. It's a vital science because of the role insects play in our lives, both positive and negative. Entomologists, with their knowledge of insects and insect habits, can be very important in trying to control the devastating damage insects can do to crops and the role they play in transmitting diseases.

How can I use the Bug Smart species section?

You'll be able to observe many of these small critters by turning over a log, looking closely at the surface of a pond or just bending down to examine the grass. In the shade of the forest on a hot summer's day, they'll probably find you! Some simple tools will help you to get close to this miniature world. A magnifying glass is great for looking at earthworms, centipedes and other critters you'll uncover under a decaying log. A sweep net made out of a pillow case sewed or pinned onto a round wire attached to a broom handle is great for capturing flying insects that are resting or hovering around plants. Just gently swing the net on and above the plants and you will have spiders, caterpillars, grasshoppers and others to look at. A bug box, a plexiglass square with one side as a magnifying lens, is a great gadget to see one specimen up close. These are inexpensive tools available at a nature store. If you are going to be near a pond, a white margarine tub will be handy. Dip it into the water and again use your bug box or magnifying glass to see what you caught. Also, a gallon jar makes a good aquarium but don't put too many things into one jar and keep it in the shade.

With over a million named insects and a myriad of spiders and other small creatures, you may not find the exact creature identified in the species section but you should be able to find out what type of critter it is and learn something about it. Look at its general shape and count its legs (six for insects, eight for spiders) and count its wings (two for flies and four for dragonflies).

Check out the size and shape of antennae. Compare your observations with those described on the following pages. Release any captured bugs after your study. Be careful not to harm their delicate wings or legs and always release them in the general area they were caught so they can return to established homes and feeding sites.

Guide to Identifying Species in Bug Smart

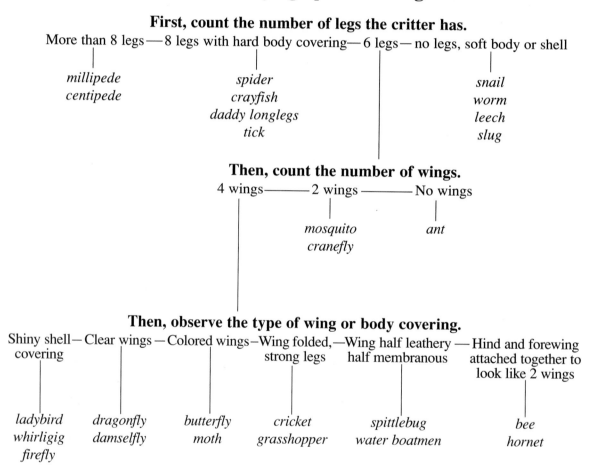

First, count the number of legs the critter has.

More than 8 legs — 8 legs with hard body covering — 6 legs — no legs, soft body or shell

millipede
centipede

spider
crayfish
daddy longlegs
tick

snail
worm
leech
slug

Then, count the number of wings.

4 wings ———— 2 wings ———— No wings

mosquito
cranefly

ant

Then, observe the type of wing or body covering.

Shiny shell — Clear wings — Colored wings — Wing folded, — Wing half leathery — Hind and forewing
covering   strong legs   half membranous   attached together to
                                                       look like 2 wings

ladybird
whirligig
firefly

dragonfly
damselfly

butterfly
moth

cricket
grasshopper

spittlebug
water boatmen

bee
hornet

DRAGONFLIES

Black-winged damselfly   *Calopteryx maculata 1¼- 1¾" (3-5 cm)*

Often confused with dragonflies, damselflies have bodies which are much thinner and slightly smaller. To tell them apart, look for the way they hold their wings when at rest. Damselflies fold their wings over their backs, while dragonflies hold them out to the sides. Black-winged damselflies spend their first two years underwater as nymphs, breathing through leaf-like gills on their tails. They emerge late in the spring crawling up a blade of grass or twig to split open their outer shell, called a **casing**. They then emerge as the flying insect you often see. The females, which live only a month in their adult stage, start this process over again when they mate and then lay eggs on plants just below the surface of the water. The beautifully iridescent male and the brown female with white dots on her wing tips can be found along small and shady streams. These flying predators catch other flying insects in mid-air and return to resting spots to dine. Damselflies seen flying attached together are mating.

Green darner   *Anax junius 2½- 4" (6-10 cm)*

The green darner is one of the largest of all dragonflies with a wing span up to 4" (11 cm). It has a green thorax (where the wings attach). Its abdomen resembles a darning needle (another common name) because of its long, thin pointed body. It searches with its unproportionately huge eyes for flying insects to eat. As in all dragonfly species and many other insects, it has compound eyes and all-around vision so they can find their food. Dragonflies are excellent fliers and can reach speeds up to 30 miles per hour (48 km). They use their front legs as little catcher mitts to funnel insects into their mouths. Of all winged insects, only the dragonflies do not beat their wings up and down at the same time. While the front wings move up, the hind wings move down. As underwater larvae, they swim along by shooting water out of their bodies. All dragonflies overwinte in this stage. Relatives of the damselfly, this group of insects from the order Odonata, first appears in the fossil record over 300 million years ago. This means they have been around since before the dinosaurs. The only difference between now and then is that they were 2' (.6 m) long back then!

Twelve-spot skimmer · · · · · · · · · *Libellula pulchella 1½- 2½" (4-6 cm)*

The twelve-spot skimmer, like other skimmers, is a type of dragonfly. Dragonflies are also known as mosquito hawks. They are some of the most colorful and helpful insects in the world. Adult twelve-spot skimmers have three spots on each of their four independent wings for a total of twelve spots, giving it the common name. You can tell the difference between males and females by the background color of their wings—white for males and clear for females. At rest dragonflies hold their wings flat and outstretched, with a wingspan of 2". They can be found flying in tandem while mating and they remain locked together for hours. Look for these flying acrobats near mid-day when they are most actively flying and swooping up to 30 miles per hour (48 km) over marshes and moist meadows, catching insects in mid air. They are one of the few insects that can fly forwards, backwards and hover. Its immature stage is a nymph, which is a six-legged and wingless form that stays underwater eating small insects. It can take up to three years to mature and crawl out of the water to split its skin and emerge as a winged adult. Look for these "shells" attached to rocks and plants near rivers and lakes.

GRASSHOPPERS AND CRICKETS

American grasshopper · · · · · *Schistocerca americana 1⅝-2¼" (4-6 cm)*

You've probably been able to recognize a grasshopper since before you walked into kindergarten, but did you know that they hear with their legs? They have "thigh drums" instead of "ear drums." They need them because, unlike most insects which are deaf, they do rely on sound for communication. Grasshoppers eat plants exclusively and in large numbers they can devastate a field. This is especially damaging when some types of grasshoppers form large swarms and migrate, at which time they are referred to as locusts. All varieties of grasshoppers can be divided into two groups based on the length of their antennae. Grasshoppers with short antennae, called **short horned** because their antennae are shorter than the length of their bodies, are one group and make sounds by rubbing their hind leg on a wing. They tend to fly while making a crackling sound. Grasshoppers with long antennae, called **long horned** because their antennae are longer than their bodies, are another group. They sing or call by rubbing two wings together. All grasshoppers serve as an important part of the food chain. They are a preferred food source for many species of birds, skunks, mice and other small mammals. You don't see grasshoppers in winter because the adults lay eggs and die and the eggs overwinter underground.

Field cricket	*Gryllus pennsylvanicus ¾-1" (2-3 cm)*

Night in the warmer months just wouldn't be the same without the often musical sound that emanates from this nocturnal insect. Catching a cricket and giving it a good temporary home is a great way for you to see how this insect fiddler makes that familiar sound. It's produced by rubbing their fore wings together. (See How and Why Do Crickets Chirp?) Field crickets eat mostly plants, although they have been known to eat other insects, even other crickets. Cotton clothing is also attractive to them if they get into homes. They overwinter as eggs laid in the ground by the female in the fall.

TRUE BUGS

Spittlebug / froghopper	*Philaenus spumarius ⅜" (1 cm)*

In the spring and summer, throughout the eastern U.S., you might notice something that looks like someone has rudely spit on the stems of plants. This gross looking "spit" is actually the very safe and secure home of the larval stage of the spittle bug and gives this insect its common name. Wipe away the white foam to see one or two tiny green insects. It makes this wet home by attaching itself face down on the stem of a plant and piercing the host plant with a syringe-like mouth, sucking out the plant's liquid. Adding a bit of air, the resulting foamy spittle

91

comes out of the opposite end of the spittle bug and naturally flows down and encases the insect. As a tiny larva, it then hides itself among the bubbly, sticky juices. Inside it slowly grows, until it emerges as an adult. This method of protection is so successful that it has no known natural predators during this larval stage. The adults are jumping insects that hop from plant to plant like frogs, which is how it got its other common name, froghopper. The adults mate and lay egg masses of 1–30 in the fall. They do this on over 400 species of plants. The hardy eggs make it through the winter in this stage.

Water boatmen   *Corixa spp. ¼ - ½" (.6-1 cm)*

One of the most common water insects anywhere in North America, the water boatmen looks and acts just like its name sake. Shaped and proportioned like a row boat, these gray to brown true bugs have thin white to yellow markings across their backs. Their "oars" are their middle and hind legs. Watch for them rowing across the surface of your local pond. Front legs are used to scoop up microscopic plants, called algae, as they move across and under the water. Very capable flyers, water boatmen will visit bird baths to eat the tiny algae that grow in the stagnant water. Otherwise, water boatmen live in ponds, puddles and slow moving streams. You can also catch them at night if you shine a flash light on a white sheet and stand by with a small net. Be sure to show respect for these tiny creatures by letting them go at the end of your observations. Like all insects, water boatmen breathe through small openings in their bodies, called tracheal systems, so when they dive underwater they carry air bubbles as portable air supplies trapped under each wing. They are also covered with air trapping hairs that allow these water loving insects to stay submerged for up to 36 hours. All of this air gives these bugs a shimmering coat that reflects sunlight like a shiny coin. Females glue eggs to underwater plants which hatch in only 7–15 days.

BEETLES

Firefly   *Photinus pennsylvanicus ¼ - ¾" (1-2 cm)*

Fireflies or lightning bugs are not really "flies" or "bugs" so their names are misleading. They are soft-bodied beetles that are known for the conspicuous way they light up the night with their flashes of light. Fireflies are one of the few insects in North America that can signal with a light. Both males and females flash but the male's flash is brighter and more frequent. These flashes act as a signal for mating. Around sunset on a warm July or August evening, the males fly up to 15' (4.5 m) high sending out a pattern of flashes to stationary females—different species of fireflies send out different patterns. The "lightning" is considered a cold light and is produced by a chemical reaction that happens when oxygen is combined with a chemical called 'luciferin' in their abdomen. The light that is produced is nearly 100 percent efficient. They overwinter as larvae buried in the soil and eat other insects during their life cycle. These larvae also glow and are often called glow worms. To get a firefly to land on your hand for closer examination, cover a flashlight letting only a small beam of light through. Position your flashlight about two feet above the ground and flash the light in the same pattern as you see the firefly flashing. If you turn the light off and stand still, the firefly might land on your hand. It's very helpful to have another light in your other hand to shine on the firefly as it lands.

Ladybird beetle *Hippodamia convergens* ⅛- ¾" (.3-1 cm)

Also known as ladybugs, these beetles have become well known for the way they eat plant-damaging aphids, scale insects and the eggs and larvae of moths and butterflies. Each individual beetle has an appetite for consuming many insects every day, making them a popular biological control. Its bright red color is a warning to predators that it has toxic blood. There are 350 different species of these beetles, some with yellow, black, orange or bright red undercoats—their spots vary with each species (kind). Some species have two spots while others have 10 and even 15. The number of spots do not indicate how old the beetle is, just what kind it is. They are distributed worldwide and their common name dates back to middle ages when these insects were dedicated to women. Look for large groups of ladybird beetles each autumn swarming on logs, leaves, along beaches and at the bases of trees. They are preparing to overwinter under logs and leaves.

Whirligig beetle — *Gyrinus spp.* ⅛-¾" (.3-2 cm)

Aptly named, this water insect is the only beetle that swims on the surface of ponds and lakes, whirling around as it feeds on small insects. Look for black dots that move about in crazy eights on the surface of the water. One of their most fascinating adaptations is that they have divided eyes, the upper half of their eye is for seeing above the water and the lower half for seeing in the water. They also dive below the surface, much like scuba divers do, carrying their air supply in a bubble with them. The female lays eggs on submerged plants, where the beetle's larvae matures. Look for whirligigs in mid to late summer. Like frogs and toads, adults leave the surface to spend the winter season hibernating on the muddy bottom.

MOTHS AND BUTTERFLIES

Cecropia moth, caterpillar — *Hyalophora cecropia* 4¼-6" (11-15 cm)

These large and beautiful insects are a treasure to find in any of their stages. Like most moths, cecropias fly at night and are often seen at house and street lights. Look for large brown cocoons attached to branches after the leaves have fallen in winter. In summer look for the large stout bodied green caterpillar with yellow and orange horn-like projections lining its back. They feed on a variety of leaves including cherries, maples and willows. Their rather fascinating natural history includes the fact that the beautiful adult does not begin life with any mouth parts. The adult moth emerges from its cocoon only to find a mate and doesn't waste any time eating. To find a mate quickly before they die, the moths use their large sensitive antennae. The female releases a scent, called a pheromone, which the male can pick up from as far away as three miles!!

BUG SMART

Isabella moth, woolly bear caterpillar   *Isia isabella 1¾- 2" (4-5 cm)*

This common moth is part of a family of some 200 species. Look for this common fuzzy caterpillar (the isabella moth in its larvae stage) crawling across sidewalks and trails each autumn. The woolly bear will spend the winter as a caterpillar and metamorphose into a moth in spring. Before it hibernates under dead leaves and logs, the woolly bear feeds on green plants like plantain. In spring the caterpillar feeds lightly before it spins a chocolate brown cocoon of silk. It emerges in about 2 weeks from the cocoon as the adult moth and flies off to start the life cycle again. The size of the rust and black bands of the woolly bear have been said to predict the coming winter, but they have no way of predicting the weather. The size of the bands are a better reflection of the bands of its parents.

Common sulphur butterfly   *Colias philodice 1⅛-2" (3-5 cm)*

Sulphurs, some or our most common and familiar butterflies, have either white, yellow or orange wings. Each wing is rounded and has simple patterns of black spots or bands. These small butterflies can be seen visiting flowers or congregating at mud puddles where they gently sip moisture. Notice the bulbous ends to their antennae. Their alter-ego, the small green caterpillars, feed on plants like clover found in open fields. They overwinter as a partly-grown larva (caterpillar) or pupa (in a casing called a chrysalis) and emerge in the spring ready to mate and start the cycle over again. The male has special scales on its wings that it rubs together, releasing a chemical, a pheromone, that attracts females. If she is interested, she responds by fluttering her wings. To witness this courtship ritual, look for them in open areas around the lunch hour when they are most active. When the female is not interested, you'll see two sulphurs spiraling up into the air. They will sometimes ascend 60' (18 m) up into the air before the male gives up.

Monarch butterfly
Danaus plexippus 3½ - 4" (9-10 cm)

This beautiful member of the milkweed butterfly family (Danaidae) is one of the few true migrating insects. Each year it migrates from all over North America to overwinter in Mexico and southern California. The monarch over-winters by hanging from the branches of trees by the hundreds of thousands. When spring arrives, the monarchs head north, mating and laying eggs as they move along. Look for tiny cream colored domed shaped eggs on the undersides of milkweed leaves. In four days when the caterpillar hatches, it begins to eat the milkweed leaves which contain toxic liquid. It is unharmed by the toxic milk and uses this substance as a defense against predators. Over the next 10 days the larva molts 4 times and then changes into the chrysalis, a stage called **pupa** (pew´pa). The chrysalis is a beautiful light green shell with a gold trim attached to a branch or blade of grass. In about 12 days a very different, very wet adult monarch emerges. Three or four generations later, at the end of the summer, the young monarchs, without any guidance, make the 2000 mile (3,218 km) trip to Mexico and the cycle starts over again. As forests in Mexico are cut to raise cattle, monarch populations are threatened.

Mourning cloak butterfly
Nymphalis antiopa 2½ - 3½" (6-9 cm)

A velvety purplish to blackish butterfly with a distinctive white to yellow band on the outer edge of each wing, this familiar butterfly got its name from its close resemblance to a dark funeral shawl worn by widows. You'll see this butterfly early each spring before most other insects, because it overwinters as an adult. It chooses holes in trees or behind loose bark for hibernation. Since it spends the winter as a winged adult, its scalloped-edged wings often appear ragged when it emerges in the spring. These butterflies like to feed on sap from trees or rotting fruit. Females lay their eggs in masses around the twigs of elm, willow and poplar trees. Look for the caterpillars on these leaves in the spring. Like many other butterflies, it is considered to be a tasty meal for birds.

TRUE FLIES

Bluebottle fly — *Calliphora vomitoria ½" (1 cm)*

The bluebottle fly is a large, hairy fly with red eyes and black sides. It is about twice the size of the flies commonly seen in your home each autumn. If they do get in your house, they buzz loudly while looking for a way out. Flies form the group of insects called Diptera, which means two-winged. They actually had four wings at one time in ancient history, but the hind two wings, called **halteres** (hal-ters´), are so small that they don't function in flight. These knob-like structures act to balance the fly in flight. If we were flies, we'd put our feet in our dinner plates in order to taste our food. When the adult fly lands on sugar particles, for example, the fly first spits out a type of liquid that dissolves the sugar. This lets the fly taste with the sensors in its feet. If it's a liquid meal, it lowers its straw-like mouth part, the **proboscis** (pro-bos´is), and sucks. Another lovely trait of the bluebottle fly is that it lays its eggs on dead animals, garbage and sewage. The larvae that hatch from these eggs serve a beneficial role by eating the carcass or garbage and thereby recycling it. Bluebottle flies and other insects also contribute to the process of turning discarded plants and food into compost. Some adult flies overwinter in the cracks and crevasses of trees and buildings. This is why you see flies during minor warm-ups in early spring.

Crane fly — *Tipula spp. 1½- 2¼" (4-6 cm)*

With a wingspan up to 3" inches and very long legs, these flies are often mistaken for being giant, male mosquitoes. Often these flies are seen in the evening resting near a house light where they slowly pump their entire body up and down with long flexible legs. Like all true flies, they have only one pair of wings. Their miniature hind wings are reduced to small knobs, called halteres, which vibrate rapidly in a figure-eight pattern and act as balancing organs while they are in flight. As immature larva, they are **omnivorous** (om-niv´er-us), which means they eat both plant and animal material. At this stage they live on the bottoms of small rivers and streams. You can tell crane flies from mosquitos by how many legs each stands on at rest. Mosquitoes hold two legs up and to the rear while crane flies stand on all six legs.

Mosquito	*Culex pipiens* ⅛-½" *(.3-.6 cm)*

The unsettling sound of a buzzing mosquito in your backyard on a hot summer's evening is not designed to annoy you—it's the female mosquito beating her wings between 300 and 800 times a second. This sound is meant for a male mosquito's eardrum which is located at the base of his antennae. Males can only hear within 12–15" (30 – 38 cm). The sound causes males to pursue the source and clamp onto whatever makes the sound. Copulation occurs in the air with the males riding underneath. This relative of the fly bites rather than stings and only the females of certain species can make one miserable on a hot summer's day—the males stick to plant juices. You can tell male mosquitoes from females by the male's long feather-like antennae. The adult female mosquito has a needle-like mouth, called the proboscis, which can prick the skin of mammals and birds (all of us included) and suck up a meal of blood. She uses the protein in the blood to help nourish her eggs for reproduction. Mosquitoes lay eggs in shallow water, which is why some species are more numerous in rainy years than in dry years. Their eggs stick together in masses and are like rafts floating on the surface of the water. They are tan in color. They hatch into tiny larvae which cling to the underside of the water surface and breath air from tubes that are attached to the ends of their bodies. They eat tiny plants and are a favored food of ducks. Larval mosquitoes continue to molt (grow and shed skin) until they turn into a pupa. It is the pupa that hatches into the adult. Many species of ducks and other animals depend on mosquitoes and their larvae for food. Programs to control the mosquito population by poisons affect the food supply of these species.

ANTS AND BEES

Little black ant	*Monomorium minimum* ⅛" *(.3 cm)*
Black carpenter ant	*Camponotus pennsylvanicus* ⅛-½" *(.3-.6 cm)*

Ants come in one of three colors: black, brown or red. They are all small powerhouses that prey on other insects for the majority of their diet, but they will drink nectar from flowers and eat other sweet things. There are nearly 2,500 different kinds of ants found just about everywhere on earth except near the North and the South Pole. They are all social insects, meaning that each member of the colony has a specific assignment. Most ants have two special eyes. Each is made up of from 6 – 1,000 individual eyes and is called a compound eye. The ants overwinter in a colony that consists of a queen and her worker ants, which are sterile females, and a few male ants. The only egg laying is done by the queen each spring. The eggs hatch into larvae and then pupate into adults. Although ants are not known to have wings, some ants do develop into winged males and females which fly about and mate, starting new colonies. Some of the worker ants live to be six years old with queens living as long as 15 years. Look for small or large mounds of soil which were built with the excavated soil from the colony. Most ants will attack if disturbed and will bite, so be cautious around the large ant hills. The main purpose of their nests is to raise their young, store food and survive winters.

Bald-faced hornet   *Vespula maculata ½ - ¾" (1-2 cm)*

This insect lives in a large house, up to 2' (.6 m) in diameter. It contains hundreds or sometimes thousands of individuals. These nests start out with a single, fertilized queen who builds a small, paper nest to raise the first group of workers. As more workers are hatched, the nest is expanded until, at the end of the summer, a large gray nest is complete. The outer shell is made from a papery material and protects hexagonal cells inside, which is where the hornets lay their eggs. The hornet chews up wood pulp, mixes in saliva and then uses its antennae as a measuring stick to see if the hexagonal shape is correct. No matter how large the nest becomes, they only occupy it for one year. As winter arrives, all of the hornets die except for the fertilized queen. The queens spend the winter under loose tree bark or underground. Left behind is a remarkably large paper-like nest that suddenly becomes visible when the leaves fall off the trees. These hornets feed on other insects, dead flesh, nectar and rotting fruits.

Bumblebee   *Bombus spp. ½" (1 cm)*

Contrary to popular belief most bee species are solitary, not living in colonies. Honeybees and bumblebees, the fatter and fuzzier versions of honeybees, are the only bees that live in colonies. Wasps, yellow jackets and hornets are in a different group than bees. Both types of bees sting, but the bumblebees can sting repeatedly whereas the honeybees die after they sting once. Bumblebees have long tongues, called a proboscis, that allow them to reach nectar in deeper flowers like snapdragons. They stay underground in loosened soil or in old dens of animals. To start an underground home, the queen builds a wax honeypot and fills it with the nectar she has collected. Pollen is also collected and is left for the new emergent bees who are too weak to fly outside at first. During the summer months, all of the bumblebees that hatch from the queen's eggs are infertile females and function as workers. Large and fuzzy, bumblebees are better insulated against cool mornings than other types of bees, so you'll see them start feeding earlier in the day. With the onset of winter, each fertilized female crawls into her own hibernation chamber in an underground mouse nest or animal burrow.

Honeybee   *Apis mellifer ½-¾" (1-2 cm)*

We owe much to these social and busy insects which can produce up to 500 pounds of honey per hive in one year. There is a division of labor in the bee colony. The queen bee lays eggs, the worker bees (infertile females) clean out the hive, feed the young, make the honey and gather the nectar and the drones (male bees) live only to mate with the queen. Honeybees make wax in their abdomens and have a special honey stomach for the production of this much coveted substance. The phrase "busy as a bee" probably came from the fact that in order to produce one pound (.4 kg.) of honey, about 20,000 trips must be made to nectar-producing flowers. The scouting bees communicate the location of pollen-loaded flowers by performing a bee dance. The angles of their dance correspond to the angles of the sun to the flowers. Honeybees spend the winter as adults feeding on the honey they made during the season in order to survive. Because bees produce so much honey, beekeepers can remove some of it without hurting the colony.

SPIDERS AND TICKS

Crab spider   *Misumena vatia 1½" (4 cm)*

Unlike the orb weavers, the various species of crab spiders do not spin web snares. Instead, the crab spider perches on a flower waiting for an unsuspecting insect to come for the flower's nectar. The crab spider can slowly turn color from white and pink to bright yellow in order to remain camouflaged on its chosen flower. In one quick movement it grabs its dinner. It is called a crab spider because it holds its front legs outstretched and moves sideways like a crab. It hunts with its gripping forelegs and injects an enzyme into its victim which digests the insides of the bug. Later the spider sucks out the contents of its prey. Spiders eat often. A typical spider can increase its weight tenfold in two weeks. Like most spiders, male crabs are much smaller than their female counterparts, and can be identified by their longer legs. The female spider deposits her eggs in a silken sac and attaches the sac to the underside of a leaf. She will stand guard over the eggs until they hatch. Examine the blossoms of the common yarrow and you may see a crab spider eating a fly.

Common garden spider (orb weaver)   *Argiope spp. ½-2" (1-5 cm)*

These large black and yellow spiders are just one of a group of approximately 2,500 species of orb weavers that are found all over the world. Also known as common garden spiders, these orb-weaving spiders are known for their remarkable webs. This group of spiders get their name from the spiral orb web that the females weave. The orb weaver can construct its classic shaped web in about an hour and often decorates it with a "Z" shaped weave that reflects ultraviolet light right in the middle. This fools flying insects into thinking the "Z" is an ultraviolet light reflecting flower. Despite having eight eyes like other spiders, Orb weavers don't see well. They don't need to because with their sensitive feet, they feel the tension of their

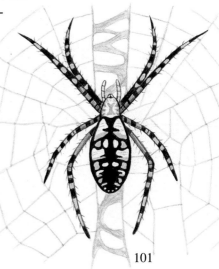

webs and pick up vibrations caused by colliding insects. Orb weavers set up their webs between twigs or long tall grasses and then sit back and wait. If they feel something other than a trapped insect, they drop to the relative safety of the ground. When something like a fly becomes entangled in their web, the orb weaver spider darts out and immediately wrap its prey into a tidy silk package to be fed on or hung up for later consumption. The spider doesn't get caught in its own web because it has an oil-like substance on its feet and it avoids the sticky strands of the web. In the fall orb weaver females lay hundreds of eggs in small packets. Some overwinter this way and others hatch in the fall and overwinter as little spiderlings. All spiders grow by molting or what is called **ecdysis** (ek´di-sis). When it grows, it casts off its tight-fitting outer body cover (exoskeleton) after it forms a new flexible one underneath. The new flexible outer covering will soon harden so the spider has to expand and grow quickly.

Daddy longlegs   *Leiobunum vittatum 1- ½" (4 cm)*

Daddy longlegs look like spiders and are in the spider group called Arachnida, but are not true spiders. There is a whole group of real spiders called daddy long legs but they are not as common. They have several differences. They have a flat oval body similar to a spider, but the cephalothorax is joined to the abdomen giving the appearance of only one body part. A less visible difference is that they have only two eyes instead of the usual eight of spiders. Like spiders, they don't have antennae. However, they use their second pair of legs, which are longer than their other legs, like antennae. If you watch them for awhile, you'll see that they do not spin webs. Their particularly long legs act as sensory organs, helping them to negotiate uneven terrain and to find unsuspecting insects. They are most active at night feeding on other insects, like flies, aphids and leafhoppers. They have odor glands on their bodies that make them distasteful and therefore undesirable to predators. They lay eggs in the fall which hatch into tiny daddy longlegs. Then they molt (shed their covering) and grow in stages, 7 – 8 times in 10-day intervals until they are full-sized adults. In northern states, daddy longlegs don't survive the winter. The female will inject a single egg into the soil where it will wait until spring. In southern states they live up to one year. Because they're more abundant in the fall, they are also called "harvestmen."

BUG SMART

Wolf spider	Lycosa spp. ½-2" (1-5 cm)

With over 2,000 species, wolf spiders are some of our most common spiders. A small spider with eight dark eyes of unequal size, they are gray-brown with a sparse covering of hair. Males are half the size of females. Like the crab spiders, the wolf spiders make no webs. They run along the ground to catch their prey of insects. They have good vision and a highly developed sense of touch and they only hunt at night. The females of some species carry around the egg sacs containing the young on their backs for up to six months. They overwinter in a burrow in the ground.

Deer tick	Ixodes spp. ½" (.3 cm)

Ticks are some of the most patient of all animals. Females are in need of blood to nourish themselves to produce and lay eggs. These creatures crawl out to the end of a blade of grass and wait with their front legs outstretched to grab the first animal that walks by. It is not uncommon for a tick to wait all summer in one place, eating nothing until an appropriate donor happens along. Once it attaches to its host, it begins to fill with a meal of blood. After it feeds, the female tick falls to the ground and lays thousands of eggs in 4 – 10 days. The eggs hatch in a month and the six-legged larvae look for their first blood meal. Soon they molt into eight-legged larvae which also look for a blood meal before they turn into adults. In some species, the male doesn't feed at all and only mates with the female. The deer tick is so small, about the size of the head of a pin, that it is hard to detect until long after it has done its damage. Some of these ticks in some areas carry Lyme disease, a serious arthritis-like ailment, that can be best cured in the beginning stages by large doses of antibiotics. The tick's mouth parts, called palps, are covered with sharp backward facing teeth that make them difficult to remove.

Wood tick
Dermacentor spp. ½" (.6 cm)

These large ticks, about ³⁄₁₆" across (2 – 3 mm) have distinguishing male and female characteristics. Tell the two apart by the male's suspender-like stripes down its back and the female's necklace-like stripe. Only the females go for the blood meal. The males are only looking for females and in some species, may not eat at all. When the female is engorged with blood, she can be as big as a ½" (13 mm) long and looks gray-blue instead of her usual brown tone. Both adults live from three months to as long as three years. The larvae, which have only six legs and are only ¹⁄₄₀" (.6 mm) long, feed on the blood of small animals such as mice. They molt to an eight-legged immature nymph stage and then after feeding, they become adults. This process can take up to two years. Adult ticks seek larger animals and that is why we find them on ourselves after a walk through tall grasses on a summer's day. A quick but thorough tick check prevents them from using you for a blood supply.

"SQUIRMS"

Earthworm
Lumbricus terrestris 2-8" (5-20 cm)

Who hasn't picked up earthworms after a warm summer rain? You use them for fishing or know that they are somehow good to find in a garden. Important recyclers, earth worms are marvelous animals. They actually are critical for our own food supply because they make soil rich by eating fallen leaves and depositing rich organic soil. Their tunnel systems make it easy for water and air to pass through the soil which aides the plants' growth. Earth-worms are sightless nocturnal creatures spending most of their time swallowing earth below the surface and depositing it around their burrows in the form of castings. In loose soil they just push soil aside, but in hard soil they actually ingest it. They are one of the few critters that breathe through their skin. They also don't have any eyes but can sense light with their skins. Tell the front from the back of a worm by the thick band, called a **clitellum** (kle-tel´um). It is found in the front quarter of the

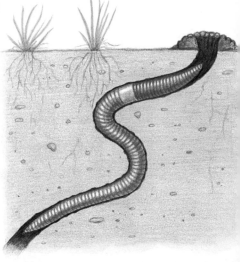

worm and produces mucus to keep the rest of the body moist. Earthworms join at the clitellum when mating. Worms are **hermaphroditic** (her-maf´re-dit-ik), which means that they have both male and female reproductive organs and only need to find another worm in order to exchange cells. An earthworm moves by contracting each segment of its body. Four sets of bristles on each segment, called **setae** (see´tee), help move or anchor the worm within its tunnel. That's why you can't easily pull an earthworm out of its tunnel.

Leech — *Helobdella stagnalis ¼-3" (2-8 cm)*

They are used as bait and even as tools of medicine to stop blood from clotting. Most leeches are simple animals that make a living feeding on the blood of other animals. They do this with a suction cup-like mouth that has small teeth that cut the skin and start the bleeding. Once it's attached and the blood starts to flow, the leech produces an anticoagulant which inhibits the blood from clotting. Most leeches attach to fish and other water animals. Leeches are slow moving animals so you can handle them briefly without worry.

Common tadpole snail — *Physa heterostropha ½-1" (1-3 cm)*

These common snails are found throughout ponds, lakes and streams. They are easy to identify because they have small shells with pointed ends and large flared openings when viewed from underneath. To see this, turn the snail over—the opening should be on your left side. Each shell can range in color from yellow to brown. Even though they live in water, these snails breathe oxygen from the air. They surface and gather one oxygen bubble that they store in a sac-like cavity on the back. They spend their days feeding on small plants like algae. Young snails hatch from their eggs which are laid on cattails and other water plants. Snails' eyes are located on short stalks, which are like their antennae. As adults, they overwinter underwater, buried in mud. Snails are an important food source for fish, raccoons, egrets, Herons, muskrats and more. See if you can't find a few next time you visit a pond.

Slug
Philomycus carolinianus ½-1" (1-3 cm)

Slugs are closely related to snails. In fact, the only difference is that slugs have small hardened bony plates on their backs, called a **mantle**, instead of a full shell for protection. They easily squeeze into small places, hiding under moist leaves and logs to keep from drying out during the day. They emerge at night and feed upon green plants, much to the distaste of many gardeners.

They breathe through an air hole located on their back (looks like a breathing hole of dolphins) and they see and smell with their antennae. They have several antennae, some for sight and others for smell. Night critters, they move about on a large single "foot" that leaves a slime trail. This helps them creep along and negotiate rough and dry terrain. Look for these trails early in the morning while the track is still fresh. Even though each slug has both male and female parts, referred to as hermaphroditic, they still need to find a mate to reproduce. Each slug lays hundreds of eggs which hatch in three weeks.

Centipede
Lithobius spp. 2" (5 cm)

These small flat bodied critters are fast and ferocious hunters. In Latin *centipede* means one hundred legs. Though there are many types of centipedes, none have fewer than 30 legs. In the class of animals called Chilopoda, centipedes have a pair of legs on each body segment. On their first body segment is a pair of jaw-like claws that carry a poison intended to paralyze their insect victims. They are good controllers of insects. Centipedes have a flat body with two legs per segment, whereas millipedes have a round body with four legs per segment.

Millipede
Callipus spp. 1-5" (3-13 cm)

Millipedes are long cylindrical-shaped animals that are closely related to spiders. They have many body sections called segments. Each segment has two pairs or four legs. Though their name means thousand-legged, the common millipede has only 115 pairs of legs, two pairs for each segment. This is about twice the number of legs of the centipede which has one pair for each segment. Look for these amazing creatures under logs and piles of leaves. Millipedes feed mostly on decaying plants, unlike centipedes which are carnivorous. Their tiny eggs are laid in a nest and guarded by their mother. Even though they have more legs than a centipede, they are slower, perhaps because they don't have to "catch" their food—plants. Millipedes grow by adding groups of three or more segments after each of their molts.

Crayfish   *Cambarus bartonii 2-5" (5-13 cm)*

Living in ponds, lakes and streams, crayfish are in the crustacean family and are relatives of the lobster. They have a hard shell covering called an exoskeleton and long jointed legs. Distant relatives of insects, they have two sets of antennae. The long whip-like antennae help the crayfish keep track of what's going on in front and behind as well. The smaller, branched antennae are used to feel objects up close. Both sets of antennae are sensitive to touch and smell. Its pincers help it to defend itself as well as to get food. Crayfish are omnivorous, meaning they eat both animals and plants. They'll scavenge for dead water critters as well as eat algae and other plant material. A very fast swimmer, crayfish swim backwards to get away from predators like raccoons, frogs, turtles, otters, minks and wading birds. Their quick backward get-aways are facilitated by having eyes on top of little stalks, raised above their heads. They can quickly see what's all around them so they won't back into something dangerous. Because the crayfish is a favorite food for so many, it lays hundreds of eggs in the spring. The female attaches the eggs to small projections, called **swimmerets**, on the underside of her abdomen. The young continue to hang on after hatching. To grow it must molt its hard outer shell, which it does by splitting its back and crawling out. A new shell, soft and pliable underneath, hardens and the crayfish continues to grow. Crayfish spend the winter as adults under the water and mud. To find crayfish, look in soft mud along the shores of rivers and lakes. You can often see hollow, chimney-like structures made out of mud which the crayfish leave as they dig their tunnels. These chimneys can be up to a foot high (.3 m) and the tunnels they make can be 2 – 3' (.6 to .9 m) deep. You can tell the males from the females by the male's larger claws and thinner bodies.

Because the illustrations in the species section are enlarged to show detail of the bugs and "squirms", we've included these drawings to show their relational sizes.

Crayfish   *Cecropia moth*   *Earthworm*

Green Darner   *Twelve-spot Skimmer*   *Monarch*   *Mourning Cloak*

Clouded Sulfur   *Grasshopper*   *Cricket*   *Blackwing Damsel*   *Isabella/ Wooly Bear*   *Leech*

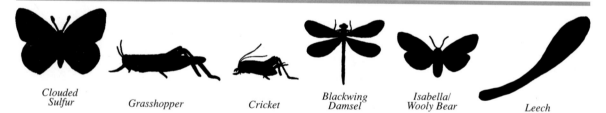

Millipede   *Centipede*   *Orb Weaver*   *Wolf Spider*   *Cranefly*   *Daddy Longlegs*   *Slug*   *Honeybee*   *Bumblebee*

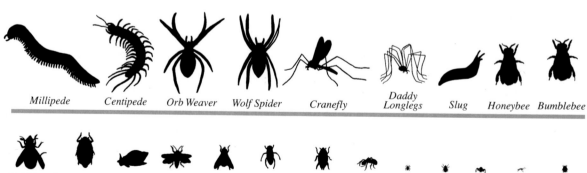

Bald-faced Hornet   *Whirligig*   *Tadpole Snail*   *Firefly*   *Bluebottle Fly*   *Water Boatmen*   *Spittlebug*   *Ants*   *Deer Tick*   *Tick*   *Crab Weaver*   *Mosquito*   *Ladybird*

Critter Smart

With a sharp rat-a-tat, a Downy Woodpecker announces its presence from atop an aspen tree, a well-furred cattail sways in the breeze and an iridescent dragonfly flashes in the sunlight. As a nature enthusiast, you are alert to all such displays. Still, you are most eager to catch a glimpse of a muskrat threading its way through the bulrush; you long to be startled by a woodchuck scurrying for its home. Why do we measure the success of an outdoor excursion by our encounters with mammals? Although we are surrounded by natural wonders, many are subtle and easily overlooked. Some, such as the complex and invisible process of photosynthesis that takes place within leaves, are truly miraculous. Nonetheless, it is the black bear lumbering unexpectedly across the trail ahead that leaves our hearts racing.

Since prehistoric times, people have been fascinated by mammals. We know that critters such as the bison and musk oxen were an integral part of the lives and spiritual practices of early peoples. Ancient cave paintings and etchings of these animals have been found all over the world. Later, people named constellations after the significant mammals of their era. For example, Ursa Major is the bear constellation.

When we talk about mammals, we are literally talking about ourselves and our relatives. All mammals have hair covering part or all of their bodies, nurse their young and are warm-blooded, meaning they have consistent body temperatures. We share the planet with about 4,000 other species of animals in every habitat imaginable. About 400 species live in North America.

The fact that both mountain lions and bats are mammals reflects the diversity of this class of creatures known as **Mammalia**. Mammals have evolved remarkable adaptations to meet the challenges of getting food, finding shelter and defending themselves. Some mammals such as deer, have adapted to eating only vegetation. These are called **herbivores** (hur´be-vorz). Others, such as the wolf or bobcat, eat only other animals and are called **carnivores** (kar´ne-vorz). Bats have yet another type of diet consisting solely of insects; they are called **insectivores** (in-sek´te-vorz). Animals such as bears eat plants and animals and insects and are called **omnivores** (om´ne-vorz). This variety in the diet of mammals have made them very adaptable and have contributed to their success. Mammals are diverse and unique in other ways too. Bats have a sophisticated sonar system for capturing tiny insects in complete darkness. Beavers are famous for their construction skills. The defense mechanism employed by skunks is legendary and has undoubtedly played a role in its survival.

Scientists simplify matters by classifying mammals into more manageable groups called orders. Humans are primates and are therefore most closely related to other primates, the order of monkeys and their relatives. Rodents include the whole range of mammals from mice to muskrats, with jaws designed for gnawing plants. Other orders include lagomorpha, which contains all of the rabbits and hares, and carnivora, which includes foxes, wolves, bears, raccoons, weasels and cats.

As diverse as mammals are, there aren't nearly as many species of them as there are of other animals. Even so, scientists have thoroughly studied only about one percent of them. For that reason, their more intricate behaviors often remain a mystery. Those who study mammals are called mammalogists, and the science itself is called **mammalogy**. Our knowledge of mammals, their numbers and behaviors, is of significance, because so many are threatened by habitat destruction, and what threatens one eventually threatens all. On-going research is being conducted to help us understand more about mammals.

Although small mammals existed during the last part of the dinosaur era, they didn't become dominant until about 63 million years ago. No one knows for certain why dinosaurs died out, but many experts believe that, for some reason, the earth's climate changed suddenly and drastically. Because mammals were more agile and able to withstand great changes in temperatures, thanks in part to their fur and their ability to regulate their body temperatures, they may have been able to thrive in a climate that eliminated the less adaptive giant reptiles.

After the demise of the dinosaurs, mammals took over the dinosaurs' place in the natural order and eventually became the dominant animal species on earth. From whales in the oceans and squirrels in the trees, to moles underground and bats in the air, mammals occupy every niche, every life-supporting place.

An individual mammal tends to stay within a given area or range throughout its life. It roams this home range thoroughly, and knows its hiding places and food sources well. The size of a home range depends on the type of mammal. Larger mammals tend to have larger ranges. Typically, mammals that need large, wild ranges, such as the cougar, are most threatened. Mammals that exist on smaller parcels of land are not as severely disturbed by human activity. Indeed, some of them are thriving. Deer, for instance, are doing so well that their increasing numbers create problems in some areas. With their voracious appetites, they sometimes strip all available vegetation.

Such damage lowers the quality of the land on which they roam. Even so, we thrill at the sight of a deer grazing at dusk. More often, however, when we seek out mammals, they elude us. We have to be satisfied with finding their homes, or identifying their tracks, **scat** (droppings), and other signs. As you become more familiar with these signs, you'll know which critter's territory you've entered.

Is there a difference between the words animal and mammal?

Yes! When we hear the word *animal*, we think of lions, deer and other big mammals. But actually, the term animal is much broader. Insects, birds, fish and other creatures are also animals. *Mammals* are a type of animal with backbones and hair or fur; they also nurse their young. They are warm blooded, maintaining a constant, warm body temperature by trapping their body heat in layers of fat or hair or both.

Whose house is this?

There is nothing like a deep dark hole in the ground or in a tree to pique the nature-lover's curiosity. Here are some factors to consider in determining who the occupant might be. The specific habitat in which you find the home is the most telling clue. For example, gophers prefer open fields, while wood-chucks select wooded areas for their building sites.

Consider also how the hole was made. Some critters are messy diggers, while others carefully remove any evidence of their digging. Chipmunks are neat, and you won't find piles of soil outside their holes. Gophers leave large mounds at the entrances to their tunnels. Also, their tunnels are too deep to be seen from above ground. In contrast, moles create long shallow tunnels that leave a rumpled track just below the earth's surface. The diameter of the hole is also significant. Most animals make an opening that is tailored to their own size. A snug fit keeps larger predators out.

Identifying a hole's inhabitant becomes confusing when one mammal takes over the home of another. Foxes are known to dig out woodchuck homes to make their own enlarged dens. The presence of fox tracks and scat around the entrance are good evidence of this occurrence. Or, let your nose tell you if a fox is nearby; foxes have a distinctive, musky odor, easily confused with skunks. The difference is that foxes leave a trail of scent to mark their recent presence, while skunks spray only in defense situations.

How do mammals navigate in the dark?

If we tried to run through the woods at night, we would most likely be full of bumps and bruises. But **nocturnal** mammals, those active at night, navigate with ease. That's because they have highly evolved adaptations.

Often their eyes have many more of the light-gathering receptors called rods. They also have larger pupils to let in as much light as possible. Starlight, moonlight or the low glow of a far away city provides sufficient light for these mammals to see on their evening prowls. Most mammals have night vision that is at least twice as acute as that of humans. While we are lost in blackness on a moonless night, nocturnal mammals can see as well as if there were a full moon.

In addition to utilizing their highly evolved night vision, nocturnal mammals often simply know from memory where they are going. It's critical to their survival to know their territories intimately. Bats, for example, have the passageways of caves memorized, which helps them navigate in complete darkness.

Bats have developed another unique means of maneuvering at night. They send high-pitched clicking sounds into the darkness ahead of them. The time it takes for the sound to return as an echo tells them how far away an object is, so they can avoid collisions. This navigational tool, called **echolocation**, was used as a model by scientists in the development of sonar devices for ships.

A nocturnal mammal's sense of smell also aids its night maneuvers. An animal follows pathways it has previously marked with scents. The scents are made in special glands and excreted with urine. The whitetail deer is one of many mammals to utilize this technique.

The ability of mammals to negotiate in darkness may seem mysterious to humans, even though our earliest ancestors probably moved under cover of darkness in a similar fashion. Most likely they were tree-dwelling animals who jumped from branch to branch in the dark. However, as human beings evolved, they became adapted to an exclusively **diurnal** (die-ur´nl), or daylight existence. Not so for our fellow mammals. Rarely are they strictly nocturnal or diurnal. Rather, most mammals are active during the hours of dawn and dusk; they are **crepuscular** (kri-pus´kye-ler).

> **❝If you talk to animals they will talk with you and you will know each other. If you do not talk to them you will not know them, and what you do not know you will fear. What one fears one destroys.❞**
>
> CHIEF DAN GEORGE
> TEL-LAL-WAH
> COAST SALISH

Why do animals' eyes shine at night?

If you have ever caught a deer in your headlights while night driving, you've seen a deer's eyes shine or appear to glow with the reflected light. While there can rarely be too little light for nocturnal mammals, there can be too much. Nocturnal mammals have larger retinas than we do. This expanded retina captures more light and allows better vision at night. A thin membrane at the back of the retina, called the **tapetum** (te-pe´tum), acts like a mirror and reflects light back through the retina toward the light source. Because the deer's nocturnally oriented eyes contain only the rods designed for black and white vision, they are limited to perceiving the world in shades of gray. Thus, when confronted by bright lights, deer are momentarily blinded. Naturally, they stop in their tracks, appearing to be paralyzed. The intensity of the light floods their eyes and temporarily overwhelms their vision. It's similar, no doubt, to the way we respond when a camera flash bulb goes off directly in our faces.

Why are some mammals active at night?

In the complex world of nature, each animal fits into a specific niche. Some animals are small, quick and active only during the day; others are the opposite. It's all a matter of food. All animals need to eat, and most spend the majority of their waking hours either eating or hunting for food. Competition for food forces different animals to hunt at different times and places. They have adapted to hunt best at one of three times: night, day, or the in-between hours of dawn and dusk. Nocturnal mammals have claimed the niche of night when much of the competition is asleep. On the other hand, hunting brings animals out of hiding places, putting them at risk of being stalked by other animals. Adaptation to darkness provides the effective protection of cover.

How do mammals survive harsh winters?

Mammals have evolved a variety of adaptations for surviving the harsh conditions of winter. Food is scarce during the winter months, so one way to survive is to require less. Many animals reduce their need for food by slowing their body's functions. They lower their breathing rate, body temperature and heart rate, thereby conserving energy. This allows them to live off food and water stored in their body fat. Different species do this at different rates. The deepest sleepers are the true **hibernators**. They stay in their sleep-like state all winter. The woodchuck, for example, lowers its body temperature to between 38 and 57° F (3 and 14° C). It slows its respiration to one breath in six minutes. Other mammals, such as raccoons and skunks, go in and out of what might be called a temporary hibernation. When the weather becomes colder, they become inactive, conserving their body fat. As it warms up, they become more active again.

Critters that remain active throughout the winter employ a variety of strategies for survival. They grow thicker coats, some of which can turn white for extra camouflage. Their guard hairs are hollow which aids in insulation by trapping warmth next to their bodies. In addition to storing fat in their bodies, some mammals store food in caches in the ground or in trees. Often they change their diets to foods that are more available in winter. For instance, rabbits, which consume green leafy plants during summer, readily turn to a diet of bark and branches, supplemented by a certain type of their own droppings. This unusual habit is called **coprophagous** (ko-prof´e-ges).

Only large mammals are able to withstand extreme cold. Smaller mammals, such as shrews, voles and mice, have such small body masses relative to their body surface that their metabolism cannot maintain warmth. Instead of hibernating, they snuggle under snow, where the temperature rarely drops below 15° F (-9° C). The lack of this protective blanket during cold, snowless winters takes a great toll on their populations.

Why do some mammals change the color of their coat for winter?

Some mammals exchange their summer fur for a winter coat of white, which camouflages them against the white background of snow and ice. Camouflage is an advantage in two ways: It helps hide an animal from predators, and it also disguises them as they sneak up on their own prey. The cue for them to change their color is triggered by a combination of shortened periods of daylight and an internal clock. This autumnal change sends a signal to the animal's brain to stop producing pigment, called **melanin**. As the animal's hairs are replaced with new ones, which is a constant process, the new hairs lack the pigment and the coat becomes white. The lengthening of the day in the spring signals the mammal's brain to resume the production of melanin, and the new hairs which contain color replace those without.

How do water-loving mammals avoid getting cold?

Water-loving mammals are covered with two types of fur: short underfur and longer guard hairs. This thick, double layer of hair is an effective insulator. These mammals also have special oil glands that waterproof their fur, so cold water never reaches their skin. With this combined protection, water-loving mammals are well adapted to their cold and wet environment.

Beavers are included in this category. During winter, they swim under water and obtain oxygen from air holes in the ice, as well as from air trapped in pockets between the ice and water. In addition to storing body fat as an energy reserve, beavers store food or tree limbs which often are stuck underwater in the mud, next to their lodges. This provides an easily accessible meal for these water-dwelling creatures.

Do mammals sleep for long periods as humans do?

No. Research has shown that most mammals sleep in a series of short spells. Like the typical house cat, most mammals take "cat naps." Sleeping for a prolonged time in one spot would make an animal vulnerable to predators. Also, mammals need to wake and eat often in order to maintain a steady rate of metabolism. For these reasons, sleep cycles of frequent short naps increase a mammal's chances for survival.

How do mammals defend themselves?

Different mammals use different key strategies to defend themselves. Fleeing a dangerous situation is a successful strategy for many prey species, such as deer. Rabbits sometimes run, but they often choose the opposite tactic; they freeze. By sitting motionless, they blend in with the background and avoid detection. Skunks spray their unfortunate victims with an extremely offensive scent from their musk glands. Chipmunks and woodchucks escape into the safety of their holes. Climbing into the refuge of high branches works well for tree squirrels.

66What is man without the beast? If all the beasts are gone, man would die from a great loneliness of spirit, for whatever happens to the beast soon happens to man. All things are connected.**99**

CHIEF SEATTLE

Other strategies are further examples of how animals would rather avoid a fight than have one. Some mammals, including raccoons, fluff up their fur to appear larger and more menacing to scare off their opponents. Both raccoons and foxes will turn sideways to appear wider. Other animals scream or make other threatening noises. Raccoons hiss, and rabbits shriek, while chipmunks chatter to frighten an attacker. If these tactics don't scare away a predator, they may confuse them long enough for an escape.

How close together do mammals live?

Every critter lives within a limited area, called a home range or territory. Within its home range, it finds the essentials of life: food, water and shelter. When too many of the same species try to live within that range, their chance of survival decreases. They are all competing for limited resources.

For that reason, many mammals go to great lengths to mark and defend their territories. For example, when humans raise orphan raccoons and release them, they often find later that their charges have been killed. The dominant male raccoon in the area kills them, as he would kill any competing raccoon in defense of his territory.

Territory size usually corresponds to the size of the mammal. The larger the mammal, the larger the territory. The amount of food available also affects the size of a home range. Abundant food will enable an animal to remain in a smaller area. The reproductive cycle affects territory size, as well. In search of a mate, mammals roam greater areas, often ranging beyond the normal boundaries of their territory. During the period of raising their young, mammals become increasingly protective of their more densely populated home range.

Some species, such as the gray squirrel, overlap their home ranges. In contrast, foxes don't overlap much, preferring to establish consistently spaced territories. Together, a number of wolves occupy an area in packs. Because bears do not spend their lives in social groupings, they require large individual ranges. All these factors affect the number of mammals in a given area.

The following list indicates the size of an average home range for some common mammals:

Muskrat—a circular area about 100 yards (91 m) in diameter
Porcupine—a few acres in winter; 200 acres (81 ha) in summer
Coyote—5 to 25 square miles (1300 to 6500 ha)
Red Fox— one to five square miles (259 to 1300 ha)
Raccoon—10 acres to several square miles (4 to hundreds of ha)
Mink— one-half to three square miles (125 to 775 ha)

Are all mammals helpless at birth?

Newborns in the mammal world vary in their degree of independence. Mammals such as the opossum, are extremely tiny and helpless at birth and must live in their mother's pouch for several months. These mammals belong to a group called **marsupials**. Others, including squirrels, rabbits, and foxes are born without fur and with their eyes closed. Still others, such as the white-tail deer and hares, are well-furred and more fully developed at birth. Although they need to be nursed, they are much closer to maturity than marsupial mammals.

What kind of hairs make up a mammal's coat?

Most animals such as deer and opossum have two kinds of hair covering their bodies. The entire body is covered with a dense layer of short hairs called an **undercoat**. This comprises the majority of the animal's hair and gives it it's overall color. Evenly spaced and protruding beyond the undercoat are the **guard hairs**. They are long, hollow, coarse hairs that stick out beyond the undercoat. They often give the animal's hair its streaked, mottled or camouflaged effect. The guard hairs function in several very important ways. First, they are a good defense against sticks, twigs and other disturbances during normal activities of the animal. They are great insulators because they are hollow and trap air next to the body for extra warmth. Guard hairs are usually shed in spring in favor of a lighter summer coat and are regrown in autumn. These hairs often are inadvertently pulled out when the animal brushes up against twigs and branches. Look for them along well-worn deer trails.

How can I track animals?

Animal tracking is an ancient art going back thousands of years. It was a necessary skill for early hunters because without weapons such as rifles, they needed to get close to their prey for capture. This lost art of tracking can be a fun way to spend a winter afternoon in the woods or a warm spring morning on the mud flats of a nearby river. The impressions in the earth tell a complete story. When examining tracks, first look at one individual track, then look at the pattern that several tracks together make. Note the surrounding habitat which will provide clues as to the animals that would likely be there. Finally, look for any other clues of the activity of the animal.

In looking at the individual track, note the general shape, determine if there is a heel pad and if so, what it looks like. See if there are there are any toes, count them and determine whether they are all on the same side of the track. Birds have four toes, three forward and one hind. Tracks that look like tiny human hands seen along a creek usually belong to a raccoon.

After examining one track and any additional signs, look at a group of tracks to see the pattern of movement of the animal. Becoming familiar with a few terms will help you describe the different kinds of tracks and their patterns. Terms like alternating and registering are ways that trackers describe where a single track falls in a sequence. For example; when a fox walks, it moves the front and back foot on the same side at the same time. The hind foot will step directly where the front foot had been, giving the impression of only one track. This is called direct registration. **Direct registration** helps an animal such as a fox stalk its prey silently. Each front foot is placed carefully so as not to snap a twig or crinkle a leaf. The hind feet fall into the same step behind, assuring the same quiet placement. Each track is a register. Animals such as dogs have **indirect registration**. The hind foot registers just outside the front track. Our domesticated dogs' ancestors had direct registration. After thousands of years without a need to stalk prey, their gait has become "sloppy" and your family dog has indirect registration. Tracks like those made by raccoons will have alternating hind and front tracks which is called an **alternating pattern**. Other terms like **bounding** and **hopping** are used to describe a complete set of four tracks. Hopping and bounding tracks left by such as squirrels and rabbits will be in groups. A continuous line of tracks are left by walking animals such as opossum and raccoons.

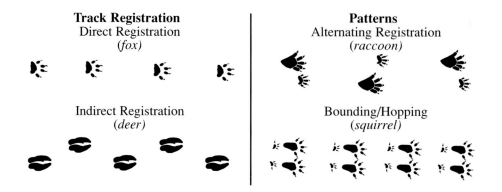

Track Registration
Direct Registration
(*fox*)

Indirect Registration
(*deer*)

Patterns
Alternating Registration
(*raccoon*)

Bounding/Hopping
(*squirrel*)

Don't overlook tracks made by the tiny animals like worms, frogs, toads and small birds. Small birds that visit your bird feeder will most likely have pairs of hopping tracks. Worms leave interesting serpentine patterns in mud puddles after warm summer rains. Toads will leave slight smudges in garden soil and depressions where they have backed themselves into loose dirt to wait for an insect meal. Frogs will leave triangular shaped tracks in the mud around ponds and lakes.

Next, note your surroundings and look for other clues. If you are in the woods and see hopping tracks that start and stop at a tree, they will most likely belong to a squirrel. Birds often leave some of the most interesting tracks found. Occasionally along their foot tracks, you'll see markings left by the tail or wings of a bird. Shore birds leave distinguishing tracks in the sand or mud while they search the shore for insects. Birds like Pheasant have especially large tracks which can be followed at great length. Look for wing tracks in the snow where these birds take off or land.

A wavy line between the tracks could be a sign of opossum or mice which drag their tail leaving a characteristic mark. Some of the most exciting tracks to see are those made by Owls or Hawks. Often you can see tracks of small rodents such as mice moving across the surface of the snow. Suddenly the tracks end in an irregular shaped depression where an Owl or Hawk has swooped down to capture the animal. The end of the trail is usually punctuated with a pair of wing tracks left by the bird of prey. Some other more playful animals, such as the mink or otter, create one long depression on the side of a hill when they slide on their bellies just for the fun of it. Often you can see tracks leading back up to the top where they take another ride down.

For a fun activity, consider making a tracking stick. Any old broom handle will do. First remove the broom part then using a magic marker, lay your stick next to a set of clearly identifiable tracks and mark off the distance between two of the tracks. Record the tracks of a squirrel, rabbit, skunk, raccoon and more and label each one with the animal's name. The next time you are out tracking and the tracks are not clearly visible, you can use your stick to help identify the unknown tracks just by the distance between them.

How can I tell which way an animal is traveling by its track?

Fresh tracks with clearly defined toes are usually enough to tell which direction the animal is traveling, but what can you do if the track is not so clear? At times, snow has blown into the track or a mud track has dried and cracked, masking the toes and the direction of travel. Often the general shape of the individual track will be enough to follow the direction of travel. Walking animals like foxes and dogs will have a track with a pointed and rounded end. Just like your own foot the toes are pointed and the heel is rounded.

For hopping animals like rabbits, look only at one group of four tracks. Two large hind feet will be in front of the two small front feet. These animals hop in a manner that has their hind feet land in front of their front. This might seem confusing but stop and watch a rabbit or squirrel to see for yourself. The larger hind tracks point the direction of travel.

Once you have determined the direction of travel you can use **back-tracking.** This is a tracking method that will help you learn what the animal does or where it travels in its natural state. If you are at all close to the animal, it probably knows you are there and you'll never catch up to it to see it. In addition, because it probably sees or smells you, it may use escape behaviors or distraction techniques to throw you off track. To see what it was doing and where it was before you came, follow its tracks backwards. You'll see a more natural line of travel and if you track far enough, you may even discover its home.

Why do squirrels chase each other?

Squirrels chasing each other, round and round a tree trunk is a common site. Often the lead squirrel will stop and jump on the pursuing squirrel only to break apart and continue the chase. What is this "squirrel tag" all about? Chasing is a behavior that serves several different functions. One reason for a chase is dominance. Squirrels live in social groups that usually include all the squirrels they come in contact with, much like an extended family. Within this social group, the squirrels have home ranges in which they spend most of their life. These ranges are broadly overlapping, approximately one wooded acre each. Both the males and females travel freely for food and water between the home ranges. A chase can occur when a smaller younger male squirrel enters the home range of a larger older squirrel. The older one will assert his dominance and chase the younger squirrel. This is not a territory chase since squirrels don't defend territories.

Another reason for chasing is mating. These not so romantic chases occur usually between 6:00 and 9:00 A.M. either on the ground or spiraling up and around a tree trunk and ending in the top branches. Several dominant males from the area can pursue a single female. Listen for a "chuckling" sound made by both the males and female during the chase. At times, the pursuing males will stop to fight amongst themselves before returning to the chase. Watch for the females to stop and turn on the males briefly before running off. It is usually the oldest and largest males that end a chase by successfully mating with the female.

What is a squirrel highway?

In the same way that you know your neighborhood and which street leads to the corner store, squirrels know every branch of the trees they call home. A thorough knowledge of the "squirrel highway" is key for a squirrel to travel at great speeds from tree to tree to escape predators, locate food or to interact socially with the neighbors. Each highway has markers along the way, in the form of scent markers, like we have highway signs. Look for a squirrel pausing to sniff or rub the sides of its face on a limb. It is either smelling or leaving a scent marker from glands located near the mouth. Also, squirrels have favorite paths and branches that they use to jump from one tree to another. Watch and see if you can identify these "interstate" highways of the squirrel world.

How does a squirrel bury nuts and find them again?

The average squirrel can bury up to 50 nuts per hour. For each nut the squirrel digs a hole three to four inches (10–12 cm) deep with its front paws. The nut is often husked before placing inside the hole. It is nudged into place with the nose which might serve to push the nut down or mark the nut with a scent gland located near the mouth. The excavated earth is scraped back into the hole and any leaves and grass are pushed back into place. Soft, gentle patting from the front paws tops off each site. Memory plays a small part in locating these buried treasures later but the scent left by the squirrel or the smell of the nut guides them to the exact spot. The squirrels do not find all the nuts and the result is new trees.

Where do all these animal trails go?

Day after day millions of people travel on roads to get to work and school. Can you imagine society without our elaborate network of roads? How would you get to the grocery story or bank? In nature, animals use "roads" to get to places that have water or food. A trail is established by animals that are traveling to the same places. They simply take the path of least resistance around fallen trees, brush and other obstacles. The typical animal trail is a narrow path about 6 to 10 inches (15–25 cm) wide and meanders through the woods or criss-crosses open fields. At first glance you might think these trails wander aimlessly. But each trail leads to a specific place of importance for the animals. Most animal trails lead to food and water but they can also serve as emergency escape routes. Some trails are only used in winter while others are exclusively summer trials. In the northern states when the snow is often deep, an established trail takes less energy to travel. There is some evidence that animals that are active at night, such as deer, have memorized the trails. This memory probably helps them navigate in the dark.

Many kinds of animals such as deer, fox, woodchuck and skunk will share the same trail. Some main trails are used for decades and new trails are created all the time. New trails are often extensions from an existing trail leading to new locations of food and water. Many small "sub-trails" break off the main trails and lead to underground dens or **forms**. A form is a shallow cup-like depression on the ground where an animal such as a deer or rabbit rests, sleeps or waits out bad weather. The next time you see an animal trail, take a minute to look for tracks. Better yet, follow the trail and see where it leads.

If you want to see the animals that made the trail, choose a spot near a main trail and conceal yourself behind a fallen branch or tree. The best time to do this is at dawn or sunset when most animals are active. Sit back and wait to see who comes by.

What is a deer yard?

Each winter, in colder climates, deer will congregate in herds up to approximately 30 or more animals. They choose a spot in the forest that has a dense stand of evergreens or is sheltered from wind and snow. Ideally, it would also have a southern exposure to take advantage of the sun's warmth. These areas are called deer yards and can be up to several acres in size. During winter, deer change their diet from fresh green plants and flowers to woody plants and evergreens. In the north, white cedar seems to be favored over red cedar, pine or spruce. During the day, the deer typically stay bedded down in these areas. At twilight they head out on a well established network of trails to eat but they always return to the yard at the first sign of daylight. They also use the yards during bad weather, sometimes staying for several days until the weather improves.

How and why do beavers cut trees and build dams?

Beavers cut trees for two main reasons. One reason is to eat the leaves, buds and the growing part just under the bark called the cambium layer. The second is to use the logs for building their domed lodges and dams. A typical lodge is made of tree limbs, mud and debris and usually has one inner chamber that is about three feet (1 m) across and two feet high (.6 m). The den is dry with only one underwater entrance that is used for both coming and going. The lodge is safe from most predators since it is very strong. Typically, a lodge can easily support a person's weight and may even be bear-proof. Should an intruder attempt to get in, however, they always have a quick, underwater get-away.

A good habitat for a beaver is a quiet part of a river or lake that is deep enough for it to come and go from its underwater passageway and that is surrounded by trees such as the beaver's favorite, the quaking aspen. When a beaver can't find water that is deep enough, it creates its own. A stream that runs through a grove of young aspens is a prime target for the beaver's handiwork. Within two to three days, a pair of beavers working at night to build a dam can transform the area into a pond. Should there be a leak in the dam, the beaver will listen for rushing water to find the holes. They'll repair it using their front feet to pack mud into the area and not their tails like we've seen in cartoons. They use their tails as rudders and to slap the water to warn others of danger.

Can opossums hang from their tails?

Opossums have long, naked **prehensile** (pre-hen´sel) tails that are shrouded in mystery and myth. Many anecdotal stories abound about the opossum using its tail like a monkey. All of these are false. These stories appear to have originated from a single painting by a Frankfurt artist Maria Sibylla Merian some 250 years ago. Her painting depicted an opossum using her tail as an anchor for her young to hold onto. Over the several hundred years that followed, this painting was used by other artists and taxidermists for reference in poses for opossums. Each artist's conception slowly changed with each new rendition and eventually showed the opossum using its tail like a monkey. While the tail of the opossum ranges from 18 to 20 inches (45 to 50 cm) long, and it can use it to stabilize itself briefly while maneuvering or climbing, the opossum only has the ability to hang by its tail for a very short time. An opossum hanging by its tail will quickly fall to the ground.

How do skunks spray?

The smallest of children know, probably from cartoons, that skunks spray their enemies with an awful spray. Other animals in the **mustelid** family also have scent glands but they don't use them the same way that skunks do. They use them for communication in marking trails and territories. Skunks develop an initially odorless fluid secretion from their anal glands at 4–5 weeks. In several more weeks it turns into one of the most awful and sustaining natural smells ever. Skunks do not choose to use their spray as their first line of defense. While most nocturnal animals are dark and camouflaged, skunks have colors that stand out at night which warns others of their presence. If their color does not deter an intruder, they use another line of defense. The striped skunk will begin drumming the ground with its front feet several times and the spotted skunk will do a handstand. If you see these behaviors, get out of the area fast as their next line of defense is the spray. They can spray with amazing accuracy and they will always aim for the face. The skunk will lift its tail and turn its head around to see the intruder. Without moving, it can spray straight back or to the side up to a distance of ten feet (3 m). This is done by using two anal glands and a squeezing sphincter muscle that releases the awful smelling fluid in a rapid succession of seven or eight sprays. The fluid is a yellow oily substance which is actually harmless to the skin but nearly impossible to remove from clothing. If it lands in the eyes, it can be very painful. The only time this incredible defense system of the skunk is not effective is against large birds of prey, especially the great-horned Owl, because they have no sense of smell.

Can I raise a baby raccoon as a pet?

Attempting to make pets of any of these wild critters is not recommended. As babies, they may be appealing, but as adults, they are likely to resort to their instinctively wild behavior. Raccoon pets have been know to rip curtains to shreds, and even de-scented skunks never respond to your commands as dogs can be trained to do. Domesticated animals make the best pets. Wild animals deserve to be respected for their wildness. The greatest satisfaction comes in observing these critters in their natural environment and working to protect it in order to preserve their future.

What environmental problems affect mammals?

Habitat loss is a serious problem, especially for animals that need large, undeveloped territories. Much habitat loss is due to development and urban sprawl. Wild places give way to bulldozers as more people escape the confinement and stress of the inner city in search of the beauty of open spaces. Some critters have found ways to survive in close proximity to human development. Rabbits, deer and squirrels adapt so well to human neighbors that they are considered destructive to cultivated as well as native vegetation. Others, such as wolves, cougars and bobcats, because of their requirements for specific foods in large quantities and adequate shelter, do not thrive near humans. Wolves used to live throughout North America. Now they can be found only in Canada and certain areas of Minnesota, Wisconsin and Michigan in the U.S. All of the wild cats, including bobcats and cougar are in decline because of habitat loss.

How do I use the Critter Smart species section?

Your first sighting of a bear or deer in the wild is a thrilling and memorable experience. Being mammals ourselves, we can relate to their movements, their fears and many of their habits. To increase your chances of spotting mammals, remember that most are active during the early morning and early evening hours. Also, remember that they are skittish; most have senses much more acute than ours. Sitting quietly in a prime wildlife viewing area is more likely to provide satisfying results than hiking at a fast clip. Binoculars are a must for mammal viewing, because you are not likely to get close. The mammals described in the species section that follows were selected because they are the ones you are most likely to encounter. Even if you don't see the actual critter, it's rewarding to come upon its track. We have included a discussion of tracks in the species description to assist you in identifying any animal that has recently passed or may be behind the next tree.

Badger   *Taxidea taxus 22" body (56 cm) 12" tail (30 cm)*

front

hind

The badger is a squatty weasel, with a well-deserved reputation for being a powerhouse of strength. Originally found no farther east than just east of the Great Lakes, its habitat now includes all of the continental U.S. and Canada. They can be found in open areas with sandy soils, as well as in wooded areas, as long as the soil is not too heavy for their prodigious digging. Badgers are mostly carnivorous, feeding on gophers, mice, prairie dogs, rabbits, woodchucks, moles, lizards and snakes. An extremely aggressive critter, the badger will take on animals twice its size, even a bear, but will also feed on the remains of dead animals. The badger's long claws are perfect for digging not only insects, eggs and snails out of hiding, but great quantities of dirt, as well. The badger can dig at a faster rate than a person with a shovel, causing dirt to fly as far as 4 – 5 feet (1 – 1.5 m) in the air. They create a series of underground dens within their home range, which is about one square mile (259 ha) for females and two-and-a-half square miles (648 ha) for males. A den is marked with a bare spot of dirt with several well-worn trails leading away from the entrance. Each spring, around April or May, mothers give birth to 1 – 5 (usually two) young in a soft, grass-lined den. In the northern part of their range, badgers accumulate body fat to sustain them during extended stays in their burrows. However, these periods of prolonged sleep are not actually hibernation, as the badger will wake up occasionally to seek a meal. Because a badger's legs are so short, its belly drags on the ground as it walks, leaving a shallow trench-like depression in the snow between its tracks. Notice the claw marks with each print. It walks somewhat pigeon-toed. Notice how the shorter claws of the hind feet don't show as well as the forefeet.

Bat   *Myotis spp. 1-2" body (2-5 cm) 6-12" wing span (15-30 cm)*

Bats have the undeserved reputation as spooky Halloween creatures that fly into people's hair and spread awful diseases. From a scientific perspective, bats are fascinating as well as beneficial creatures. Because many bats are insectivorous, they serve as important natural control of mosquitos. Bats also have the distinction of being the only mammal capable of true flight. Their precision in locating small flying insects by **echolocation** has made bats the subject of great interest to the U.S. Navy in the development of sonar systems used to detect submarines. Bats emit ultrasonic sounds, called **cries**, pitched at a higher frequency than humans can hear, bouncing the sound off an object in order to locate it without seeing it. When a cry is given, a tiny muscle in the bat's ear contracts for an instant. This closes off the ear momentarily and prevents the bat from hearing its own cry. The returning echo is received by an inner ear. A bat in flight emits cries at the rate of 8 – 15 per second. It can increase that number to more than 200 per second as it narrows in on the location of its prey. Although they spend much of their time in darkness, bats are not blind; their eyesight is as keen as our own. There are typically two kinds of bats, "tree" and "cave" bats. All tree bats migrate to the tropics during winter. Generally, the farther north you travel, the fewer bats you'll find; the farther south, the more bats. The little Brown Bat is the most common bat and is considered a cave bat. It hibernates hanging upside down in limestone caves throughout the winter months. Female bats give birth each year to only one offspring, called a **pup**. Their low reproductive rate and the destruction of their caves has led to much of their demise.

Black bear   *Ursus americanus 6' long (1.8 m) 3' high (1 m)*

front

hind

Once common throughout the Eastern U.S. and Canada, black bears are now found only in sparsely populated areas. Hardly anyone has a hard time identifying the American black bear. Weighing up to 300 lbs (15 kg), they are the smallest of all bears but the most common. Black bears are not always black. They can range in color from cinnamon brown, blond, to rust colored. However, the face is always brown and they have a conspicuous white patch on their chest. Black bears live solitary lives coming together only to mate. They are omnivorous meaning they eat meat, fish, fruits, berries and green plants.

Each winter, black bears enter dens and sleep until spring. This is not a true hibernation. Waking several times during warm weather, mothers give birth to two cubs during the sleep, usually in January or February. Each baby weighs only 8 oz. (226 g).

Bears mark their home ranges by clawing at prominent boundary trees. Unlike grizzly bears, black bears have no problems climbing a tree.

Rarely dangerous, only a few cases of attacks on humans have ever been reported. While you are not likely to see bear tracks in the snow due to sleeping during winter, at other times of the year look for large pads with distinct claw marks on both hind and front paws.

Beaver — *Castor canadensis 25-30" body (63-76 cm) 10" tail (25 cm)*

The beaver is the largest member of the rodent family in North America. Its coveted fur made it the most prized pelt during the fur trade of the late 1800's because it was processed into a felt and made into the tall top hats so popular in Europe at the time. For the beaver's sake, it was a good thing that the hats went out of style before nature's carpenter became extinct. In primitive times, there were an estimated 60 million beavers that lived throughout North America, with densities of 50 per square mile (259 ha). By 1900, trapping and civilization had eliminated beavers from the east and south. Re-introduction and regulations have helped to re-establish the beaver in its former range within the limits of available habitat. Natural predators include coyotes, bobcats, otters and minks.

The beaver's continually growing front teeth are its most significant tool for felling trees. Beavers are well suited for an underwater existence. They have flaps of skin which automatically close to keep water out of their ears, nose and mouth. They have webbed back feet and a multi-purpose tail designed for balance, steering, warning intruders and storing fat. Their inner two toes on their hind feet are for distributing the oil secreted from glands near their tail through their fur for water-proofing. Their fur has a thick underlayer of insulation covered by longer and coarser guard hairs. The beavers' diet is strictly vegetation so they get ready for winter by stashing freshly cut tree limbs near their lodge so that they don't have to travel far for food. They remain awake all winter. The breeding season starts early in the year, around January and February, by pairs who probably mate for life. They have only one litter each year consisting of an average of 3 – 4 young, called kits. These kits are born fully furred with their eyes open and they are able to swim. They live with their parents for two years and are then encouraged to leave to start their own families.

front

hind

Eastern chipmunk *Tamias striatus 5-6" body (12-15 cm) 9-13" tail (10 cm)*

Chipmunks actually are small four ounce (113 g) ground squirrels that live in wooded areas. This mammal's scientific name offers a fitting description: *Tamias* is Greek for "a storer," and *striatus* is Latin for "striped." The common name of chipmunk comes from an Native American word, "chitmunk", that refers to the animal's chit-like alarm call. They have several other calls, as well, the most common being a single high-pitched call repeated at a rate of about 130 per minute. Chipmunks can produce these calls even with their cheeks stuffed full of sunflower seeds. While gathering a store of food for winter, chipmunks utilize their roomy cheeks as temporary storage until they deposit their cache below ground. During the process of tunnel excavation, chipmunks also fill their cheeks with the soil that will eventually be carried out and dumped elsewhere. A chipmunk's underground home, or burrow, is used for several years and can be quite complex, extending up to 20' (6 m) and containing many chambers and alternate exits. Storage chambers are filled with nuts and seeds. Unlike the woodchuck with its obvious deposit of excavated soil at the hole opening, the chipmunk removes tell-tale soil from the entrance. This extra effort helps to camouflage the chipmunk's dwelling from such potential invaders as weasels, snakes, and foxes. Chipmunks are not true hibernators, because they occasionally wake and venture out during warm spells. In the open, the chipmunk is also prey to Owls, Hawks, and house cats. Each year the females give birth to four or five young, which stay together most of the summer. Chipmunks are entertaining subjects for observation and are easy to spot, because they are active during the day. Look for chipmunk tracks around summer mud puddles. Natural hoppers, chipmunks leave four small prints close together.

front

hind

Eastern cottontail rabbit *Sylvilagus floridanus 14-17" (35-43 cm)*

Quite common in urban areas, the cottontail does not change color for winter, nor does it hibernate. It survives winter by eating twigs, buds and berries. You can tell if a deer or a rabbit has been gnawing on a twig by the type of cut that has been made. Rabbits produce a sharp, slanted cut, while the dull teeth of a deer leave shredded ends. In summer, the cottontail will eat almost any kind of plant. They thrive in suburban areas where predators are limited to house cats and cars. Also, rabbits produce multiple litters, making them abundant in most areas. Mating occurs as early as mid-February, with the first litter being born in mid-March. In warm climates they breed year round. Each female can have 2 – 4 litters each year, with 3 – 6 young per litter. This abundance supports the food chain in wilderness areas, where both adult and baby rabbits are prey for many predators including Owls, Hawks, Eagles, foxes, wolves, bobcats and mountain lions. Cottontail nests, called forms, are usually well-hidden in a hole or depression in the ground and covered with leaves and grass. After giving birth, mother cottontails give the young little attention except for nursing. By the time the young are fully furred and have their eyes open, they are ready to leave the nest. Well-meaning people who find tiny rabbits, perhaps 4 – 5" (10 – 12 cm) long, often search in vain for a nest. These youngsters probably are living on their own. Rabbit tracks are easy to find and follow in the snow. Look for a hopping pattern of tracks that show the long oblong hind feet landing ahead of the front feet. The hind feet clearly indicate the direction of travel. Cottontails can run at speeds up to 18 mph (30 kph).

Coyote — *Canis latrans 4' body (137 cm) 16" tail (40 cm)*

More common than you might think, the coyote is found throughout much of Eastern U.S. and Canada. Smaller than the average large domestic dog, the coyote is usually active at night. Overall, coyotes are buff gray with whitish bellies. They have characteristically pointed noses and ears with unproportionately long legs. Their bushy gray tail is often tipped with black. Sometimes confused with wolves, the coyote weighs only 50 lbs. compared to the timber wolf which weighs 100 lbs. or more.

You may not readily see a coyote, but listen for high pitched howls and barks at night. They usually run carrying their tail low. They hunt small mammals like mice, voles and birds. In summer, the coyote will eat fruit and berries along with frogs and grasshoppers.

129

Solitary travelers, coyotes come together for mating only. Females give birth to 6 – 7 pups in an underground den. Coyotes can take small cats and dogs but often shy away from domestic animals. Even though they are hunted in many states, the coyote seems to be growing in population. Similar to dog tracks, the coyote has four toes on the front and back. Look for a wandering pattern of tracks.

Muskrat *Ondatra zibethica 10-14" body (25-35 cm) 11" tail (28 cm)*

This beaver-like rodent is a great swimmer with unique adaptations for an existence in the water. Skin flaps protect its ears, nose and mouth from water, while clear eyelids act as protective swimming goggles. Its common name, muskrat, comes from the mammal's characteristic "musk" odor, and "rat" for its naked tail. Its oiled reddish-brown fur keeps its skin dry, and its webbed feet keep it swimming steadily at about two miles per hour (3 kph). Muskrats feed on water plants, snails and small fish. Although smaller than the muskrat, the mink is its fiercest enemy. The muskrat constructs its home out of mud and cattails with an underwater entrance. Dozens of these domed homes can be seen in shallow lakes and ponds. Muskrat dens double as habitat for nesting geese atop the mounds. A pair of muskrats will raise two to four litters of seven or eight young each in a single season. Keep an eye out for a muskrat during the day as it crosses a marsh or lake forming a V-shaped wake on top of the water. Muskrats are active day and night, and they don't hibernate. You will rarely see muskrat tracks because their winter activity is carried on underwater and inside their dens.

front

hind

Opossum *Didelphis virginiana 15-20" body (38-51 cm) 9-13" tail (23-33 cm)*

On this continent, the closest relative of this shy mammal can only be found in zoos. Otherwise, you'd have to travel to Australia to find their kangaroo cousins in the wild. Both kangaroos and opossums are **marsupial** mammals, meaning they carry their young in pouches outside their bodies. Litters are composed of as many as 15 young called "kits." They are tiny, kidney bean-sized, helpless baby opossums, that must be nurtured in the mother's pouch. After emerging from the pouch, the young ride on the back of their mother for several weeks. Offspring produced as early in the year as February are weaned *front*

hind

by May, so females can produce a second litter. Catching a glimpse of an opossum in the glare of your headlights is a common way to encounter this nocturnal critter. They spend each night searching for grasshoppers, crickets and other bugs, beetles, berries and even dead animals. They have no trouble with this highly variable diet because opossums have 50 teeth, more than any other North American mammal. Opossums don't hibernate, but they will sleep for several days during periods of cold weather. Their enemies include dogs, foxes, coyotes, bobcats and even Great Horned Owls. Opossums will climb trees to escape danger, but when frightened, they will play dead, hence the term "playing possum." They are solitary animals, preferring woodlands and areas near streams. They sometimes take over the abandoned homes of other animals or seek out cavities in rocks, brush piles, trash heaps, hollow trees and old logs. After locating a cavity, they prepare a lining of leaves and grass. An opossum picks up its nesting materials with its mouth, takes it with its front paws and passes it under its body to the hind legs, then transfers the material to a loop in its bare but dexterous tail. In this fashion, the opossum can easily transport materials to build its nest and it will often build a new nest every night. Opossum tracks have a distinctive, opposite, thumb-like toe that juts out to one side. Pairs of tracks alternate in a bow-legged waddle with a "tail-drag" pattern between.

Raccoon   *Procyon lotor 30-45" body (63-100 cm) 12" tail (30 cm)*

front

hind

From an early age you could identify this masked critter of uncanny skills. These adaptive mammals are more common now than ever. They are omnivorous which means they take advantage of all food sources, including bird feed, bird and turtle eggs, small mammals, crayfish, fish, as well as berries and other plant materials. They grow heavy fur coats for winter, and although they are not true hibernators, they are known for sleeping in trees during the daytime. These behaviors undoubtedly remind you of another well-known mammal. Believe it or not, a raccoon's closest relative is the bear. Unlike bears, raccoons are nocturnal critters.

131

You are most likely to sight them beside a stream in early hours of dawn or with your headlights at night. Only the female is involved in raising the four or five young they produce each year. Often, to her host's dismay, the raccoon chooses to locate her nest in people's chimneys or under deck porches. It is the amazing dexterity of their paws, so similar to our hands, that makes raccoons so fascinating for people to watch. Experts offer various theories as to why raccoons appear to wash the food they take from a pond or stream. One theory is that this action sensitizes their paws, thereby increasing their sense of touch. Another is that it is learned behavior taught to each young raccoon by its mother as a method of removing sand from snails and crayfish. It was thought at one time that raccoons needed to wash their food because they had no salivary glands, but this isn't true. They have very active salivary glands and do not wash the berries or mice they eat, only the food taken from the water's edge. Certainly it's not a matter of fastidiousness, for given a choice, raccoons will put their paws in muddy water as frequently as in clear water. For now, the purpose of this signature behavior of raccoons remains a mystery to us.

Red fox   *Vulpes vulpes 42" body (106 cm) 16" tail (40 cm)*

In all seasons, the red fox, a member of the canine or dog family, can be found circling its territory. Because they do not hibernate or migrate or store food, foxes are constantly roaming the open fields and woodland habitat in search of food. Although it's known as a hunter of rabbits, mice, pheasant and other small animals, the fox relies on a wide range of foods, including fruit and seeds. During winter months, their diet consists of as much as 75 percent vegetation. Surprisingly, red foxes are not always red; they can be black, gray, brown or yellow. A white-tipped tail identifies the red fox, while its tree-climbing cousin, the gray fox, has a black-tipped tail. Foxes communicate by scent. The scent glands located near their tails enable them to release the skunk-like smell to mark their territory. Red foxes have expanded in number and range in recent years. Historically, wolves and coyote have preyed on the fox, but with those populations diminished, humans are the main predator of the fox today. Believed to mate for life, foxes dig underground dens in which to raise their young. They prepare multiple den sites, so that in case of danger, they can quickly relocate their offspring. The female gives birth annually to one litter of six or eight babies, called kits or pups, which both parents

front   hind

help to raise. Fox tracks are easy to recognize: look for a straight line of dog-like prints. The hind foot of the fox falls directly in the track left by the front foot, giving the appearance of a single line of tracks.

Striped skunk   *Mephitis mephitis 18" body (46 cm) 10" tail (25 cm)*

front   hind

    As familiar as this mammal is, you may not know that it is a member of the weasel clan known as the mustelid family. All weasels have the smelly musk glands, but the skunk is the only one that can squeeze the glands at will and spray it on its enemies. A fat-bodied weasel, the skunk cannot climb trees to escape danger, so it warns its enemies with its bold black and white coat. Turning its back to a perceived enemy, it begins by stamping the ground with its front legs while hissing, growling and waving its tail. If this display isn't enough discouragement, only then does the skunk use its ultimate defense. The skunk can spray its oily, extremely foul-smelling fluid up to eight times per encounter and hit a target up to 10' (3 m) away. The odor travels about ½ mile (.8 km) in the wind. This means of defense is effective with most predators, except those such as the Great Horned Owl, which does not have a developed sense of smell and is not bothered by the spray. Because skunks prefer open areas to forests, they have adapted well to living in close proximity to human dwellings. In some cases, skunks have become so abundant they have devastated populations of ducks and turtles with their omnivorous appetite for a varied diet of eggs, insects, mice, shrews, carrion and vegetable matter. They are not true hibernators and will wake during spells of warm weather to hunt for insects under logs. Mothers give birth to 4 – 7 babies in a den that is lined with soft plants usually within a tree cavity or if you're unlucky, under the deck of your house. When old enough, babies will follow their mother, learning how to forage for food. With five toes on both front and rear feet, skunks leave alternating matched pairs of prints along a meandering track.

Fox squirrel *Sciurus niger 10-15" body (25-38 cm) 9-14" tail (23-35 cm)*
Gray squirrel *Sciurus carolinensis 8-10" body (20-25 cm) 8-10" tail (20-25 cm)*
Red squirrel *Tamiasciurus hudsonicus 7-8" body (18-20 cm) 4-6" tail (10-15 cm)*

There are 60 different kinds of squirrels scattered from the Arctic to the tip of Florida. Their scientific name, *Sciurus*, combines the Greek word *skia*

grey squirrel

for "shadow" and *oura* for "tail" to indicate that they are the only animals that sit in the shadow of their own tail. A squirrel's tail is functional in many ways: it is used for balance when climbing, or as a parachute when jumping to slow their descent in preparation for landing. It's also used for warmth, like a blanket, and as a communication device to signal warning. The more agitated a squirrel is, the faster it flicks its tail. When extremely upset, it combines this action with a loud raspy cry. Squirrels have the classic, gnawing type of continually-growing front teeth that are typical of members of the rodent

family. They eat a varied diet of some 100 different plants, including nuts from oak, hickory, walnut and elm trees. While you've undoubtedly seen squirrels busily burying nuts in the ground, you may not realize that they use their noses to relocate the nuts later on, even under a foot of snow. These common critters live everywhere from dense forests to cities, to parks and backyards. They build several nests and move frequently if one nest is damaged or to escape bad weather or

red squirrel

predators. A typical squirrel's nest is constructed of leaves in the fork of a tree branch. This is in contrast to a large bird's nest, which is similar in size, but is made of twigs. Mothers give birth to

fox squirrel

3 – 5 blind and naked babies. She can have several litters a year in warmer climates; winter litters are usually born in a tree cavity while summer litters are born in leaf nests. Babies will nurse for up to two months. Tree squirrels live out their lives in and around one area and rarely go farther than 200 yards from home. The exception to this rule occurs during mating season when males may range more widely in search of a mate. Females have their babies in the nests, and

front *hind*

whole families return there nightly to sleep together. All members of the tree squirrel family have four toes on the front feet and five toes on the hind feet. Look for their tracks in snow and mud. Because squirrels hop, the 5-toed hind feet register ahead of the 4-toed front feet. Watch for groups of tracks containing these four prints. The toes of the wider and larger hind feet clearly indicate the direction of travel.

Whitetail deer — *Odocoileus virginianus 3-4' tall (.9-1.5 m)*

Because of a lack of natural predators such as wolves and cougars, the population of these hoofed mammals is greater today than at any other time in history. Due to increased numbers, many deer have been drawn out of their wilderness homes and have adapted to habitats created by humans. Deer thrive near cornfields, on the edge of woodlands and in suburban parks, where their habit of eating 7 – 10 pounds of leaves and twigs a day has a profound impact on the local plant and animal life. Deer are active all year long and can be seen early in the evening and on into the night. They use their sense of smell to help negotiate well-worn paths. Thanks to their perfectly counter-shaded coats with white underparts, deer are very well camouflaged. To the human eye, a deer standing on snowy ground among the trees is nearly invisible. The male deer, known as a **buck**, grows antlers every year to spar with other bucks for domination of a herd of females, called **does**. In the fall, males mark their territories by rubbing their antlers against small trees. Such "rubs" often damage the tree to a fatal extent. Antlers are shed annually in the late winter. These discarded trophies provide a rich source of calcium for mice and other rodents. In their first year of life, does can have twin offspring, which allows for rapid reproduction of the species. Sometimes, depending on the health of the mother, deer have triplets or even quadruplets. Because deer walk on their toes, they leave a distinctive track that looks like two halves of an upside down heart. Each half is a toenail that sinks deep into snow or mud. The pointed end of the track indicates the direction in which the deer is traveling.

front   hind

Woodchucks *Marmota monax 16-20" body (40-51 cm) 7" tail (18cm)*

With 45' (14 m) or more of tunnels per home at depths of 3 – 6' (1 – 2 m), this member of the rodent family is truly a champion digger. In loose soil, it can dig itself out of trouble from such pursuing predators as foxes, coyotes and weasels in a matter of minutes. When a woodchuck is approached by any creature that poses a threat, it will give a loud whistle and run directly to the entrance of its home, thus giving it another common name, whistle pig. Also known as a groundhog, this true hibernator appears on television news each February 2. On this day, according to legend, if the groundhog sees its shadow, six more weeks of winter weather will follow. Folklore aside, woodchucks are strictly herbivorous, eating grasses, leaves, nuts and berries. It is not uncommon to see a woodchuck perched high up on the end of a branch eating the young leaves of a tree. Similar to the squirrel, the large front teeth of the woodchuck grow continually and need to be ground down by gnawing to prevent becoming too big. The number of woodchucks increased as forests were cleared during European settlement of the U.S. Breaking up the heavily forested areas created more of the woodland edges that comprise the preferred habitat of woodchucks. Just four weeks after mating, two to five tiny babies are born blind and hairless. They grow quickly and are ready to venture out of the burrow after one month. The adults live a solitary life, driving away their young in the late summer of the same year the babies are born. Then they fatten up for the October to February hibernation where they spend the winter tucked deep within their dens. Males are usually the first to awaken each spring and begin searching for a new mate and looking for leftover berries and new greenery.

front

hind

Herp Smart

Life surrounds you in a marsh. Herps hop around you, peek at you from behind trees and sun themselves on rocks in the heat of a summer day. So what are herps? They are turtles, snakes, lizards, frogs, salamanders and all of the critters that can be categorized as reptiles and amphibians; the word herp refers to all the animals in both categories. It comes from the Greek word *herpeton*, meaning to creep. **Herpetology** is the study of reptiles and amphibians. Since scientists study these animals together, we are grouping them, too. There are several thousand species of reptiles and amphibians in North America. As adults, they live in a variety of places: fresh and salt water, forests, prairies, deserts and, if you are lucky, in your backyard! They are all cold-blooded, needing the sun's warmth to maintain their body temperatures during the summer, and they hibernate during winter. Although they are studied together, reptiles and amphibians are actually completely different. In general, **reptiles** are the only group of vertebrates (animals with backbones) that have scaly skin and lay their leathery-shelled eggs in the ground. Some snakes, however, do give birth to live babies and are still considered reptiles. **Amphibians** are the only group of vertebrates that live part of their lives in water in one life form and then change to live another part on land. Their eggs are not covered with a shell but are laid in jelly-like masses in shallow water.

Reptiles are a primitive group. They are simple animals, but they have been very successful. In fact, they've been around for hundreds of millions of years, much longer than the dinosaurs and longer than people. The word reptile is Latin, *repere*. Like the Greek word *herpeton,* it means to creep, which very well describes how these animals get around. Reptiles are grouped into four categories: turtles, snakes, lizards and crocodiles. In Herp Smart, we'll look at only the common turtles and snakes in Eastern North America. Although the two seem quite different, turtles and snakes have much in common. They both lay eggs and have a protective covering of plates or scales instead of fur, skin, or feathers and most are considered carnivorous, meaning they eat other animals.

The word *amphibian* is often incorrectly thought of as meaning an animal that lives on both land and water. It comes from the Greek words *amphi*, which means both and *bios*, which means life. What it really means is that these critters have two separate stages of life. Like butterflies, amphibians undergo a transformation that is so incredible it has to be seen to be believed. Frogs, toads and salamanders start life as tiny eggs that hatch into larvae. In the case of frogs and toads and some species of salamanders, these larvae are commonly called tadpoles. At this stage, the tadpoles have gills and live only underwater. As they grow, they develop lungs to breathe air. Even more remarkable, they also grow legs, which carry them out of the water and onto land. Amphibians are divided into three groups: frogs (which include toads), salamanders and caecilians, which are legless, worm-like animals of the tropics. In Herp Smart, we'll talk only about frogs, toads and salamanders.

When you find a herp, you've probably found a healthy environment. Herps cannot live in polluted areas. They need the many insects and small animals that are normally found in a healthy habitat. A pond that has been treated to kill mosquitoes, for example, is missing an important food source. A healthy pond will support a large number of reptiles and amphibians which provide natural insect control. In turn, herps themselves are preyed upon by larger animals such as raccoons, Hawks, foxes and Owls. All are a part of the food chain.

Herps fascinate and sometimes even frighten us with their unfamiliar shapes. They are often considered ugly or useless creatures and have been scapegoats in many a myth and story. Historically, snakes have represented the dark side of humanity; biblical accounts associate snakes with the devil, such as the snake tempting Eve in the Garden of Eden. Toads and newts are associated with witchcraft and were once thought to be ingredients in magic potions. Like misconceptions about many other curiosities of nature, these bad reputations were born of misunderstanding of just how special these animals are.

Why do turtles and snakes sunbathe?

Unlike humans, they're not sitting in the sun trying to get a tan! These critters are **cold-blooded**, a term that confuses many people. They think it means that a reptile or amphibian's blood or body is cold. Actually, being cold-blooded means having a body temperature that changes with the outside temperature. All animals need to regulate their body temperatures to survive. Mammals, including humans, who maintain a relative constant body temperature, do this by eating food and then converting it into energy. This energy fuels our muscles. The activity of our muscles, including those of our internal organs which are active even at rest, produces heat internally, just as a furnace produces heat in your house.

Reptiles and amphibians lack this internal furnace so they need sources outside their bodies. They warm up by sunning themselves and cool off by shading themselves. To picture this, imagine putting 50 blankets on a snake.

While you would feel hot and sweaty under those blankets, the snake wouldn't get any warmer. Being warm-blooded, you make heat and then trap it next to your body with the blankets. Since snakes don't produce heat (and they don't have electric blankets), they must get it from the sun. That's why you see snakes and other herps absorbing the heat of sun-warmed roads and trails, or sitting on a rock; they are **basking**. When they become too warm, they go underground or under leaves to cool off.

Unlike snakes, frogs and toads must not only keep their bodies warm but they need to keep their skins moist, too. If they were to stay in direct sunlight, they would dry out too quickly, so they stay near rocks and leaves that have been warmed by the sun. Here they absorb some warmth but they are out of direct sunlight and away from the drying wind.

How do tadpoles change into frogs and toads?

Just as butterflies go through changes, frogs and toads undergo **metamorphosis**, a dramatic transformation that we find amazing. Each spring, female frogs and toads lay masses of a hundred or more eggs in warm, shallow ponds. When the eggs hatch, tiny tadpoles appear. They spend their time swimming, eating and, most importantly, avoiding predators. Within a few days to a week of hatching, tadpoles start to grow legs, first back legs and then front legs. Their tails are then absorbed into their bodies as they enter the adult stage. During this metamorphosis, many changes also take place inside these critters. Tadpoles eat mostly microscopic organisms, or tiny plants, but they become insect eaters when grown. Because of this change in diet, their intestines need to shorten. In addition, almost all amphibians change from using gills in order to breathe oxygen underwater to developing and using lungs to breathe oxygen from the air.

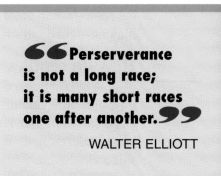

"Perserverance is not a long race; it is many short races one after another."

WALTER ELLIOTT

You can observe this change from eggs to tadpoles by going to a pond near you in the spring and looking for eggs. The eggs are clear and jelly-like and are in a round mass about the size of a softball in the case of frogs or a string-like mass in the case of toads. Take some of these eggs and place them in an aquarium that is unheated and aerated. Within about two weeks, you'll see tadpoles emerge. Observe the eggs change from light to dark and watch the development within the egg. As you watch them, try to realize that as adults, they'll look nothing like they do now. They'll develop lungs, lose their tails and grow legs! Once they've hatched, quickly release them back to the pond where you found them to let them complete their life cycles. Who knows, by the end of the summer you may even meet one of these very critters again as a land-loving, jumping toad or frog!

How long do frogs and toads live?

Most frogs and toads live only five to ten years. That's a short time when you consider that in some parts of the country, they spend up to half of the year underground in hibernation. So why do critters with such short life spans have such complicated life cycles? Probably because changing from swimming creatures to hopping creatures allows them to obtain more food. Most frogs and toads live on the edges of ponds, lakes and marshes. These bodies of water are a relatively good source of food, but for a tadpole in a small pond, the food resources are still limited. Its "frog" stage may have evolved simply as an efficient way for it to reach new ponds and other, more abundant food sources.

Adding to the struggle for life, many other animals (besides children!) hunt frogs and toads. Frog and toad eggs and tadpoles are eaten by fish, while grown frogs are eaten by fish, raccoons, herons, snakes, foxes, owls and snakes. Because they are a favorite food for many, frogs often live short lives but reproduce in great numbers. Without this rapid reproduction, these animals may have died out many years ago.

How do reptiles and amphibians survive winter?

What do herps do when the wind blows from the north and the temperature dips to freezing? Birds fly south and mammals add layers of fat and extra fur—but not herps! Reptiles and amphibians take the low road and head underground. While most are well adapted to cold climates, winter is still a challenge.

The first step in surviving winter is choosing suitable shelter. Turtles burrow into the mud or sit on the bottom of lakes, rivers and ponds. Salamanders and snakes crawl under decaying logs, rocks or into the hollows of trees. Snakes also slither into established cavities underground with other snakes. Toads crawl into burrows, natural crevasses in the ground or they just dig themselves down into the ground. Some will bury themselves up to 12 inches (30 cm) deep. Tree frogs crawl under fallen leaves, while pond frogs burrow into the mud at the bottoms of ponds and lakes.

Once in their respective places for the winter, herps experience a complex chemical reaction that is key to their survival for the winter. Not much is known about this reaction but it is thought that normal body functions stop or are at least greatly reduced. The water normally found within the cells of the body is replaced with a glucose or glycol substance (a sugar-based solution) that lowers the point of freezing. It also helps to reduce dehydration. Without this substance, the water in the cells would crystallize upon freezing and the pointed ends of these crystals would puncture the cell walls, ultimately destroying the cells and the critter. Even with this substance, some frogs, toads, snakes and turtles partially freeze. In fact, some studies have found that up to 30 percent of an individual reptile or amphibian freezes each winter. Amazingly, the animal still emerges each spring undamaged. Much still needs to be learned to understand this process.

While winter winds blow through the bare branches of trees, herps lie in suspended animation underground, waiting for spring. Then, as they have for the past several million years, they respond to external and internal stimuli and the antifreeze process is reversed. Slowly they come back to life and each in its own way heads for sunlight and its reviving warmth.

What's the difference between frogs and toads?

There are many types of frogs, including green frogs, tree frogs and toads. All are considered frogs. It might seem confusing, but a toad is simply a type of frog. All frogs share common characteristics: the ability to jump or hop, a tongue that is attached to the front of the mouth instead of the back and an absence of claws. Frogs range in size from the tiny spring peeper, that could sit on a dime, to the large bullfrog, which can grow to eight inches (20 cm) in length. In most species of frogs, the females are bigger than the males.

Toads have thicker skins than other frogs do, so their skins resist drying and can retain water longer. This characteristic allows toads to live further away from water, in places like your garden. As adults, toads generally stick to the land, while frogs are generally water lovers. Toads have smaller, less powerful legs, so they can only hop, not jump like other frogs. Frogs and toads are both most active during warm summer nights, when they can avoid the excessive heat and dryness of the day. They feed on insects by sitting still and waiting for the insects to fly or crawl near. In a split second, their mouths open and their long sticky tongues dart out to capture dinner. Gardeners are happy to have toads in their gardens to keep insects in check.

How many kinds of frogs and toads are there?

The ancestors of frogs and toads were among the first vertebrates, or animals with backbones, to evolve. Frogs and toads evolved during the dinosaur era. Although we don't know exactly how many species exist worldwide, the number is probably about 3,500. They are most common in the tropics, but they can also be found within the Arctic Circle, right up to the permafrost line, where the earth is frozen all year.

Why do frogs sing?

There are many sure signs of spring each year and one of them is the first evening trills of frogs and toads. Following the silent evenings of late winter, their choirs begin suddenly one spring day around dusk. The intensity of their singing decreases slowly throughout the summer until autumn, when the evenings once again grow silent. The voices you hear belong to male frogs that gather in large groups in ponds and marshes to sing a chorus in order to attract mates. Both male and female frogs have large ears, providing them excellent hearing. That's why it's so hard to sneak up on them.

Each frog species has its own distinct song. Some quack like ducks. Others croak or ring like a bell. So why is "ribbit" the sound we most commonly associate with frogs? Ribbit is the call of the California tree frog, which is found near Hollywood. It seems filmmakers there imitated its call in Hollywood movies.

Why do frogs have air sacs that inflate?

Think of these as an amplifier. The sounds made by frogs originates in their larynx or voice box. The frog takes air into its lungs and closes off its nostrils. The air is then forced up and out. The air rushes past the larynx to produce the sound. The air sacs on the outside of the frog then inflate. These act as a resonating chamber and the effect is that it intensifies the sound.

How can I get a better look at frogs while they're singing?

To see frogs calling, take a flashlight and follow their sounds to a pond near you. Don't be discouraged if they stop calling upon your approach. All you need to do is be still for just a moment. You can get the males to start calling again by making a hushed, high whistle or by rubbing two stones together to make a soft, rubbing sound. These noises will trick the male frogs into believing that other male frogs have started calling again for mates. They won't want the competition to get ahead of them, so they will all start to sing again. Continue approaching the frogs until you are at the water's edge. Scanning the shallow part of the water with your flashlight should reveal the singing frogs.

Can you get warts from toads?

The answer to this one is easy—no! If they did give us warts, all those curious children who touch them routinely would be covered with warts. Most toads do have a bony ridge called a **cranial crest** on their heads and two swellings called **parotid glands** behind their eyes. These may look like warts but they aren't. These bumps are glands that provide a defense against predators because they secrete noxious fluids that cause vomiting. These fluids are not poisonous to people, although if your child happened to kiss a toad, there may be a localized reaction. The poison works when an animal, like a fox or raccoon, catches a toad in its mouth. The secretions taste bad and the animal drops the toad unharmed. If your family dog has ever caught a toad, you have probably witnessed this reaction.

cranial crest

parotid glands

Why do I sometimes see frogs on my windows — are they trying to get in?

They probably don't want to get in! These are tree frogs and they are simply doing what comes naturally to them—climbing. The tree frogs have little adhesive-type pads on their toes. This allows their feet to adhere to trees, windows and anything else they want to climb. They are climbing to get to insects. The light from your windows attracts bugs and the bugs attract the frogs.

How do frogs get insects with their tongues?

Frogs and toads have unique tongues that play a large role in obtaining their dinner. They simply sit and wait for a tasty meal to fly or crawl by. They then quickly extend their very skillful tongues and touch the bug. Their tongues have sticky pads that catch the bug and it's brought into their mouths. Once they have caught something, the eyes of the frog do something very unusual. To assist in swallowing the prey, the eyes actually drop into the mouth cavity, helping to push the food down their throat. Catching insects on the fly takes skill, patience and some unique talents—all things that frogs seem to have!

How many salamanders are there and where do they live?

On warm spring and summer nights, deep within the woods, salamanders meet at the edges of ponds to mate and lay eggs. Salamanders who inhabit the woods are the most common species of salamander. About 350 known species live throughout the world, except in Antarctica and the North Pole. Some live entirely on land, while others live entirely in water. Either way, the adults are all carnivores whose main food is insects. Salamanders are common in the eastern U.S. and Canada because of the numbers of streams, lakes and ponds. More species live in North and South America than on any other continent. Because of their secretive lifestyle, many more species are probably still unknown to scientists.

How can you find a salamander?

A salamander can't vocalize, so you won't hear one and you'll rarely happen across one. To find a salamander, turn over logs and look under rocks. Your search will be most productive on warm spring or summer nights after rainy days. Salamanders are easy to identify because they have four legs and a tail. They are covered with dark, smooth, wet skin with no scales, that has spots or stripes. Lizards, by contrast, have rough, dry and scaly skin. Salamanders are also much slower than the quick moving lizards. Different species of salamanders range in size from one inch (2.5 cm) to a foot (.3 m) long. Put on your boots and grab a flashlight and head out to your favorite woodland to look for these secretive critters. Remember to replace any rocks or logs you moved to their original positions.

Sadly, salamanders are decreasing in numbers. Loss of habitat is the biggest threat to them, though many are killed when crossing roads to reach breeding ponds. Because of their sensitive skins, salamanders suffer from pesticides, herbicides, acid rain and other toxic wastes, which directly affect their reproductive rates.

> **Now I see the secret of the making of the best persons. It is to grow in the open air, and to eat and sleep with the earth.**
>
> WALT WHITMAN

How many kinds of turtles are there?

Turtles might be slow but they have been around a long, long time. Any reptile with a bony shell and a toothless, beak-like mouth is a turtle. There is no other animal quite like it. North America has nearly 50 species of turtles and worldwide there are about 250 species.

Turtles evolved about 250 million years ago. The earliest turtle fossils date back 180 million years. They were around long before the dinosaurs emerged, but they have changed very little in all those years. Maybe there is something to the saying "slow and steady as a turtle." The word **terrapin** (ter´a-pin) is sometimes used to describe edible turtles, but it has no scientific meaning.

How are turtle eggs hatched?

Generally, turtles rarely come on land except to lay eggs. Females travel to areas with soft soil, dig deep holes with their hind legs, deposit their eggs and leave. The sun does the incubating. Turtle eggs generally lack sex chromosomes. It is the temperature of the nest that determines the sex of the young of most turtle species. A cool incubating nest that is in reduced sunlight will produce males. A warm nest in direct sunlight will produce female hatchlings. Laboratory experiments have determined that the threshold temperatures are 88° F (31° C) or higher for all females and 77° F (25° C) or lower for all males. Nests that incubate at temperatures between 77 and 88° F produce some males and some females.

The turtles' habit of leaving the eggs to hatch on their own is risky and the majority of turtle nests provide foxes, skunks and raccoons with a nourishing meal. The young that do hatch often become food for larger animals; only a small percentage of baby turtles live to maturity. If they survive without being someone's meal when they are young, turtles can live 20 to 50 years, which is relatively old, compared to most birds, fish and mammals.

What do I do if I see a turtle laying eggs?

Late each spring, mother turtles all over North America haul themselves out of the water to dig a nest to lay their eggs. The female searches out a place with soft soil, usually on a hillside, anywhere from 100 feet to several miles from the lake or pond where she lives. She uses her hind feet to dig out a hole as deep as her hind feet can reach. Slowly and methodically she scoops out the soil to make a nest. While these mothers are concentrating on digging, they are vulnerable to predators and even family dogs and cats. Once the nests are made, many are raided by skunks and raccoons. If you have observed a turtle laying eggs, you can help to protect the incubating eggs by encircling the nest site with a sturdy fence or you can tack down some strong chicken wire over the site. This will protect the eggs from other animals. Mark your calendar to see how long the young take to hatch. You might want to take the soil temperature to guess the sex of the offspring.

How long do turtle eggs take to hatch?

Depending upon the species, a mother turtle will lay 4 to 40 white, leathery eggs at a rate of two per minute. After the eggs are laid, she covers them with the soil to incubate in the sunshine. The time it takes to incubate the eggs depends upon the warmth of the surrounding earth which is heated by sunlight. Usually the eggs take up to three months to hatch. If incubation progresses rapidly, the young will hatch just before winter. If the incubation is slow or taking place in more northern climates, the eggs will remain dormant until the next spring. Sometimes the young hatch in autumn but remain in the underground nest until spring, when they dig themselves out.

Do turtles bask, too?

Often when you approach a small pond or river you can catch sight of several turtles just before they slip into the water. Just as snakes need to bask in the sun to maintain their body temperature, so do most turtles. Turtles tend to bask in the same spot every day, which makes them easy to observe. They prefer sites well out in the water and in a position to give them a good view in all directions, so they can watch for danger. When sites are limited, they often climb onto the backs of other turtles to get more sun. Turtles almost always bask in the morning, presumably to warm up after a cool night. Larger turtles bask longer, probably because they have a greater mass to warm. The next time you approach a pond, walk slowly and quietly; you might get to see these sunbathers before they slip off into the water.

Can turtles leave their shells?

Cartoons often show turtles leaving their shells whenever they wish, but in reality, turtles can't do this. The two halves of a turtle's shell are fused to each other by a bony bridge, creating a safe and permanent home. The upper half is called the **carapace** (kar´a-pace); the lower is the **plastron** (plas´trahn). Both are made of bones and covered with plates that give the shell its color and design. The turtle's body is attached directly to the shell on the inside; in fact, their backbone and ribs are part of their shell. Turtles were the first animals to evolve a bony covering, a remarkable development that has served them well.

Although they can't leave their shells, some turtles can withdraw deep inside these marvelous structures. They pull their heads in by curling them back with their necks in an "S" shaped curve. They can also withdraw their legs. Some turtles such as the box turtle, have a semi-flexible bottom shell which helps to protect the turtle after it has withdrawn. When the turtle withdraws, the lower shell partially closes at the openings where the head and tail protrude, making it harder for a predator to reach the turtle inside. When turtles leave the safety of water they often take with them a small reservoir of water, which keeps them moist. This water is found inside the small space around the front and back edges of their shells. If you pick up a turtle, try to keep it level so this tiny reserve won't spill out.

Snakes — evil serpents or good rodent control?

Few animals have received as much bad press as the snake. A snake's physical attributes and natural behaviors may be partly responsible for such a bad reputation. Consider the following natural characteristics. They have an un-winking stare because they don't have eyelids; this stare has even been thought to have hypnotic powers. Some rare species of snakes, even though they are small, can kill a grown person with one bite. A snake has no vocal chords so it is eerily silent. It sheds its skin in a unique way. They have no legs, but move quickly across the ground. And, in eastern North America snakes live mostly underground, coming out only to sun themselves. It's no wonder they make many of us uncomfortable and seem a bit untrustworthy! In some states, venomous snakes are worth more dead than alive because the states still pay a bounty. Besides killing the bounty snakes, people often mistakenly kill other snakes for which there is no bounty. Bounty hunting has reduced snake populations and has even led to extinction for some snakes in certain areas.

Besides feeding on frogs and toads, snakes eat mice, voles, worms and insects, making them great for controlling the population of rodents. They have no trouble following these small critters into their hiding places for a meal. The next time you see a snake, try not to think "vile serpent" but instead "great rodent controller."

How many kinds of snakes are there and where did they come from?

There aren't many fossils of snakes, but they probably evolved from lizards about 150 million years ago. Today there are approximately 2,000 kinds of snakes in the world. They inhabit all kinds of terrain, from the tops of cold mountains to burning deserts. Some even live in shallow oceans. Still, several countries, such as Ireland and New Zealand, don't have any snakes.

How do snakes move without legs?

Snakes are so agile they can slither along the smallest branches, slip easily across loose sand and swim in or at the water's surface. They do this in one of three ways. The first way is called **lateral motion** and it is the method you are most likely to see. The snake pushes against the ground with its belly and slithers forward. The entire length of the snake touches the ground at the same time. This produces quick forward motion. The second method is called the **concertina** because the snake mimics an accordion. It bunches up its body, anchors its tail and then pushes forward. This motion is used in tight places where the lateral slithering doesn't work. Unlike lateral motion, only parts of the snake's belly touches the ground at the same time with this motion.

The third is **sidewinding**. The snake arches its back up off the ground so that its head lurches forward. As the head lands, the rest of the body loops high in the air, repeating the pattern. The snake touches the ground in only one small spot at a time and very quickly at that. For that reason, snakes use this method when crossing loose sand or hot places. Most snakes of the desert use it regularly.

All of these movements are attributable to the snake's backbones. A snake has somewhere between 200 and 400 vertebrae in its back. Between each vertebrae is a joint that allows the snake to be flexible. Incidentally, we have only 33 vertebrae in our backs.

Why do snakes shed their skins?

Snakes are reptiles and all reptiles are covered with a protective layer of scales. This type of body covering goes back to the age of the dinosaurs and before; most of them were covered with scales. Scales don't grow, so as the snake does, this protective cover soon becomes too small and the snake has to grow a new one. To do this, it has to **molt**, or shed the old covering of scales first. When it comes off, the old covering looks like a paper-thin "skin." It is not really skin like yours, but it is the top layer of scales and is often called skin.

All snakes molt at least once and sometimes as many as several times per season. Younger snakes grow faster than older snakes and, therefore, molt more often. The common garter snake molts several times per season, depending on its age, how often it eats and on how long the warm weather lasts. Most snakes shed all at once rather than in small sections, with the whole process taking about two to three days to complete.

Snakes don't have eyelids, but instead they have a clear scale covering their eyes. When it's ready to molt, a snake's eyes become clouded, indicating new scales forming under the old. The snake also stops eating. It usually remains hidden away from any danger, until the molt is complete. The skin around its head pulls away first. The snake may help remove it by rubbing its jaw against a rock or twig. The remaining scales are shed when they catch on brush or rocks as the snake winds its way through the undergrowth, peeling off the skin as you would peel a sock off your foot. Therefore, when you find a snake skin, it is almost always inside out. Pick it up and take a closer look. It will be dry and easy to handle, not gross and slimy as some would think. Each species of snake has a set number

> **Making new paper from old paper uses 30 – 35 percent less energy than making it from trees and reduces air pollution by 95 percent.**

of scales in a specific pattern, which makes shed skins easy for naturalists to identify. See if you can detect different patterns on the skins you find.

Why do snakes stick out their tongues?

Unlike humans, a snake doesn't use its tongue to move food around and help it swallow, but it does use it to taste and smell. A snake's sense of smell is many times more sensitive than our own. To smell, the snake first protrudes its tongue to pick up scents wafting on air currents. The fork at the end of the tongue adds to the surface area that can pick up these scents. The tongue then transfers the scents to an organ in the roof of the mouth called **Jacobson's organ**, where the scent is analyzed and passed on to the brain.

Snakes also lack external ear openings. They "hear" by feeling vibrations on the ground. Some snakes have special heat detectors that can sense the body heat of warm-blooded animals. These look like pits between a snake's eyes and nostrils. Because these snakes can sense an animal's heat, they can easily locate prey, such as mice and other rodents, even in dim light.

How can snakes swallow a mouse whole?

Snakes swallow their occasional dinners whole. This is possible because a snake's lower jaw can unhinge from its skull, letting its mouth open extra-wide for prey that would normally be too large to swallow. Strong tendons bring the jaw back into place after the prey has moved into the snake's throat. Snakes really don't eat much and they don't eat often; chances are you haven't seen one eat. Because snakes are cold-blooded and they don't derive their warmth from food, they don't need to eat very frequently. Most snakes in our area eat only once every other week during the active months of summer. They don't eat at all during winter unless kept in captivity in warm quarters.

How do snakes capture food?

All snakes are carnivorous, meaning they eat other animals. They capture their dinner in one of several ways. One way is **constricting**—a snake will grab the prey in its mouth, coil around it and squeeze it tight until it suffocates. The bull snake uses this method. In capturing small prey, coiling and suffocating may not be necessary. The garter snake captures prey in its mouth with one quick strike and the prey suffocates on the way down the snake's throat. Snakes have sharp teeth that are slanted backwards. These hook and hold very well. Once a snake has a grip on its prey, the victim rarely gets away.

Some snakes have developed additional strategies for capturing dinner. The rattlesnake, for example, has fangs that can inject a poisonous substance that either paralyzes or kills their prey. Just about every state and province in the U.S. and Canada have some populations of the famed rattlesnake.

Why do my hands smell after handling a garter snake?

The snake is probably trying to tell you it prefers to be left alone! In defense, a snake will usually dart for the cover of water or thick vegetation when you approach. If no cover is available, it will sometimes hide its head under its coiled-up body. If you succeed in capturing it, be aware that garters will bite if handled roughly so grasp them gently just behind the head and support the rest of the body with your other hand. Be prepared for the snake to discharge its anal contents, which is a clear pungent fluid. This strong musk really isn't very effective as a defense against predators, but it seems to work well to deter humans. The smell lingers even after washing. To avoid this encounter of the smelly kind, handle the snake gently and keep your fingers away from its anal opening. These snakes are easily tamed and will not be aggressive after just a few minutes of handling.

Are all snakes venomous?

Only about one third of the 2,500 species of snakes are venomous. The potency of snake venom is often highly overstated and encounters with venomous snakes are rare. Ask around in your area to determine if poisonous species exist. They are more prevalent in some areas than others. To determine the habits and dangers of venomous snakes, check out a field guide or consult your local nature center. Not all snake venom is detrimental. Some venoms are actually useful in the preparation of medicines. Cobra venom has been used as a pain killer. Other venoms have been used to treat epilepsy and current research is experimenting with snake venom to treat asthma and arthritis.

Do all snakes lay eggs?

Even though snakes are well known for laying eggs, only two-thirds of all non-venomous snakes lay eggs to reproduce. The other one-third, including the common garter snake, carry the young within the mother's body and give birth to live young. Our common garter snake breeds in the spring and two to thirty young are born live in late summer. When born, they appear like miniature adults and care for themselves right away. Females mature in two years and can produce one brood a year. With the exception of two, all venomous snakes lay eggs.

How long do snakes live?

Snakes are similar to other animals when it comes to life expectancies. Usually the larger the animal, the longer it lives. Bears can live over 20 years. Larger snakes, such as the anaconda, boas and pythons, can live to 20 years. Smaller snakes, such as the common garter snake, live an average of five to ten years. Keep in mind that snakes are slow and don't have much of a defense against predators. They end up as food for many animals, from eagles and hawks to coyotes and foxes. In the wild, most snakes don't live out their life expectancy.

How are frogs and turtles affected by the environment?

Reptiles and amphibians are considered by scientists to be an **indicator species**, which means they indicate the relative health of a specific ecosystem. Quite often people of older generations ask "Where have all the frogs or toads gone?" These animals have decreased in overall numbers in the past 50 years and their decline is related to the decreasing quality of our environment. Soil and water pollution and the practice of draining wetlands have had a large impact on these species. The latest evidence points to the increase in ultraviolet light due to a decrease in the ozone layer, affecting frog and toad populations. Light-sensitive eggs are being destroyed by the extra sunlight and millions of eggs are left unhatched in our ponds and lakes.

Also, with our increased traffic, every spring many frogs, toads, salamanders, turtles and snakes are killed crossing roads getting to breeding areas. In many parts of the U.S. and Canada, citizens have put up signs indicating frog and toad crossings to protect them at this critical time. Finally, today's monoculture yards, the ones that only have grass and frequent fertilizer applications, don't provide the habitat needed for frogs or for the insects that they feed upon. If we planted a variety of plants in our yards and provided areas free from human disturbance, we could accommodate these critters and help restore their numbers.

Turtle populations are also declining all over the world. Experts point to the commercial collection of eggs, collection for pet stores, wetland drainage and limited nesting habitat as some of the reasons. The rise in raccoon and skunk populations have also negatively impacted the turtles' reproduction. These predators feed on the buried eggs of all kinds of turtles. Much can be done for these ancient animals. Saving even the smallest wetland can help. So can controlling predators such as raccoons whose numbers have exploded in our urban areas. Taking the time to move turtles off roadways will help protect vulnerable females as they search for places to nest.

How can I use the Herp Smart species section?

This special group of animals is unique so it is worth spending extra time to search them out. Once you have spotted a turtle, snake or frog, resist that urge to grimace with disgust. Fear of these creatures is a learned behavior and is not based on fact. Snakes are not slimy and frogs and toads won't give you warts. Bring along a net and binoculars on your next nature walk to get a closer look at these creatures. Use your net to capture frogs and turtles without harming them. When approaching ponds and marshes, walk quietly, hide behind shrubs and use binoculars to get a better look at turtles and other herps. Open fields are great places to turn over rocks in search of snakes. Do this only in areas where there are no known venomous species. If you know that there are even some venomous species in the area, avoid seeking any snakes. Always replace overturned rocks to their original position to preserve these established shelters. Fallen logs and branches shelter salamanders in the woods and are always worth turning over to see what's underneath.

You are ten times the size of these creatures and your size alone is enough to frighten these timid animals. Handle them only if you are confident that you can do so without harming them or yourself. Replace all captured critters to where you found them. Moving these animals out of their territory denies them established shelters and food sources. Do not keep them captive. It is best to leave them right where they are to be sure they and any future offspring will survive. Lastly, most animals will defend themselves when threatened. Keep your fingers away from their mouths—especially turtles. Do not get too close to snapping turtles. They can sometimes grow as large as 40 pounds and will latch onto anything and not let go. If that happens to be your finger, you may lose it.

HERP SMART

American toad   *Bufo americanus 2-4" (5-10 cm)*

The American toad is a familiar creature in suburban gardens and yards. This thick, warty-skinned toad grows up to 4" (10 cm) and lives up to 10 years. It has shorter legs than other frogs and hops rather than jumps. They can be found looking for their food much further away from water than frogs. Because their skin is thicker and they don't dehydrate as quickly, they do not need to stay as close to water as the frogs. Each evening during the breeding season, males will give a high musical trill lasting 10 – 30 seconds. Look for a bony ridge, called a cranial crest, running across the top of the head, along with two glands behind the eyes, called parotid glands, that secrete a toxic fluid used to fend off predators. Most active at dusk and into the night, the American toad eats insects which it catches with a tongue that is attached to the front of its mouth. It can even be flipped out to catch flying insects. American toads are gray or brown while males can be identified by a dark throat patch. They lay eggs in long strands in the spring. Each autumn, American toads migrate to underground chambers or dig their own burrows to spend the winter.

Bullfrog   *Rana catesbeiana 4-8" (10-20 cm)*

The largest of all North American frogs, the bullfrog grows as large as an amazing 8" (20 cm) long. This smoothed-skinned frog has large tympanums (eardrums) and lives in large bodies of water. A large green frog with a white belly, the bullfrog calls with a deep hoarse "jug-o-rum." Bullfrogs are daytime hunters and are known to eat mice and snakes, along with other frogs and crayfish. These large frogs live up to six years, with females laying up to 20,000 eggs per round, floating mass. You may see this as a softball-sized group of clear, jelly-like eggs floating in the shallow end of a pond. After hatching into tadpoles, they spend the next year and a half to two years before they metamorphose into frogs. They overwinter underwater in lakes, ponds and rivers that are deep enough to have an adequate oxygen supply through the season.

Gray treefrog
Hyla versicolor 1½-2½" (4-6 cm)

The gray treefrogs are a small, chubby nocturnal frog (1¼" or 3 cm) with slightly warty skin and a distinctive white mark below its eye. They live in trees and shrubs but are never too far from water. What distinguishes treefrogs from other frogs are small adhesive toe pads, called **disks**, which enable these frogs to climb trees. These pads work so well that many report these frogs clinging to windows. It is from this vantage that you can see a yellow or orange patch on the inside of the hind thigh. Early on a spring evening, male gray treefrogs call from shallow woodland ponds or from perches in trees and shrubs. You can see these night-time critters by following the uniform trill or call with a flashlight. Adult gray treefrogs overwinter beneath leaves, logs and rocks and have the ability to withstand freezing temperatures up to -20° F (-29° C) for short periods of time.

Green frog
Rana clamitans 2-4" (5-10 cm)

A medium-sized, smooth-skinned frog of ponds, wetlands and streams, the green frog usually lives a solitary life and ranges in color from pickle green in northern regions to tannish brown in the South. No matter where you see this frog, look for its large disk-like eardrum, called a **tympanum** (tim´pa-num), just behind its eye. Males have larger eardrums, along with a yellow throat patch, while the female's eardrums are smaller and she has a white throat patch. Green frogs give a call that sounds similar to the plunking of a banjo. They eat snails, slugs and other water insects and spend the winter buried near the bottom of ponds where there is oxygenated, ice-free water. Green frogs are known for giving a series of chirps or yelps when picked up or startled.

Northern leopard frog
Rana pipiens 2-5" (5-10 cm)

This is the common green or brown pond frog that's covered with large, round, dark spots like the spots of a leopard. Look for these frogs in damp fields and along ponds, lakes or streams around dusk, when they become active for the night. Males and females look similar with females (3½"or 8.2 cm) slightly larger than males (3 ¼" or 7 cm). Although these are pond frogs, most of their hunting is done on land for things such as grasshoppers, crickets and spiders. Male leopard frogs have two vocal sacs, one near each front arm, which produce a "croaking" sound followed by a "clucking" sound. Males make calls to attract females in spring. Leopard frogs overwinter on the bottom of lakes and ponds. They cannot withstand freezing like some frogs that spend the winter on land.

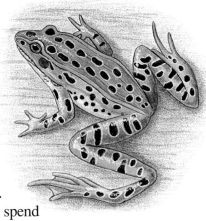

Common garter snake   *Thamnophis sirtalis 1-4' (.3-1 m)*

The garter snake is probably the most common snake in North America. It's stripes resemble the markings on the fancy garters used to support a gentlemen's socks. This non-venomous snake grows to about 4' (1 m) in length with females larger than males. You can tell the difference between the sexes by noting the length of the tails. Measure between the anal opening underneath or where you can see a slight bulge from above, and the tip of the tail to determine the sex. Females have shorter tails and larger bulges. Both sexes are brown with three yellow or red stripes down the sides and back. Though many snakes lay eggs and leave them to hatch on their own, garter snakes keep their young inside their bodies in a clear sac until they give birth to them

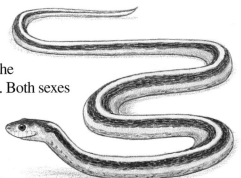

live. Sometimes one can witness a female giving birth to as many as several dozen pencil-thin snakes in late summer. They can live to about ten years of age. Garter snakes don't venture far from home, spending their entire lives within a two acre range (.8 ha.). All garters are most active in spring when they look for mates. Be on the watch for a writhing mass of snakes on the ground called "mating balls" during this time. Mating balls usually consist of one female and up to four dozen males. Only one will be successful in mating. Logs and rocks are favorite shelters during hot days and cool nights. They hibernate underground in well established dens used by hundreds of snakes. Note that they are not called gardener snakes, as many people mistakenly call them.

Eastern hognose snake   *Heterodon platyrhinos 1-4' (.3-1 m)*

The most obvious feature of this snake is its upturned nose, which gives it its common name. Hognose snakes are thick-bodied snakes of dry, sandy, open woods where they hunt for frogs, toads and insects. They grow up to 4' (1 m) in length and can be highly variable in color. They can be tan or brown, but most are yellow-brown with square blotches on the back and round blotches on the sides. Females are thicker and longer than males, but both have a dark line extending across and down the sides of the head through the eyes and terminating at the corners of the mouth. It uses its unique nose to root through the grass looking for food. Hognose snakes are the actors of the woodlands. When frightened, this non-venomous snake will act like a venomous snake and hiss, puff-up its body and vibrate its tail. If this doesn't scare off the offender, it will roll over and lay in a loose coil, playing dead. Here it will stay until the danger has passed. It will then roll over and slither away.

Red-belly snake   *Storeria occipitomaculata 1-1½' (.3-.5 m)*

Although these snakes have stripes, they are not considered one of the striped snakes as garter snakes are. Red bellies are light gray to black or brown with very faint dark stripes along their sides and three light red spots at the base of their head. A small, often described as cute, non-venomous snake reaching only about 1½' (.5 m) in length, red bellied snakes have a striking red or orange underside which is not easily seen without turning it over. Red-bellied snakes call the woodlands home where they hide under rocks, logs or bark and hunt for insects, earthworms and slugs. They bear up to 15 live young, each about 3 – 4" (7 – 10 cm) long.

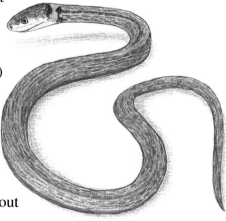

H E R P   S M A R T

Eastern box turtle — *Terrapene carolina 4-8" (10-20 cm)*

This high-domed, black or brown turtle has a pattern of yellow rays bursting like sunlight on its shell. The Eastern box turtle lives not in the lakes and ponds, but in the habitats of eastern prairies and woodlands. It is a very long-lived turtle, living up to 50 years. It is active during the day and can be seen slowly making its way across the forest floor. The front and rear openings of its shell are somewhat flexible, partially closing to enable this turtle to completely withdraw into its shell. Distinguish males from females by the longer tails of the males and reduced hind claws that are noticeably curved. Also, males usually have red eyes while females have brown eyes. Each autumn, box turtles eat a variety of plants and animals, in preparation for hibernation which is spent in holes or depressions in the ground.

Painted turtle — *Chrysemys picta 4-9" (10-23 cm)*

North America's most wide-ranging turtle, the painted turtle is considered a true "basking" turtle; look for painted turtles sunning on logs and rocks in the early morning hours. These small turtles prefer shallow, freshwater ponds with half-submerged logs on which they sun. The olive green carapace (upper shell) helps them stay camouflaged as they expose themselves to potential danger while basking. The smooth, olive plastron (under shell) has red bars and crescent marks along the edge. Yellow and red stripes mark their legs, long neck, face and head. Females grow larger than males but the males have considerably longer front claws. Painted turtles stay close to their aquatic homes and leave only for mating and laying eggs. Look for females crossing roads to lay eggs in sandy soils. They eat a variety of plants and animals, such as algae and small fish and snails. Each autumn they bury themselves in the mud at the bottom of lakes and ponds and hibernate through winter. They are long-lived turtles, averaging 10 − 15 years of age and are able to reproduce after about five years.

Snapping turtle — *Chelydra serpentina 8-24" (20-61 cm)*

A large turtle, the snapping turtle has a well-deserved reputation for being rather grumpy if cornered. The combination of a having somewhat of a temper and sharp, powerful jaws makes them creatures to respect from a distance. The thick neck and legs are so large and the plastron is so small that this turtle is unable to completely withdraw into its shell. They are usually seen floating at the surface or resting on the bottom of small lakes and rivers. They are most active at dusk and night so use a flashlight to spot them in shallow waters. Snappers will eat just about any plants or animals that are found in water. To catch fish they go fishing much like people do. Some species sit and wait on the bottom of the pond, dangling a worm-like projection from their tongue. They snap up an unsuspecting fish as it approaches the fake lure. The tail of the snapper is longer than just about any other turtle. Look for large triangular plates lining the tail and shell of these pre-historic creatures. These large turtles live about a half a century and begin breeding at about 5 – 7 years of age. Like painted turtles, snappers will bury themselves in the mud at the bottom of ponds and lakes to overwinter.

Tiger salamander — *Ambystoma tigrinum 6-13" (15-33 cm)*

Whether covered with brown, olive or yellow body markings, these non-vocal salamanders are easy to identify. Geographic variations account for the different colors. These large salamanders have long tails, stout bodies and short legs and live up to 25 years. Look for salamanders under logs and rocks during the day or traveling between shallow lakes and ponds at night. Often salamanders become trapped in window wells and swimming pools where they can easily be removed to a safe location. Tiger salamanders eat a wide variety of insects and worms and in turn, are food for turtles, herons and even snakes and otters. Each spring tiger salamanders emerge from underground cavities and crevasses and migrate to shallow ponds for mating. Females lay hundreds of eggs in large masses. In 3 – 5 weeks the eggs hatch into water-dwelling larva. By mid-summer, the larva become adults.

Mushroom Smart

On a morning walk through the woods, birds sing above your head and dew glistens in the eastern glow of the sun. You notice something unusual on the forest floor, something sprouting. You think it's a mushroom, but what kind of mushroom is it? Is it edible? What good do these mysterious organisms do? Mushrooms do indeed seem mysterious. Thousands of them, in every size, shape and color appear each year. There are those who spend a lifetime studying mushrooms, but even the casual nature explorer can learn to identify some common mushrooms and some of the important roles they play.

Technically, a mushroom is the visible, or above ground, portion of an underground or wood-dwelling organism, called a fungus. The organism is not an animal, of course, but it's also not a plant—it is a fungus. At one time, mushrooms were classified as plants, but modern **taxonomy** (the way we name and classify organisms) has placed mushrooms in a kingdom of their own called **Myceteae** (my-ce′tae). Also in this kingdom are rusts, molds, mildews and yeasts which don't produce what we would typically think of as a mushroom. These organisms are usually so small that unless you use a microscope you will never see them. For that reason we do not cover them in this chapter. Even though the word **mushroom** technically refers only to the visible portion of a fungus, we will use it in the more general way, referring to the entire organism.

The study of mushrooms is called **mycology** (my-col′ogy). The term comes from two Greek words: *mykes* for mushroom and *logos* for discourse, or study. A person whose hobby is hunting "edible" wild mushrooms is called a **mycophile** (my′ko-file), and a scientist who studies mushrooms is called a **mycologist** (my-call′o-jist). In the past, the word **toadstool** was used to describe a poisonous or inedible mushroom. Toadstool is a slang word that is not used consistently, and we would like to discourage its use. The word mushroom is thought to come from the French word *mousseron*, which came from the word *mousses*, or moss. It was thought that moss and mushrooms were similar, but we now know that one is a plant and the other is a fungus.

Mushrooms are the marvelous recyclers and assistants of life. They are responsible for breaking down fallen logs, branches, leaves and other non-woody plants and animals and returning them to the soil. One might say green plants and mushrooms are the ying and yang of the natural world. Plants give

159

life by producing seeds, leaves and oils that feed all living things. Then, after these plants and the animals that feed on them have died, mushrooms convert them into fertile soil so that new plants can grow. In doing so, they help continue the cycle of life.

Mushrooms influence an amazing number of everyday things, from medicine to agricultural practices, from architecture to the culinary arts, from biohazardous waste cleanup to biological warfare. For example, the miracle drug of this century, penicillin, is produced from a fungus. And the latest technology in hazardous waste clean up employs a fungus to convert toxic substances left behind by manufacturing, into harmless compounds.

To the best of anyone's knowledge, there are about 250,000 different species of mushrooms. Most are small and not seen. If you diligently search them out, you can expect to see a couple of hundred different kinds. If you are a casual mushroom hunter, you may find a few dozen kinds. One thing is sure: no matter where you travel, some type of mushroom is sure to be there. A mushroom's reproductive spores are carried by the wind and travel worldwide, making mushrooms one of the more successful and wide spread organisms on earth.

Are mushrooms plants?

No, they are not plants and they differ from plants in many ways. Most importantly, mushrooms don't have chlorophyll, which means they are not green. Also, mushrooms cannot produce their own food like plants, therefore, they are dependent upon plants or animals for a source of organic food. Unlike a plant, a mushroom takes up water and nutrients directly through its body. Lacking a vascular system like plants, once the water and nutrients are within the mushroom, they are passed from cell to cell in a sponge-like fashion. Finally, mushrooms don't have flowers like plants, but instead, reproduce by producing spores or by budding. **Spores** are microscopic cells that are capable of growing to reproduce themselves. **Budding** is a process where a small portion of the fungi breaks off and grows to reproduce.

What is the difference between a mushroom and a fungus?

The confusion between mushrooms and fungi is really one of terminology only. In one sense they are the same thing; the mushroom is simply a part of the fungi. What we call a mushroom is the fruiting or reproductive portion of the fungi. It might help to think of picking a mushroom as you would pick an apple from a tree; both are the fruiting, reproductive body. The only difference is that the "tree" portion of the fungus is underground or within a log. A fungus sends up the mushroom for the sole purpose of providing a vehicle for the dispersal of spores, the equivalent to a plant's seeds.

160

What are the parts of a mushroom?

Any mushroom can be broken down into several parts. The most visible part of any mushroom is the **cap**. Caps come in many sizes and shapes, including round, pointed and flat. Each of these caps has either gills or pores underneath. The **gills** or **pores** hold the microscopic structures that look like sacks which produce the spores. A stalk or stem usually holds up the cap, although some mushrooms have stems that merge into caps, giving the appearance of no cap or stem and others have no stem at all. Generally, the stem can be thick and strong or thin and weak, long and flexible or short and brittle. Either way, the stalk serves to get the cap up into the air so the gills or pores can release their spores. Stems may have a ring or "skirt" around the stem, which is called the **annulus** (an´u-lus). During the development of the mushroom, the annulus covers the gills, protecting them while they mature. Some mushrooms originate from a round ball-like structure that breaks open and appears like a "cup." The portion of the mushroom you don't see underground or within wood is called **hyphae** (hi´fee). Thin, string-like, white or brown threads intertwine to form a continuous mat. Individually each thread is called hyphae but combined in a network or continuous mat they are referred to as **mycelium** (my-see´li-um). At points along the mat of mycelium, mushrooms spring forth.

cap

gills

annulus
(skirt)

stalk
(stem)

Amanita
(poisonous)

What is a spore?

Just as a raspberry shrub produces a raspberry, a mushroom produces spores. A new shrub grows from the seeds of the raspberry and in the same way, fungi grow from the spores of the mushroom. From underneath the caps of some mushrooms, within pits of others or sometimes from inside a mushroom, spores are made and stored to be released when ripe. Tiny sack-like structures hold two, four or more spores waiting to be released when the mushroom matures. Mushrooms are prolific spore producers; each releases hundreds of thousands of spores each day. The smallest spores measure about 1 micron (about the size of bacteria) so you can't see them without a microscope. The largest are about 300 microns and visible to the naked eye. Most spores are so small that thousands can fit on the head of a pin. You can see spores by placing a cap of a fresh mushroom on a piece of white or black paper with the gill or pore side down. Cover both the paper and mushroom with a cup or bowl to block any air currents. After a couple of hours, enough spores will have fallen onto the paper to make them visible. This is called a **spore** print.

Spores usually drift on air currents, but they can be carried by birds, rodents, insects or water currents. They endure drying, freezing and long periods of dormancy and still retain the vigor to sprout new life, but only a few land in a place where they can grow. If they all grew into new mushrooms there would be no room for any plants or animals.

Spores have irregular sizes and shapes, some having wing-like projections, spikes or knobs. Because of these shapes, they fall with surprising slowness in still air. However, the air is rarely, if ever, completely still. Spores take advantage of this and ride air currents high up into the air and to all points of the earth. In fact, the air is always filled with tiny spores. Some are carried more than a mile (1.6 km) above the earth. A single spore can travel up to 2,900 miles (4,666 km) on a 20 mile-an-hour (32 km) wind if blown to the height of one mile (1.6 km). Rain storms flush many spores from the sky, thus aiding spore dispersal. They land in every conceivable place—on trees, on crops, and even on people. In controlled experiments, "marked" or "tracer" spores have been released in a room on the first floor of a four-story building and recaptured five minutes later in a room on the fourth floor. You can run, but you can't hide from these tiny packets of reproductive power.

How many mushrooms are there?

Mushrooms have existed since Precambrian times (about 1.2 billion years ago) but the kinds of mushrooms we see today didn't evolve until 350 thousand years ago. Currently they are a diverse group with about 250,000 distinct species living in salt water, fresh water, soil and wood throughout the world; they can even live on your feet as athletes' foot. They are so wide-spread that they are considered to be one of the most successful forms of life on earth— and one of the oldest. It would be fair to say that every square inch (centimeter) of soil on the earth has a species of mushroom growing in it. The reason you don't see mushrooms popping up all over the place is that many spores require very specific conditions to send up a mushroom. Of those that do, some produce inconspicuous, small mushrooms, while others send up very large ones.

How do mushrooms suddenly pop up in my yard?

Mushrooms seem to mysteriously pop up overnight, a perception that has contributed to many untruths and myths. If you suddenly see a mushroom where you didn't before, chances are the fungus had been growing in your lawn for years and only when the conditions became just right did it send up a mushroom. The rapid growth of mushrooms themselves are related to the fact that mushrooms are 90 percent water. Once the right conditions of temperature and moisture are met, the mushroom simply pumps water into its cells and away it goes. Mushrooms have been known to push up right through asphalt driveways and tennis courts. This display might attest to the power of hydraulics.

What do fungi do?

Mushrooms perform three main functions. The first is to break down dead matter. Green plants feed the earth's creatures with their leaves, flowers and seeds, but they are so prolific that they produce more than animals can consume. Fungi break down the excess plant material. If they didn't, our planet would soon be covered with dead plants, choking out any new growth. The majority of mushrooms live on dead plant material, such as dead trees, branches and leaves, and some live on dead animals. As mushrooms eke nutrients from this matter, they break it down and recycle the nutrients back to the earth. These mushrooms are called **saprophytes** (sap´ro-fites).

Other fungi subsist on living plants and animals. Their lifestyles are similar to that of the saprophytes and serve a similar purpose, but they slowly kill their host. They are called **parasites**. Lastly, one group of fungi actually benefits some plants. These fungi live among the roots of nearly all trees and shrubs. They are called **mycorrhiza** (my-ca-rise´a) and enable a growing plant to absorb water and essential minerals more easily than if the plant were not associated with the mushroom. In fact, most plants require these fungi to live. In turn, the mushroom draws nutrients from the plant's roots. This relationship is not clearly understood. We do know that in some of these **symbiotic**, or mutually dependent relationships, either partner would die without the other. The word mycorrhiza literally means fungus root.

> **What is life? It is the flash of a firefly in the night. It is the breath of a buffalo in the winter time. It is the little shadow which runs across the grass and loses itself in the sunset.**
>
> CROWFOOT

In addition, some fungi have formed partnerships with insects. For example, it's not the termite that digests the wood it eats, but instead, it's a fungi growing in the termite's stomach. Also, leaf cutter ants don't eat the leaf wedges they cut, but rather, they feed the leaves to a fungus they keep in their underground nests. They cultivate and feed on the fungus, not the leaves.

How do fungi help humans?

Volumes could be written on the effects mushrooms have had on humans throughout history. Various species are used in making many medicines and foods. Using mushrooms in medicine is not something new. The first mention of mushrooms used in medicine was in the fifth century B.C. in the writings of Hippocrates, who recommended using mushrooms to cauterize "nervous parts." While some mushroom spores are quite flammable in themselves, the mushroom was also soaked in a flammable substance, and then dried. After drying, the mushroom was set on fire and as it smoldered, it was applied to the affected part. This process is still employed among some remote primitive tribes. The Greeks and Romans also ate mushrooms as a universal remedy.

In September 1991 the frozen remains of a man were excavated from an ice field in the Austrian/Italian Alps. This unfortunate soul had been encased in ice for the past 5,200 years. Otze, as he was named, represents the oldest man and most complete remains of any human of that time. He carried a small leather bag that contained a ball of mushrooms known to have antibacterial properties; presumably it was used to treat minor wounds. Otze demonstrates just how humans have depended on fungi for centuries.

The common blue and green molds we so frequently see on fruit, cheese and bread in our neglected refrigerators are actually fungi whose profuse spores typically float in the air and dwell in the soil. This mold is one of many species of *Penicillium* and is used in the production of the antibiotic drug penicillin. Some species of Penicillium are used to control other fungi that cause skin disease. Blue cheese and Italian Gorgonzola contain Penicillium and it is what gives Roquefort and Camembert cheese their highly prized flavor. Mushrooms are also important in the production of wine and beer. Various kinds of alcoholic drinks are fermented with sugar and starch using yeast, a single-celled fungus. The yeast feeds on the sugars and starches and in the process converts the ingredients into alcohol. This process has been employed for thousands of years as just about every major civilization has used alcohol for medicinal purposes or for pleasure. These same properties of yeast are what causes bread to rise.

How do fungi hurt humans?

It is thought that the hallucinogenic properties of some parasitic fungi known to attack grains, played a role in the witch hunts of Salem. It seems some villagers unknowingly consumed tainted bread and suffered from the delusion that others were witches. Many innocent people died because of the lack of understanding of this mushroom contamination. Now grains are inspected for any of this contamination, making them perfectly safe for our consumption.

Mushrooms have also been responsible for considerable damage to crops while they grow or when they are stored. "Field fungi" can stain or discolor seeds, shrivel seeds before they are harvested, or reduce the chance that seeds will sprout. "Storage fungi" can turn kernels of corn, barley and wheat black, and reduce its value. Whole grain elevators can become infected and worthless.

Finally, the timber industry can be harmed by fungi as several thousand species of mushroom-producing fungi live exclusively on wood, causing decay and rot. When wood becomes wet, fungi move in, causing rot. Mushrooms are constantly attacking moist wood, whether the wood is in a tree or lumber. Lumber is treated to keep out water and fungi.

Are mushrooms edible?

This is probably the most common question about any mushroom. **Mycophagests** (my-co-fa´jists) are people who eat wild mushrooms. While some wild mushrooms are edible, some are not; in fact, they are poisonous. Hopefully, the mycophagests know the difference. The vast majority of mushrooms aren't poisonous but are inedible for a variety of other reasons. Either they are too small, too hard, or they don't produce a typical, visible fruit. People have eaten mushrooms since prehistoric times. Undoubtedly, early gatherers tried many kinds of wild mushrooms and learned which were edible though trial and error—sometimes deadly error. We recommend that if you are not 100 percent sure whether a mushroom is edible, don't eat it. (When in doubt, throw it out!) To learn more about edible mushrooms pick up a field guide and take a class. You might want to join your local mycological society. Their members are always glad to share their knowledge.

Edible mushrooms are nutritious. They are low in calories unless they are cooked in butter or other high calorie substances. They contain some protein, vitamins (A, B, C and D) and several minerals. They are low in fat and contain no cholesterol. Overall, mushrooms compare favorably to vegetables and can be a delicious, healthy food.

How do I avoid poisonous mushrooms?

It has been known for centuries that some mushrooms are toxic but yet every year some people are poisoned by them. The majority of mushroom poisonings occur when young children pick small mushrooms in their yards. Make sure children understand that mushrooms can be dangerous. You can't get rid of the underground portion of mushrooms growing in your lawn, but you can pick any you see before children play.

Mushroom poisonings are not common in North America; in fact more people are struck by lightning than die from eating poisonous mushrooms. The exact number of people suffering from non-fatal mushroom poisonings in the U.S.

and Canada is unknown. Some states don't record these poisonings, some people don't report them and in some cases, the poisoning is not known to be caused by mushrooms. You can learn which mushrooms are safe and which are poisonous, but if you're at all unsure, you are better off considering them all poisonous.

Of the 250,000 species of fungi found in the world, most mushroom poisonings stem from about 20 species. Fewer than ten species are deadly poisonous. Most deaths in the U.S. and Canada come from eating the deadly amanitas, a group of large, fleshy mushrooms. The first symptoms of amanita poisoning don't appear until 12 to 24 hours after this latent killer has been consumed, so a doctor may not link the symptoms to the mushroom. In a typical scenario, someone mistakenly eats an amanita and becomes ill 12 hours later. He or she is seen by a doctor just as the symptoms subside. The patient is sent home, but then the symptoms return and become even more severe. In the meantime, the patient's kidneys have been damaged. It's now too late to save them, and the patient dies within several days, not within minutes, as is seen in the movies.

> **❝If everybody would learn always to think in terms of what he or she could do to protect the environment, it would have a massive ripple effect that would spread from our homes and local communities all across the nation.❞**
>
> RACHEL CARSON

Why are mushrooms shaped and colored the way they are?

Mushrooms are distinctly functional organisms yet it is hard to match the stunning beauty of a colorful sulfur shelf mushroom or the intricacies of an earthstar mushroom. Mushrooms are as varied as fish and birds, coming in just about every shape imaginable. They are cup, shell, club and umbrella-shaped and some appear like nests, cones, hair, corals, lumps of jelly, balls or rings. Why so many different shapes? In the same way that each plant has evolved to take advantage of certain insects, wind currents or other environmental conditions to reproduce, mushrooms have evolved to take advantage of ways to release their spores. The main objective of any mushroom is to effectively release as many spores as possible. Some mushrooms release spores that float easily, taking advantage of wind currents. Other spores are carried by insects or are eaten by animals that transport them to distant places.

All mushrooms that have gills or pores need to release their spores without the spores being caught up internally. Some of the shelf mushrooms that grow on the side of a tree will have their pores facing down to effectively release the spores. These mushrooms are **geocentric**, which means they are able to grow right side up, no matter what their position. If the tree the mushroom is living on should fall down, these mushrooms will grow new spore surfaces so that the spore surface is facing down. Next time you see a downed tree in the woods look for these twisted mushrooms.

Mushrooms that grow on the ground need to get above the surrounding vegetation to release their spores. Most ground-dwelling species have a long stalk to get their cap, which contains the spores, up into the air currents. Some ground-dwelling mushrooms have devices from which to shoot or puff out their spores so that they can clear any obstacles. Some species have a mechanism that uses water pressure to shoot packets of spores as many as several yards away. Others have structures that make use of raindrops which land in a cup and wash out the spores. Still others develop mushrooms, called puffballs, which are round and can be as large as the size of a basketball. When raindrops fall, they exert pressure on the outside skin of the mushroom, forcing spores out of any crack in the skin of the mushroom. Small puffballs have a hole at the top of the ball that releases thousands of spores in a single puff with the impact of a rain drop or the poke of your finger.

The colors of mushrooms vary as much as the shapes. Pink, vibrant red, green, coral white, gray, jet black, yellow, orange and of course brown, are some of the colors on the mushroom palette. Color plays an important role for many living things, but in mushrooms, the function of the colors is not so apparent. Some of the most brilliantly colored mushrooms are not poisonous, while the most drab or white mushrooms are deadly poisonous. Some mushrooms use scents to attract insects. The stinkhorn emits a foul smell that tricks flies into thinking it is rotting meat. They land to feed and lay eggs, only to find nothing to eat. Then they fly away with their feet covered with spores.

How do I use the Mushroom Smart species section?

Just about any walk in the woods in spring or autumn can reveal a wide variety of mushrooms. There are 250,000 known mushroom species with an untold amount yet to be discovered. This species section does not intend to help you identify each of these. Instead we have included five categories or groups of mushrooms based on characteristics that they share. While you may not be able to identify a particular species, you will probably be able to place it in the group in which it belongs. The illustrated mushroom shows a specific species of mushroom that we have chosen to represent the group.

For example, if you find a mushroom that looks like one you would buy in the store and it has gills under the cap, read about the gilled mushrooms. That is likely what you have found. Cup mushrooms are ones that don't have gills or pores but have pits or one, large, cupped surface. Just about any mushroom growing on the side of a tree is considered a shelf mushroom. If you have ever seen a small or large, white, round mushroom, you have found one of the puffballs. Jelly mushrooms are so named because they look and feel like jelly but do <u>not</u> taste them. Even if you can't identify the exact species of the mushroom you have found, you will learn to distinguish the characteristics that place it in a category.

This section is written so the reader can experience mushrooms on all but a culinary level. There are many good field guides to show which ones you can eat and which ones you should not. If you want to learn which mushrooms are edible, we suggest you join your local mycological society, pick up several books on edible mushrooms and go out into the woods with someone who knows what they are doing. A word of caution: never eat a mushroom that you are not 100 percent positively sure is edible. Also, always wash your hands after handling unknown mushrooms. Some are so toxic that even a tiny remnant left on your hand can make you sick if your hand touches your mouth. Don't place unknown mushrooms in coolers with your food. Pieces can break loose and become part of your lunch.

Use this chapter to learn more about the characteristics of mushroom groups and to experience the sight, feel and odor of mushrooms. When you first come upon a mushroom look where it is growing. Is it on wood or the ground? What color is it? Is it dry or wet, smooth or rough? Is there more than just one? Does it change color when touched, How does it smell? It is worthwhile to stop and examine each mushroom to marvel at its beauty.

GILLED MUSHROOMS

These mushrooms usually have a well defined cap with thin page-like gills beneath.

Amanita
Amanita spp. 4-8" (10-20 cm)

Amanitas are deadly poisonous mushrooms that have similar characteristics, making them easy to identify. Look for them growing on the ground in woodlands. From mid-summer to autumn, they start out looking like a small, white-colored egg on the ground. From this form pops the familiar mushroom with a hamburger-bun-shaped cap on a single stem. They are 4 – 8" (10 – 20 cm) tall. Caps are usually white, but yellow and red are common. The egg form doesn't disappear but takes on the shape and look of a cup, called a volva from which the mushroom emerges. All amanitas have white gills and a cup or volva and most have a skirt or ring, called an annulus, around the middle of the white stem. They live in a mycorrhizal relationship with trees, exchanging nutrients that help both the tree and mushroom. Just about all of the amanitas are very poisonous and must be avoided. If you do touch them, wash your hands before touching your mouth or eyes. They are classically beautiful to photograph, just don't touch.

Inky caps
Coprinus spp. 2-6" (5-15 cm)

Inkies are some of the most common gilled mushrooms you will see. They grow in parks, woodlands and even backyards. They can be found just about anytime of year and are only 2 – 6" (5 – 15 cm) tall. Inky caps grow on wood chips, tree stumps or even in your lawn, depending upon the species. They are called inky caps because the cap turns to a black, inky, liquid mess when it matures. Most inky caps are white, while a few are brown. Some of the inky caps are edible, while others are toxic when consumed with alcohol. Look for black "ink" in your lawn where these mushrooms were growing. If there appears to be enough "ink," try getting some on the end of a stick and writing with it.

169

Oyster
Pleurotus spp. 3-6" (7-15 cm)

This is a very common, gilled mushroom that always grows on wood. They are called oysters because of the shape of the soft, flexible cap which is oyster or clam-shaped. The caps are from 3-6" (7-15 cm) across and attractively overlap one another. These mushrooms can be found anytime of year. They are white to yellow and have large white gills which extend all the way to the attachment at the wood. Oysters help to breakdown dead branches or fallen trees. Look for small, black beetles that like crawling around the gills of this mushroom. Sniff the mushroom to see if it smells like anise.

CUP MUSHROOMS

These singular mushrooms are large and dish or cup-shaped. They are often thin and flexible but some have many small pit "cups."

Morels
Morchella spp. 2-6" (5-15 cm)

The morel is probably the most sought after mushroom by mushroom hunters. Morels are about 2-6" (5-15 cm) tall and grow only in early spring on the ground. They are easy to miss because they are often camouflaged by last year's leaves. They are considered a cup mushroom because the cap is covered with pits or "cups" where the spores are produced. All morels have a hollow stem and cap. The over-all appearance is a tan-colored stem with a cap that looks like a sponge. Look for them singularly or in groups on the ground.

Scarlet cup
Sarcoscypha spp. ½-2" (1-5 cm)

This small mushroom, about ½- 2" (1-5 cm), makes up for its size with a brilliant scarlet color. This is a true cup mushroom that grows on fallen branches or rotting wood. It is one of the first mushrooms in spring, making it easy to see and identify. Scarlet cups have no gills; the spores are produced on the inside surface of the thin flexible cup. They are not considered edible. Similar species are yellow or orange.

SHELF MUSHROOMS

Growing from the sides of trees, these mushrooms can be as hard as the wood they grow on. Some are thin and flexible.

Artist's conk   *Ganoderma spp. 2"-2' (5 cm-.6 m)*

This is a hard mushroom, having the consistency of wood, that can be seen year-round. It grows on dead trees, slowly breaking down its wood. It is flat to hoof-shaped, with a gray to brownish cap that grows several inches (centimeters) each year. The shelves can be a few inches to 2' (.6 m) across and strong enough to stand upon. The underside is white to cream and is covered with very small pores. The pores release the spores and are easily bruised. Artists etch designs on the soft, underside surface where the pores are located given its common name. After they have dried, the designs remain forever. If you find this mushroom on the ground, try using something hard to make a design of your own.

Turkey-tail   *Trametes spp. 1- 4" (2.5-10 cm)*

Turkey-tails grow in large overlapping clusters along a fallen log or on a dead, standing tree. Each cap is thin and very leathery with alternating smooth and hairy bands. These bands are also multi-colored and they resemble the tail of a turkey. They can be found almost anytime of year. They breakdown the wood on which they grow. They have no gills, but rather microscopic pores that line the underside of each cap. Be sure to touch this one to feel the soft, flexible texture.

PUFFBALLS

Puffballs come in many sizes but they all are round like a ball. Earthstars are related to puffballs having a round ball in the center of wing-like appendages, giving this mushroom the appearance of the petal of a flower. They can be found growing on both wood and soil. They are called puffballs because of the way they puff-out and become clouds of green spores when they mature.

Earthstar
Geastrum spp. 2-4" (5-10 cm)

Although not apparent at first, the earthstars are a type of puffball. The puffballs are a remarkable mushroom with a roundish "puffball" in the center of star-like rays. In some species these rays will unfold and lift the puffball up off the ground like the legs of a lunar lander (robot). They grow on the ground in leaves and other organic material. Earthstars can be seen in the summer and fall, individually or in groups. It is the "ball" that releases the spores when mature. Look for a small opening or pore in the top of the ball. If you touch the ball the spores will "puff" out.

Giant puffball
Langermannia spp. 2-20" (5-50 cm)

The puffballs range in size from the size of a marble to a soccer ball, depending upon the species. They can be found in summer to late fall. Look for them in woodlands, lawns, pastures and parks of all sizes. Most grow on the ground but some grow on wood. In either case, they don't grow on a stem. They all produce their spores within the ball. After maturing, the ball will either break open or develop a small pore in which the spores will be released. Try touching a puffball to see the spores "puff" out.

JELLY MUSHROOMS

Jelly mushrooms appear just like jelly. They can be yellow, brown or red. They are usually growing on wood.

Witches butter
Tremella spp. 1-4" (2.5-10 cm)

This is a group of mushrooms that all look like brightly colored jelly. They range in color from black to yellow and orange and they vary in texture from rubbery to moist and gelatinous. Some look like a leaf, while others are brain-like in appearance. Witches butter is golden yellow and it grows on wood, such as oaks and beech trees. It can be seen just about anytime of year. Press one and watch its jelly-like liquid ooze onto your finger.

Plant Smart

When you escape the bustle of a busy city to the calm of a woods you feel like you're entering a whole new world. The woods remind us of a time when the world wasn't full of pavement, gas stations and fast food restaurants. There tall, metal, geometrically-shaped buildings are replaced by towering, majestic oaks and maples and concrete sidewalks are exchanged for ferns and woodland wildflowers. We appreciate the beauty of plants and the fresh, peaceful feeling they give us, but we often don't think of them as being our connection to life itself. Plants are the very foundation of life on earth.

Plants help our world in many important ways. We live our entire lives influenced by them. They shelter us by shielding our homes from the hot summer sun and bitter winter winds. Plants provide habitat for animals as well as providing materials for our homes. They create oxygen and purify our air. We depend on plants, directly and indirectly, for a large portion of our diet. Also, plants beautify our surroundings, and they have inspired some of the world's best literature, art and music. All around us, from the tops of the mountains to the bottom of the seas, plants thrive. In fact, they have been the predominant life form on earth for billions of years.

Plants produce timber and coal and we use plants to manufacture many useful things such as perfumes, medicines, clothing, rubber and waxes. Even the fuel that runs our cars comes from plants. Gasoline is made from petroleum which is a product of ancient algal plants that have been buried underground for millions of years. All stages of your life are affected by plants. In fact, the clamp the doctor used on your umbilical cord when you were born was made from a plastic that was derived from a plant. When people die, they are embalmed with a fluid made from corn starch. From birth to death, we are surrounded by plants and products made from them.

Plants take in the elements of light, carbon dioxide (CO_2) and water, and convert these basic elements into energy. In that way, they make their own food. From the mightiest sugar maple to the much maligned dandelion in your yard, plants provide life in the form of food.

Green plants are living things that contain the green pigment **chlorophyl**. They include liverworts and moss as well as trees, shrubs, herbs and grasses. We don't know exactly how many species exist. There are likely many that have not been discovered by scientists, such as those that may grow in hidden places within the rainforests. The best guess is that there are approximately 350,000 species of plants worldwide, with many more being discovered all the time. The study of plants is called **botany**. Botanists help to discover new plants and to better understand the vital role plants play. Plants differ widely in shape, size and texture, but they all provide the living world with the necessities of shelter, air and food.

> **We need to develop a global ethic, one that will help individuals and societies develop attitudes and behaviors that promote a sustainable earth for people and all other organisms.**
>
> MINNESOTA DEPARTMENT OF EDUCATION

Because plants are the givers of life, any threat to plant populations represents a threat to us and all life on earth The biggest threat is that many plants are being destroyed at unprecedented rates. From the ancient forests of the northwestern U.S. and Canada to the rainforests of Costa Rica, plants are losing a battle to human development.

In this chapter, you'll to learn how to look at a field or forest and see the individual plants within it and understand their indispensable contributions to the natural world. For example, the milkweed in the field supports the life cycle of the monarch butterfly. Without milkweed, these flamboyant beauties could not survive. Every plant has a unique role that can be ferreted out with a little investigation. By learning about some of the common plants of the woodlands, wetlands and prairies, you'll be more aware of the important role that plants play in our world.

Why are plants green?

This question could be a riddle such as "What appears to be green but is not really green?" The answer would be chlorophyll. While chlorophyll is a pigment or coloring found in the leaves of green plants, it is not green as you might think. It only appears to be green because of the sunlight. The light from the sun looks white, but it is actually made up of bands or wavelengths of colored light. Usually we see these bands combined together as white sunlight. But when sunlight strikes the leaves of plants, the chlorophyll absorbs most of the bands of light. It soaks up the red and blue wavelengths and reflects back the green and yellow wavelengths. We see the wavelengths that are reflected as light.

How do plants make their own food?

Plants are unique because they don't depend on other living things for food! Why? Because they alone can make their own food from sunlight. In turn, they become food for all other forms of life. Even animals that eat other animals depend on plants, because their prey is nourished by plants. Plants are at the beginning of every food chain.

To make food, plants first capture sunlight in their leaves with their pigment, chlorophyll. Using the energy of the sunlight, they take a few basic elements such as hydrogen in water and carbon in carbon dioxide. They convert these elements to complex, energy-rich sugars and starches, in a process called **photosynthesis** while giving off oxygen as a by-product. They then convert any extra sugars into carbohydrates which are stored in the leaves or roots of the plant. We find these sugars, starches and carbohydrates in fruits and vegetables. Wheat, rice, oats, barley, tomatoes, cucumbers, squash and many other plant foods are rich in these nourishing sugars and starches.

Photosynthesis is no simple task. After years of research, scientists still don't completely understand this process that is so basic to plants. The actual amount of sunlight used by plants for photosynthesis is only a tiny part, about one-tenth of one percent (.1%) of the total amount of sunlight that strikes the earth. Yet with this relatively small amount of sunlight, plants produce about 150 to 200 billion tons of dry organic matter such as branches, stems, fruits, seeds and leaves every year. Much of that is eaten by us every year.

What is all that yellow dust on flowers?

You may have noticed bees carrying what appear to be yellow bags on their back legs. This and the dust you see on flowers is **pollen**. Before a plant can reproduce, it needs to be pollinated. Pollination happens when a plant's male cells come in contact with female cells so fertilization can occur. Within a flower are male parts that look like tiny yellow, brown or tan bananas called **anthers**; these are packed with pollen. Each anther is perched on its own even tinier stalks called **filaments**. Together they are called a **stamen**. Also within a flower are female parts. They are just as small and are made up of three parts. The round base where the seed matures is called the **ovary**. From this is a single stalk called a **style** with a sticky knob on the end, called the **stigma**. Collectively they are called **pistil**. The stigma sticks out to offer a sticky surface for the male pollen to attach to. When the stigma and the pollen combine, pollination is complete and a seed can be formed within the ovary. Pollen is transferred by wind, water, insects, birds and mammals.

Does it take two plants for pollen to work?

Not always, since it depends on whether the species is pollinated by self-pollination or cross-pollination. **Self-pollination** occurs when a flower has both male and female parts within a single flower or separate male and female flowers on the same plant. When an insect like a bumblebee lands on a flower to sip nectar, it inadvertently brushes up against the pollen from the male flower. Her pollen-coated body then by chance transfers the pollen to the sticky female stigma and pollination is complete. This type of pollination is quick and easy for the plants but doesn't produce much genetic variation which is essential for longevity of the plant's breed.

Cross-pollination occurs when pollen from one plant is "crossed" with a separate plant. This happens when pollen is transferred either by wind, birds or insects to another flower located on a different plant. Cross-pollination mixes up the genetic make-up of the plants and insures strong and healthy offspring.

Can one kind of plant pollinate a different kind?

Pollen and plants are like locks and keys. It takes a certain kind of pollen, that generated by the same species of plant, to pollinate another plant of the same species. Because this exact match is necessary, much excess pollen is produced by plants and trees to increase the chances of it landing on the same species elsewhere. In spring, some ponds and lakes are covered with a yellow film which is the "excess" pollen produced by nearby trees.

Occasionally, some pollen is effective in fertilizing other similar species of plants. This "crossing" between related species is what scientists use in producing **hybrids**. Hybrids will produce a combination of features of the two different plants. A comparable phenomenon in the animal kingdom would be the crossing of the male donkey with a female horse which results in a mule. An example of this is in the plant kingdom would be the development of different hybrid roses or various field corn hybrids. These hybrids are usually sterile. In the natural world, producing hybrids takes many years and is usually considered part of the process of evolution.

Do plants breathe?

Yes, in a fashion they do. The systems that plants use to move nutrients and exchange gases are different than those of humans. The water and nutrients from the soil are carried to the plant's leaves by a fluid called sap. Within a plant, sap moves by two pressure systems, root pressure and transpiration. **Root pressure** works when the roots absorb water and minerals, creating a solution. Having a higher concentration of solution in some parts of the roots than others causes an unequal pressure within the roots called **osmosic pressure**. This pressure forces the sap up from the roots into the main body of the tree but exactly how this works is still being debated. The current theory suggests that the loss of water from the leaves, called **transpiration**, creates a pull or tension on the sap within the plant. Sap is pulled up through the **xylem** (zi´lem) (similar in function to an artery) to the leaves which are constantly losing water (breathing) through tiny microscopic holes called **stomata** (sto-ma´ta) Therefore, the water in the leaves is continually replaced with water in the sap brought up from the roots. This flow of sap which replaces the moisture is the result of transpiration. Water is constantly moving from the bottom up in a non-dormant tree. To see how this works, place a fresh stalk of celery in a glass filled with colored water. Within a couple of hours you will see how the water has moved up the stem and stained the leaves. In a plant, when more water is lost from the leaves than is absorbed in the roots, the leaves will lose their turgor (stiffness) and will become limp and wilt. If this condition continues the leaves will die.

Do all plants come from seeds?

In nature there are very few absolutes. Not all birds fly and not all plants come from seeds. While the vast majority of plants do come from seeds, a few plants produce spores or simply clone themselves. Plants like ferns and moss use spores to reproduce. A **spore** is a small reproductive body usually consisting of a single cell. It will germinate and survive only if it happens to land in a place where conditions are just right. Plants produce spores in great numbers to overcome the great odds against their survival. Look under the leaves of some ferns for a series of brown dots which are really small structures called **sori** (sor´i) (singular, **sorus**). Within the sorus are tiny structures called **sporangia** (spe-ran'je-a). The sporangia produce spores which is the fern's version of seeds. Ostrich ferns don't have sori under their leaves but produce a tall chocolate brown frond sticking out of the center of the plant to produce spores. The frond looks like a bird's feather and has sporangia scattered evenly over the lower surfaces of the frond. Try shaking a dried frond to see the spores released into the air.

A very few other plants will **clone** themselves when specialized cells from the top of the plant are washed off by rain and carried to the ground where they begin to grow. Many of the plants in the division Bryophyta, which include liverworts, hornworts and moss will reproduce with either spores or by this asexual cloning.

Do leaves really have teeth?

A single leaf has many interesting parts to look at, including teeth. Along the edge of a leaf, called the **margin**, a leaf may be smooth or have small projections, called teeth. The teeth can be sharp or rounded. A smooth edge is said to be **entire**. Large teeth are referred to as coarse and small teeth are fine. Some leaves have small teeth right next to large teeth and are called

doubly toothed. Each leaf usually attaches to a stem by a small stalk called the **petiole** (pet´ee-ol). Look closely at the petiole for a pair of bumps at the base of the leaf. These bumps are called **stipules** (stip´yulez) although it's not clear what these small appendages do. The massive, flat, thin part of the leaf is called the **blade**. Within the blade are usually one or more major **veins** running to the ends of the leaf. A single main vein running down the center of a leaf is called a **midrib**. Several main veins are referred to as **principal** veins. Smaller veins branch off the main midrib(s) in a network fashion. All veins transport nutrients and water in and out of the leaves. To closely see the pattern of veins, try a leaf rubbing. Place a leaf under a clean sheet of paper and rub the side of a soft crayon across the paper just over the leaf. The raised veins will appear quite clearly. It's fun to compare the vein patterns of different leaves. Scattered on the top of some leaves and on both the top and bottom surfaces of others are tiny microscopic holes that the plant uses to "breathe." They are called stomata, and among other things, they take in carbon dioxide and release oxygen and water into the air. Each of these tiny holes is enclosed by a pair of specialized **guard cells** that can close to conserve water during hot weather.

Are there really male and female plants?

It's fun to think of plants as being like people. They need a mother and father to produce a seedling. Unlike people, some species of plants have both male and female flowers on the same plant. Others have just male or just female flowers. Plants, such as sugar maple trees, will be either male or female, depending upon the type of flower. These trees need a tree of the opposite sex to complete pollination. These plants are called **dioecious** (di-o´she-ous) plants. The term dioecious is Greek for "two houses", the male and female flowers grow on separate plants or "houses."

Pine trees are a good example of plants that have male and female flowers (cones) on the same plant and are called **monoecious** (mo-ne´she-ous) plants. The word monoecious also comes from Greek for "one house." These plants will have different male and female flowers on the same plant. A single flower that has both male and female parts contained within one flower is said to be a **perfect** or **hermaphrodite** (her-maf´fro-dite) flower. A plant with perfect flowers can reproduce by itself because it doesn't depend on the pollen to come from another plant. Still another kind of flower may have just male or just female parts. These flowers are called **imperfect**.

Why are some leaves in bunches and others are not?

Leaves are the kitchen of any plant. They produce the food that keeps the plant alive. Each kind of plant has leaves that are unique in shape and size, almost like your finger print—the leaf shape can identify the kind of plant. The seemingly endless variety of leaf shapes are all modifications of two basic shapes, **simple** and **compound**.

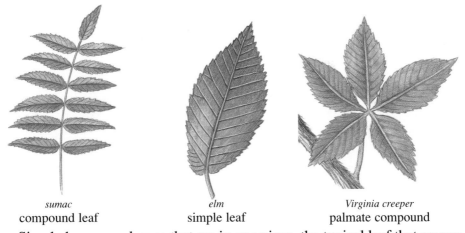

sumac	*elm*	*Virginia creeper*
compound leaf	simple leaf	palmate compound

Simple leaves are leaves that are in one piece, the typical leaf that comes to mind when you think of a leaf. Maples, oaks and curled dock are good examples of simple leaves. A simple leaf is one that is not divided into smaller leaflets. It can have teeth or be smooth along the edge. The simple leaf, such as that of a maple, has projections and indentations. The projections are called **lobes** and the indentations are called **sinuses**. Lobes and sinuses give the leaf a unique shape but it is still one simple leaf. Try to count each lobe or point, just as you would the fingers on your hand. Some leaves can have many lobes such as the maple which has five, while others such as the mulberry have two or three.

Compound leaves have two or more small leaves called **leaflets**. Examples are the rose and sumac. The leaflets can have teeth along the margin or be smooth. Each leaflet can be borne at one point or at intervals on each side of a stalk called a **rachis** (ra′kis). Where the leaflets are borne determines the type of compound leaf. Compound leaves with leaflets borne at the same point are called **palmate compound** such as the Virginia creeper. Leaflets borne opposite along a rachis are called **pinnate compound**, such as the staghorn sumac.

What are the different ways leaves are attached to plants?

No matter what the shape of the leaf, each is attached to the stem in a characteristic that is unique to the kind of plant. They can be attached in one of three ways, **opposite**, **alternate** or **whorled**. Two leaves opposite

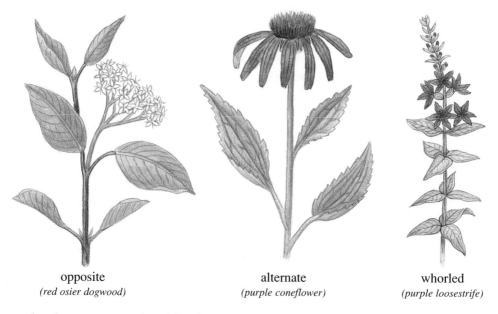

opposite	alternate	whorled
(red osier dogwood)	*(purple coneflower)*	*(purple loosestrife)*

each other on a stem is said to be opposite. Maples are good examples of this. Leaves that are attached alternately down the stem are considered alternate. Oaks and basswoods fit this description. Anytime you have more than two leaves coming from one spot on a stem they are called whorled. An example would be any of the purple loosestrife plants. Noting leaf shapes and how leaves are arranged will help you learn to identify the plants in your area.

Why do leaves turn colors in autumn?

Each autumn the soothing greens of summer explode into the brilliant colors of fall. Summer leaves are green because they contain the pigment chlorophyll. Autumn's yellows and reds are produced in two distinct processes, but both are related to the fading of chlorophyll. Chlorophyll looks green because it reflects green light. It absorbs all other wavelengths of light. Chlorophyll's ability to absorb color is more powerful than the ability of other pigments to reflect it. But in fact, leaves do contain other pigments. These include yellow and orange pigments called carotenoid (ker´o-ten-oid) pigments. At summer's end, a plant stops producing chlorophyll and begins to die. The yellow carotenoid pigments are more stable than chlorophyll and they don't break down as quickly, remaining in the aging leaf after the chlorophyll fades. With the chlorophyll gone, the carotenoid pigments get a chance to show off. They give leaves a vibrant yellow appearance in autumn.

A different process causes the passionate reds of maples and oaks. Their color comes from the brilliant red pigment **anthocyanin** (an´tho-si-e-nin). Unlike the carotenoid pigments, anthocyanin is not present in summer leaves. Leaves don't make this pigment until after they lose their chlorophyll. When the leaves start to die, sugar is trapped within the leaves. The cycle of warm days and cool nights triggers a chemical reaction with the sugars, which produces anthocyanin and the blazing fall reds.

Whether a leaf turns yellow or red, its last color is a crisp brown caused by **tannin**. Tannin is produced by plants throughout the year. It is stored in leaves and in the bark of trees. Tannin gives some leaves a bitter taste, which discourages animals from eating them and so extends the life of the leaves.

How do trees know when to lose their leaves?

Trees are not triggered as specifically as animals are to change their colors. Rather as temperatures drop and the days shorten, less and less light is available for producing chlorophyll. Also, the vessels that carry water and nutrients within leaves become clogged, just as heart vessels get clogged in humans. The clogging interrupts the transport of nutrients, which deteriorates the leaf and further interferes with its production of chlorophyll. The plant then creates a barrier of special cells, called the **abscission** (ab-szh´en) layer, where the leaf stem attaches to the tree. Cut off from the nutrients and moisture, the leaf slowly dies. The attachment either weakens and the leaf falls off, or the leaf stays on until spring, as in the case of red oaks. Another reason trees drop their leaves is to conserve moisture. In winter, when less moisture is available and in northern climates when the tree actually freezes, the leaves are a liability to the tree because of the evaporation of moisture.

How do evergreens stay green all winter?

Long after other trees have dropped their leaves, evergreens can turn on the photosynthesis process during a warm spell and shut down when the weather turns for the worse. Evergreens also can get a jump on other trees given an early spring. The needles of the evergreen have a thick waxy skin called a **cuticle**. The thick-skinned needles retain water better than the thin skin of deciduous leaves. The breathing holes in evergreen needles are slightly sunk into the surface of the needle, further reducing the amount of evaporation of water from the needles.

Why do trees have bark?

Bark can be the most interesting part of any tree. It might be smooth or rough, deeply grooved or corky. In any form, the bark is the protective cover of any tree and without it the tree will die. Scientists use the term "bark" to describe both the inner and outer layers. The inner layers are not visible until you peel away the outer bark. The slimy inner bark, called the **cambium** is the growth center for the outer bark. This is the part that beavers and porcupines like to eat. The more familiar outer bark protects the tree from insects, fungi, animals and fire. Bark is often filled with air space much like cork, making it a great insulator from fire. Many trees can survive a ground fire just because of their bark. In order to get to know tree bark, try placing a sheet of construction paper against the trunk of a tree. Gently rub a crayon across the surface which will leave an impression of the shape and texture of the bark. Each species of tree has unique shapes and lines. Compare the species to see the different patterns.

One species of oak tree, the cork oak, produces layers of cork several inches think which can be stripped from the tree without damaging it. The tree needs to mature about 25 years before the cork can be harvested. The first stripping yields "virgin" cork which is considered a low grade compared to the cork that grows to replace it. Successive crops of cork can be harvested every ten years. The older, more superior cork is used for stoppers, cork veneers and barrel plugs.

How big and deep are tree roots?

Just like an orchestra needs all its instruments to play, a tree needs to have all its "players" to function. Similar to the bass player in an orchestra, the roots of the tree are very important and are not given much attention. The roots of any tree, first and foremost, anchor the tree to the ground. Without roots, tall trees would blow over in the mildest of winds. Roots also absorb water and nutrients and in some trees, store food reserves.

There are two kinds of roots. Larger roots primarily anchor the tree, while very small roots and their microscopic root hairs absorb water and nutrients. Trees like oaks, hickories and walnuts have a single, large, deeply-penetrating **taproot**. This deep-dwelling root allows these trees to withstand drought better than shallow-rooted trees. Maples and elms have a series of nearly equal-sized fibrous roots that spread out and rarely dwell deeper than two feet deep (.6 m). These trees cannot withstand high winds and are often blown down in storms.

Root systems of trees generally extend beyond the spread of the branches of the tree. It is the ends of the roots that are the growth points and where water and nutrients are taken up. Take this into consideration when watering trees in your yard. Like the rest of the tree, all roots need oxygen to survive. Avoid driving over tree roots or black-topping over them since compaction of soil will reduce the ability of the roots to get oxygen and may seriously harm a tree.

Why do some trees flower and other don't?

To the casual observer it seems like some trees don't produce flowers while others have large showy blooms. Actually, while you may not see them, all the trees reproduce with flowers. Flowers are the first step to seeds and seeds complete the cycle by developing into trees. There are several reasons why you don't notice the flowers on some trees. Unlike the large showy flowers of the basswood, many flowers are extremely small and almost always well above your head. Many people mistakenly think the flowers are swollen buds. Actually what they are seeing are the tiny flowers in full bloom which you can see upon closer inspection. A pair of binoculars is useful to see these high-flying flowers.

These tiny flowers develop early each spring before the leaves, which are larger, have a chance to interfere with the transfer of pollen. Warm spring breezes carry pollen from the male flowers to receptive female flowers to complete the fertilization.

Are pine cones flowers?

Just like other trees, evergreen trees have flowers to reproduce but they are called cones. Each tree will have both male and female "flower" cones. Early each spring, small, yellow clusters of as many as 50 male cones, which are usually produced towards the tips of lower branches, give off copious amounts of pollen. Estimates are that each cluster produces in excess of two million grains of pollen and there are hundreds of such clusters on one tree. These cones drop off by summer and are hard to notice.

The larger "typical" pine cone is the female. These "seed cones" are much larger than the male cones. Some pine cones of the sugar pine can weight up to 5 pounds (2.3 kg). Female cones are green or purple at first and commonly take two seasons to mature into the familiar woody cones. During the first spring, the female cone is open and accepts the pollen grains carried by the wind. Each opening has a sticky drop of fluid called a **pollen drop**. Each sticky drop receives a male pollen grain, after which this fluid evaporates and the cone closes. About 15 months later, pollination is complete and the seeds develop. After this, the cone becomes woody and opens, releasing hundreds of winged seeds. Squirrels are constantly stripping cones from trees and eating the seeds within. Some cones are very resinous and don't open without some help. Jack pines have a specialized cone called **serotinous** (se-rot´a-nes) that will only open by heat. These cones usually remain closed for 20 to 30 years until heated by a forest fire, then they open to release hundreds of tiny winged seeds. Jack pines are one of the first trees to appear after a fire.

What are those big knots on trees?

Often seen on the sides of large old trees like oaks and maples, **burls** are growths that are dark, gnarly and furrowed and to some look like some kind of tree cancer. They can range in size from the size of a fist to the size of a bathtub. Burls are a good example of something that exists routinely in nature that scientists don't fully understand. They seem to be an atypical response to some kind of foreign invasion of the tree, most likely viral. It seems to affect both the rate of growth of the cells within the burl and how those cells grow. This genetic abnormality affects only the graining of the wood leaving it with a wavy pattern. Woodworkers will saw off a large burl and turn it on a lathe to make salad bowls and other products with interesting grains. Burls don't seem to compromise the growth of the tree or affect the tree's health.

Does the Woodpecker's hammering kill trees?

Many people become upset at the site of a Woodpecker drilling in a favorite tree. While it looks intentionally destructive, the Woodpecker is only looking for something to eat, trying to attract a mate, or building a nest. To find food, they drill into trees to extract tiny, wood-boring insects. Often Woodpeckers will stop on a branch or trunk and listen for the movement of insects within. If they hear something, they chisel off the outer layer and probe inside the insect tunnels with a long sticky tongue. To see this, look where a Woodpecker has been pecking. You will see a labyrinth of insect holes. Woodpeckers prefer trees that are already dying because the wood is softer and there are likely more insects. It is rare their holes alone would kill a tree, but it is possible that insects or fungi can invade the tree through the fresh holes. More than likely, if your tree is dying, it's suffering from some other disease or damage. If you have a Woodpecker drilling on the wood siding of your house, you might want to check for insect infestation. As far as we know, Woodpeckers don't drill holes for the fun of it—after all, it doesn't look like that much fun!

Why are some flowers on top of leaves and others under?

Plants position their flowers differently, usually to accommodate their pollinators, the insects and animals that visit them. Each visit is a chance to be pollinated, so it is important to present the flower in an acceptable way. Some flowers like elderberries offer large flat-topped flowers held high in the air. These flowers attract large flying insects, such as butterflies, that need a large landing platform. Other flowers, such as the trumpet vine, present tubular flowers tipped down to attract nimble, flying hummingbirds. Often, observing the shape of a flower will reveal the type and kind of visitor.

Plants in the pea family and some other plants have become very specialized and offer flowers that only open up when a specific bee lands. Honeybees, with their heavier bodies land on the larger bottom portion of the flower. This triggers the flower to open, allowing pollen-bearing anthers to be exposed. The pollen is then picked up and carried by the bee. Lighter insects would not be successful in triggering the flower to open. See this up close by pressing down on the bottom of a lupine flower (a plant found in flower gardens and roadsides), snapdragon or just about any plant in the pea family. By specializing in this way, the plant insures that only insects carrying the right pollen get in to pollinate the flower.

What are disk and ray flowers?

The flower of the common daisy or dandelion may seem simple, but take a closer look. The yellow or white "flower" you may have picked is actually several hundred flowers arranged in a head called the **capitulum**. (ka-pich´oo-lem). Each flower contains many small flowers, each called a **floret**. The outer petal-looking parts are called **ray flowers**. Pull off one of these as if you were playing the "love-me or love-me-not" game. Examine it under your magnifying glass. You will see only tiny female flower parts. Next remove one of the even smaller **disk flowers** located in the center of head. Each one of these will have both male and female flower parts protruding from the top. Each one of these individual flowers, ray and disk, will be pollinated and produce a seed.

disk flowers

ray flowers

Is there a reason flowers are different colors?

Yes, flowers are advertising to the insects they depend on for pollination that they are there waiting to give them nectar. The interesting thing is that they are not necessarily advertising in the colors that humans can see. Bees, for instance, see blue, yellow and ultraviolet. That means that flowers that appear uniformly yellow to us appear two-toned to the bee because some parts of the flower's petals reflect yellow and some reflect ultraviolet light which our eyes can't perceive. To the bee the flower looks somewhat like a target, with the center being the part of the flower that contains nectar. Spots or dots on flowers also function to guide insects to the flower's nectar and are even called "nectar guides." Red is a color that butterflies and hummingbirds can see and in places where there are few of these pollinators, there will be few red flowers.

Color in flowers is caused by pigments that are a part of the cells. For example, anthocynanins, along with other pigments called flavones or flavonals, are responsible for a whole range of colors from orange to purple and blue.

Why do some flowers smell better than others?

Flowers have a variety of ways to attract insects, birds and animals to complete pollination. While most plants offer brightly colored flowers, others offer a sweet or foul smell. Flowers that have bright colors will attract insects with good eyesight such as bees. Other flowers will offer scents designed to attract less visual insects, such as beetles. These scents come from secretory cells which are capable of secreting oils such as those found in citrus and mint. They also produce nectar for many types of flowers and secrete latex, such as the white, milky secretion produced by members of the milkweed and other families. For example, wild ginger has a very unimpressive looking flower, but it is very fragrant and attracts ground-dwelling beetles. The carrion flower has a very understated cream-colored flower that smells of rotting meat, which is where is gets its name. It is very successful at tricking flies into believing they will get a free meal. Although the fly won't be able to feed, by the time it has landed, it has already pollinated the plant. Flowers, such as roses, have a sweet smell as a by-product of the nectar they produce. The highly sweetened nectar gives off a pleasant odor only coincidentally. You might want to compare the smell of different flowers the next time you are out for a nature hike.

Why are some plants thorny?

There are many animals in the world that eat plants. Since plants can't run away from this constant assault, they fight back in other ways. Many of them produce thorns, spines, prickles and other like-minded defense systems. Each one of these appendages is designed to keep animals from eating their leaves and stems. No matter what the size or shape of the thorn, it is a modification of either the plant's leaves or stem. The spines of a cactus are modified leaves, while the thorns of the rose and raspberry are modified stems. Either way, thorns protect the plant from the ravages of plant-eating animals.

What are those ball-like structures on plants?

Some insects take advantage of plants and convert them into temporary residences. Such is the case in the hundreds of varieties of insect **galls**. In general, galls are swellings in a plant's stem or leaf. They are caused by a chemical reaction to the invasion of an insect egg. For example, some species of flies will inject a single egg into the stem of a goldenrod plant. As the insect grows, the plant's stem responds to this invasion and walls off the insect. The resulting swelling provides a protective home for the insect larvae and does not greatly interfere with the plant's function. When the insect inside completes its metamorphosis, it chews its way to the surface and flies away. Birds, such as chickadees, drill into these galls to eat the inhabitants inside. You can see hundreds of these galls in open fields and prairies. Oak trees are another common place to see galls. Large golfball-sized galls occur on oak leaves. During the summer if you cut these galls open, you'll see they are green and juicy and you may see the small white larva inside. In the autumn, the galls look brown and papery.

What are the smallest and largest plants?

Plants come in many sizes and shapes. The king of all plants is the giant sequoia. It is one of the largest living things and one of the oldest. The tallest sequoias are nearly 300' (92 m) tall, with trunk diameters of approximately 25' (7 m). These gargantuan trees grow from a seed so small that it takes 3,000 of them to make up one ounce (28 g). Each seed, about ¼" (6 mm) long, comes from a small cone that contains about 100 seeds.

Growing on the surface of your local pond or lake are the tiniest plants, the duckweeds. Some of the smaller duckweeds have leaves less than 1 millimeter (.04"). They also have minute flowers which are only .5 millimeters (.02"). Between these giant and minuscule plants are the countless thousands of plants that represent every size, shape and color. Each plant has evolved to fit into a small niche, thus avoiding competition with other plants.

Can there be too many of some kind of plants?

Yes! There are several alien species of plants that evolved in another part of the world with their own checks and balances for staying under control. Here in our area they grow out of control and crowd out native plants. This process usually means that biodiversity is undermined, reducing the overall number of plant and animal species. An example is the plant purple loosestrife. It is a beautiful plant that was brought over from Europe to adorn gardens. It "escaped" and is currently spreading through wetlands where it replaces native cattails, thereby reducing the wildlife that depend on this plant. The plant, kudzu, is an example of an aggressive invader that grows in the south.

Are some plants harmful to people?

Plants feed us, clothe us and shelter us, but they can also cause annoying allergic reactions and painful scratches and rashes. Certain individuals have allergic reactions, such as sneezing or clogged sinuses, that are caused by inhaling pollen particles in the air from trees or other wind-pollinated flowers. The production of this pollen is incidental to the plant and does not act as a defense strategy. Some plants do have other characteristics that function as defense. They can ward off predators by either being thorny or causing a rash of some sort. Poison ivy will cause an oozing rash in those people who are allergic to it. Plants like stinging nettles will give a burning sensation to anyone who brushes up against them. Ironically, if you harvest stinging nettles with gloves on and boil the leaves, it becomes one of the most delicious and nutritious vegetables that is free for the taking. Some plants can be quite toxic. For example, the water hemlock, a member of the carrot family, is so toxic that eating it can cause death. It is a common plant in wet areas along roads.

What are weeds?

There are two definitions of weeds. One is a plant growing in the wrong place, or in other words a place where something else deemed more precious is desired. For example, if a tomato plant starts growing in a yard, it is suddenly a weed. Often, the term weed is subject to the culture trend of the time. Dandelions were cultivated during early colonial times for their vitamin C value in preventing the disease scurvy and now they are the nemesis of lawn owners across the country. The other definition refers to the way the plant grows profusely without human intervention. The aspen tree can be seen as having weedy growth around an area where a prairie is desired. Most commonly, weeds are aggressive, non-woody, non-native green plants that crowd out more desirable native plants in any ecosystem.

Why is it hard to find some flowers?

While you may see daisies everywhere, it's more difficult to find lady slippers and trilliums. The requirements for growth in the case of the rarer wildflowers are just that much harder to come by. They can require a special soil type with certain types of fungus that work to prepare the soil for just the right kind of nutrients. Others depend on animals to eat and eliminate their seeds in order to prepare their seed for germination. Those that only require the wind to carry their seeds to an open spot of soil are the most prolific, whereas those that require a whole laundry list of preconditions are rarer. Still others require specific acid or alkaline soil or particular moisture conditions. For example, you will never find a cattail growing in the middle of a dry prairie. Sunlight is another limiting factor. Too much causes the plant to dry out but too little will cause it to die. Competition between plants also keeps some plants from establishing themselves.

How do we get the color in our clothes from plants?

Various parts of plants have been used for centuries for dying wool, cotton and other fibers for the making of clothing. Berries, petals, bark, nuts and even the inside part of branches have been used by native peoples for dye and are still used by indigenous peoples in some parts of the world. The boiling of the hulls of nuts, such as walnuts, will create a brown stain in the water and the fibers only need to be soaked in the water in order to take the stain. The "pith" or inside of the branches of sumac is a golden color. When it is boiled, it turns the fibers to a goldish-brown color. It takes many flower petals to make a good dye since the pigments in them are not as concentrated. To make the colors hold better and not bleed, a **mordant** is used. That is, the fibers are pre-soaked in alum, cream of tartar, vinegar or other minerals.

How many plants are used for food?

An estimated 350,000 different kinds of plants grow in the world. About 80,000 are edible by humans, though humans haven't tried most of them. About 3,000 have been eaten in different cultures at different times throughout history. Over the past thousand years, humans have stopped eating many of them. Today we use about 200 species of plants for food but only about 90 provide the majority of human food. Most remarkable, just three of those—corn, wheat and rice—supply 90 percent of the food for all the people of the world.

As you can see, the number of different plants used for food has decreased rather than increased. That's because only some plants are easy to harvest mechanically. Before modern farming began, people planted hundreds of different kinds of plants for food. These plants were collected by hand. Modern farmers prefer plants that grow to the same height and mature at the same time, so they can be harvested by one large machine.

What is tree sap?

Plants such as trees are living organisms that need to move food substances and waste throughout their system. The sap is the liquid that performs these life sustaining actions through parts of the tree called the **xylem** (zi´lem) and **phloem** (flo´em). Within the transportation system of the plant, sap flows freely. The xylem can be likened to an artery, carrying the necessary water and minerals to the body of the tree. Sap is mostly water but contains dissolved minerals and sugars important to the growth of the plant. The sap also carries any waste produced during photosynthesis.

Sap is not the same as **resin**, the yellow sticky substance usually found seeping from evergreen trees. This aromatic substance is the trees antiseptic. It prevents the development of fungi and deters certain insects from attacking the tree. Resin doesn't flow in the same canals as sap. You can often see resin oozing from a tree after it has been damaged. The resin responds to an injury by sealing up the opening into the tree. You might know resin in its petrified state as **amber**. Millions of years ago, damaged resin-producing trees oozed drops of resin. When these drops of resin fell to the ground they became buried in soil and occasionally, over million of years, were petrified into what we know as amber. Frequently, insects that were attracted to the resin drop became entangled in the resin and were entombed for eternity.

How is syrup made from maple trees, does it hurt the trees?

Maple syrup or sugar is a natural sweet flavoring of the northern wood-lands that has been used for centuries by the Native American tribes as their only source of a sweet flavoring. Maple sap begins its "run" in the late winter months when the temperatures are below freezing at night, followed by days that reach temperatures of 45 to 50° F (5–10° C). Tapping trees for maple syrup and sugar can be done year after year without hurting the trees if certain precautions are taken. For example, new holes should not be drilled within six to eight inches (15-20 cm) of last season's tap and trees that are younger and have smaller diameters can "afford" less taps in them.

To make syrup, one must concentrate the natural sugars by boiling off the water content of the sap. There are 13 species of maple trees native to the U.S. and Canada and all have been utilized for their sap at some time or another. Some maple tree species have a higher sugar content than others, with sugar maple living up to its name by producing the highest yield. The sap is mostly water, so it takes a great deal of sap to make even a small amount of syrup. If a tree's sap has one percent sugar, it will take 86 gallons of sap to make one gallon of syrup.

How do vines wrap around things?

Like all plants, vines are reaching for light and since they don't have enough support in their own stem, they cling to the branches and trunks of woody plants in order to climb to the life-giving sunlight. Some vines send out tendrils, or leaf modifications, which look like skinny curled extensions at their tips. Tendrils are sensitive to contact and turn toward the surface that it touches. The tendrils then twist around and lock on for support. Some vines have tiny adhesive disks that work like suction cups to attach onto sturdier plants and buildings, allowing them to literally climb up for support. The ivy that grows on many homes is an example of this. Some species are twiners; that is, the entire stem winds around until it comes in contact with a support. Some of these become so strong, they can actually strangle the supporting plant. Certain species are root climbers. They produce several side growths, called **aerial rootlets**, on the stems that penetrate cracks of buildings and hold the vine in place. Poison ivy is an example of this.

What is the green stuff I find on rocks or the sides of trees?

You are seeing lichens and moss. They are a part of the forest ecosystem and are not harmful to the trees. Rocks and tree bark seem unlikely candidates as growth medium, but they are quite suitable for primitive plants, such as moss and lichens, which do not require a root system. Lichens are the flat gray, green, red or orange colored growths on trees and rocks. Each is capable of actually dissolving bark or rock with a chemical acid reaction that converts bark or rock into soil for the lichens to live on. Moss is the green plant-like growth on trees. It is a bit less primitive, but also has few soil requirements and because of having no root structure, it can grow in the most unlikely places. Don't be fooled, moss grows on all sides of a tree. Many people think that moss only grows on the north side. Where it grows all depends on the available moisture. Lichens and moss were the first kinds of plants to grow on land. They prepare the area by creating soil for other more sophisticated, rooted plants to grow.

> **❝Conservation means harmony between men and land. When land does well for its owner, and the owner does well by his land, when both end up better by reason of their partnership, we have conservation.❞**
>
> ALDO LEOPOLD

Do some flowers turn to the sun?

Yes, some plants follow the sun's path across the sky. Fields of sunflowers will often have thousands of flower heads following the daily movement of the sun across the sky in unison. Other plants will orient themselves to the sun to get maximum sunlight striking their leaves, which is important for photosynthesis. A common house plant also reaches for the light of a window. The compass plant is a tall plant in the sunflower family that has leaves that are oriented in a north-south direction. One can easily tell the direction by looking at the leaves of this plant. Just why these plants do this is unknown.

Where did our present day food originate?

Every food plant of any importance to us today was discovered long ago by our ancestors. For example, the ancient Incas of Peru grew potatoes. Over two thousand years they developed dozens of varieties. Central and North American Indians grew a short, wild grass with only six to ten seeds (kernels) on each plant. They kept the seeds from the most vigorous plants each season to replant. By the time Columbus came to the Americas, the Native Americans had developed a plant containing hundreds of seeds. They called it "teosinte," or "maize." We now call this plant corn.

Tobacco, corn and potatoes were unknown in the Old World until Europeans found the natives of the Americas growing them in their gardens. Detailed records of the use of these plants were never kept, but much is known about their use after European settlement. Tobacco, for instance, was used by colonial Americans in 1774 to pay debts they owed the British, helping to free them from British rule. Maize, later known as corn, was first brought from the Americas to Europe as a novelty plant. Later it was a life saver in Africa and Spain, where people suffered massive famine until corn was grown. Many people know the story of how potatoes affected Ireland. The people of Ireland had very poor soil, making potatoes one of the few crops they could grow. They became so dependent on the potato that when the potato crop failed due to potato blight in the mid 1840's, over a million Irish people died. Another million and a half emigrated to the U.S. and Canada and the rest is history.

What are some unusual ways plants were used in early times?

Indigenous people could not afford to be as wasteful as we are in modern cultures. They depended directly on nature and needed to utilize as much of their environment as possible. The soft leaves of the mullein plant were used to line moccasins for comfort. The cattail was one of the most versatile plants. Its fluffy seed head was used for insulation and for diaper material; the reed-like leaves were used for weaving mats for lining living quarters; the root-like structures were made into a starch and the stem was cooked as a vegetable.

Willow branches have been made into whistles and birch bark was commonly used to make canoes and baskets. Plants we would never consider to be food were relished as delicacies by the people who lived in this part of the world centuries ago. The large yellow pond lily was harvested in the fall for its seeds which were roasted for food.

Knowledge of the medicinal uses of plants was passed down in an oral tradition. The medicines were administered within a spiritual, cultural context that western medicine might scoff at, but that worked for thousands of years before there were pharmacies. For example, the stem of the jewelweed plant really does work just like a first aid cream in relieving itching.

How were plants used as medicines in the past?

Plants have been used to cure what ails us since before recorded time. More than likely the discoveries followed a long process of trial and error. The first record of curative plants was carved on stone tablets in 1770 B.C. These tablets describe a number of plants used for medicine, several of which are still used today. The Chinese wrote the earliest known text about medicines. Later, Greeks and Romans contributed many plants that they used for medicine. Between the 1500's and 1700's, during the "Age of the Herbals," many German, Italian and English botanists studied plants and published stories about their healing powers. They believed that if a part of a plant looked like a specific organ of the human body, it held the cure for that organ. They called this theory the *Doctrine of Signatures*. For example, the name *liverwort* was given to a plant that resembled the shape of the liver. People thought the liverwort could cure liver ailments. At that time, many people saw the natural world only in human terms. They thought plants were placed on earth strictly to serve humans.

How do plants produce medicines?

Plants are living organisms that need water and nutrients just as we do. As they grow, they produce many products and by-products. These include alkaloids, steroids, fatty acids, essential oils, gums and resins. Most modern drugs are made from these substances. Some are essential to the plant's health while others are simply waste. Either way, plants have no way to dispose of these substances. Sometimes they store them and sometimes they link or combine them. The resulting compounds may have special qualities that people can use as drugs.

Alkaloids and steroids are the two major classes of plant extracts used for modern medicines. Alkaloids are a crystalline, organic compound made up of nitrogen and are the basis of drugs such as caffeine, morphine and codeine. In large amounts, these drugs are extremely poisonous to humans, but in small amounts they are therapeutic. Determining a safe dose has always been difficult. Patients in early times were as likely to die from a cure as from a disease.

Steroids have also proven to be a very valuable drug source. Steroids are substances that direct the functioning of tissues or organs—a kind of government of an organism's body. Birth control pills are a good example of a steroid that is synthesized directly from plant steroids.

How have plants been affected by the current environmental conditions?

Sadly, many plant species become extinct each year. Many of them die when their habitat is destroyed. Habitat in the rainforest, for example, is being lost at the rate of 100 acres a minute. Most new drugs are found in plants that live near the equator. Some experts estimate that up to 2,000 still unknown plants in the rainforest may have medicinal properties. But people may never get a chance to discover some of them. We can't over-emphasize the importance of our planet's biodiversity. For instance, the more different species of plants we have, the better defense we enjoy against virulent strains of diseases. If we depend too much on one plant or on just a few, we become vulnerable. Our world could be devastated as it was for the Irish people in the days of the potato blight. Preserving biodiversity ensures a healthy environment for people and animals and keep in mind—there is only one earth.

How do chemicals like lawn fertilizers, harm plants and animals?

Weed killers and pesticides are destructive to insect life, which means fewer numbers of insects are available for pollination of plants that require bees and the like for reproduction. Some "weed" killers are not specific enough to the undesirable plant and will kill other plants while also possibly poisoning the ground water. Lawn fertilizers have a high content of nitrogen and phosphate, which stimulates the growth of green plants. Run-off of this growth-stimulator into nearby ponds and lakes causes the overgrowth of algae and other green aquatic plants, which in turn starts a process of using up the oxygen in the lake. This is called **eutrophication** (yoo-trof´i-cation) and it potentially can kill fish who depend on the oxygen to survive. The leeching or washing out of chemicals when it rains causes them to invade rivers and eventually oceans, leading to a serious water pollution problem.

How does air pollution hurt plants?

All living things evolved in a world free of the toxic chemicals that are so prevalent today. Many of us can't even pronounce the ten most common toxic chemicals released into the environment every year. Methanol tops the list with almost 200 million pounds and is followed by toluene, ammonia, acetone, methyl chloroform, xylenes, methyl ethyl ketone, carbon disulfide, hydrochloric acid and methylene chloride. These come to us from the chemical industry in the production of solvents, paints, perfumes, gasoline, cleaning agents, pesticides, herbicides and hundreds of other sources. There are studies being done to determine exactly how they interrupt and alter the processes of living systems, but it is clear that they are not healthy for any living organisms, including plants.

Acid rain is a serious problem for plants and has caused defoliation of trees in areas where the acidity of the rain is so high that it literally disintegrates the leaves, especially at the tops of trees where they are hit the hardest. This acidity is mainly caused by the burning of coal that is mixed with sulphur. Sulfuric dioxide is released when it burns and it comes back to earth in the form of rain that can be so acidic that it has the same ph as vinegar. Smog and its major component, ozone, retards plant growth by making it difficult for the plant to breathe, just as it hurts our lungs.

How do plants help with air pollution?

With our cars and industries we are overloading the atmosphere with carbon dioxide. This results in the warming up of the planet and the potentially disastrous results that would come from the melting of the polar ice caps. During photosynthesis, green plants take carbon dioxide, which is one part carbon and two parts oxygen, from the air. Then they strip off the carbon and use it to make carbohydrates. Finally, they release the leftover two parts of oxygen. It is the two parts of oxygen (O_2) that we breathe. This process helps counteract the large amount of carbon dioxide in our air. Studies have shown that levels of CO_2 in the atmosphere have risen dramatically in the last century. This is why the combination of high rates of global deforestation with the industrialization of underdeveloped countries is such a large environmental problem.

What is the green scum on some lakes and ponds?

Each summer many lakes and ponds have large green patches or become covered with a thick green layer of scum. All of this growth is a type freshwater algae known as **green algae**. There are approximately 7,500 species of green algae. Any given pond can have many different types of green algae. Nearly all are single celled (microscopic) but are very visible when in large numbers. Some green algae are large seaweeds. They often form colonies of net-like tubes or hollow balls seen floating in the water. Although they are green, algae are not plants. They are in the kingdom Protista. They function much in the same way, taking in carbon dioxide and giving off oxygen. Most take advantage of the warm waters and abundant phosphate and nitrogen in the water to quickly multiply. Just like anything, it is good in small amounts but when there is too much, the algae will shade out many other plants. This can reduce the amount of oxygen in the water, placing stress on the fish and aquatic animals. Very often, the more polluted the water is, the more likely it is to have algae.

How can I use the Plant Smart species section?

No matter if you are walking in a woodland, wetland or prairie, if it's spring, summer, autumn or winter, plants will be there to greet you. To many people, all plants look the same or seem too confusing and difficult to identify. In the species section, you will learn to see and appreciate the differences and learn to identify some of the common plants by breaking plants into one of two simple categories. These two categories are based on the plant's stem, woody or non-woody. Plants such as trees and most shrubs have a thick or thin bark or what we call a **woody stem**. All other plants have a soft **non-woody stem**. A tree is a woody plant and a cattail is non-woody. The distinction may seem overly simple, but it works quite well. Don't be fooled by thinking that all small green plants are non-woody. Poison ivy may appear to be a non-woody plant, but look closer, without touching it, at its main stem. You will notice it has a thick, woody stem close to the ground. Once you have determined which category a plant belongs to, use the illustrations to determine its name.

We have selected 46 plants which we believe represent the major types or groups of plants found throughout the eastern half of North America. This is by no means a comprehensive list, but it is representative of many plants you are likely to encounter. With this guide, for example, you will be able to identify a plant as a rose but not necessarily which of the two dozen rose species you have found. The same can be said for oaks, pines, daisies and many other common plants of the region. The illustrated species which was chosen to represent the group has the name and height indicated. Keep in mind that all plants, and especially trees, will be found in varying states of maturity. The heights listed are for mature plants.

Even if you are unable to identify a plant that is not in this guide, you should still stop and take a closer look to note its leaf attachment and whether the stem is square or round. Crush a leaf to determine if it has any scent. The shape and color of the flower might might indicate what kind of insect pollinates it. Sometimes, to the casual observer, all plants may seem to be the same. By noting these characteristics, you'll be well on your way to appreciating the differences in plants and being able to identify them, too.

WOODY

TREES (DECIDUOUS)

Green ash	*Fraxinus pennsylvanica 66' (20 m) leaf 10-12" (25-30 cm)*
Black ash	*Fraxinus nigra 66' (20 m) leaf 10-16" (25-41 cm)*
White ash	*Fraxinus americana 82' (25 m) leaf 8-12" (20-30 cm)*

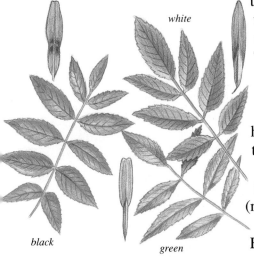

white

black

green

Here is a native tree found throughout eastern U.S. and Canada. Unlike the oaks and elms, the male and female flowers of the ash trees are on separate trees. This means only the female trees will have seeds each year. The seeds are shaped like large insect wings and, just like insect wings, these seeds can fly. When the winds of summer shake loose the seeds, each seed helicopters off into the wind to find a new home. Ash are tall, stately trees that rarely become too large to get your arms around. The bark is light gray and can be corky, scaly and usually furrowed. All ash trees have a compound leaf (many small leaflets making up one leaf). Each ash leaf has from seven to nine pointed leaflets. Each leaf is attached oppositely to the twig.

Cottonwood	*Populus deltoides 72-100' (22-31 m) leaf 3-7" (8-18 cm)*
Quaking aspen	*Populus tremuloides 39-60' (12-18 m) leaf 8-3" (2-8 cm)*
Bigtooth aspen	*Populus grandidentata 66' (20 m) leaf 2-3" (5-8 cm)*

This group of trees represents some of the fastest growing trees in the forest. These trees function to rapidly regenerate the forest after a fire or other natural disturbance, giving them the title of a pioneer tree. Quick to establish themselves, the aspens don't live a long life, about 40 to 60 years and give way to slow-growing, long-lived trees such as oaks and evergreens. Mature trees have dark, rough bark on the lower half of the trunk, with smooth gray to green bark from about the middle up. Large, heart-shaped leaves perch on the end of long leaf stems called

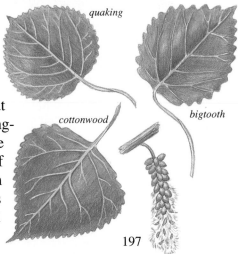

quaking

cottonwood

bigtooth

197

petioles. These petioles are often flattened and catch any breeze, causing the leaves to turn in the wind. In spring, male and female flowers mature on separate plants. The female flowers are wind-pollinated. Later in the year, the female flower elongates into hanging clusters of seed pods. Once these pods open, a storm of cotton-laden seeds emerge. The cotton catches the wind and gently floats the seeds away. Next time you see one of these cotton storms, stop and look closer at the cotton and find the small black seed.

American basswood *Tilia americana 60' (18 m) leaf 5-6" (12-15 cm)*
Carolina basswood *Tilia caroliniana 40' (12 m) leaf 3-7" (8-18 cm)*

Also known as linden, the basswood is a large native tree growing to 60' (18 m) or taller. Its trunk can be 2 – 3' (.5–1 m) in diameter, making it hard to reach around. Often a single tree will have several small young trees growing from the base of the "mother" tree. Once the main tree dies, the smaller trees will continue to grow. This is called **tilling**. Look for several trees growing around a dead stump. This will often be all you need to identify it. The bark is smooth and gray-green when young and with age becomes furrowed with narrow ridges. The leaves can be as large as a dinner plate and have an uneven or asymmetrical leaf base. They have one large vein, called a midrib, dividing this leaf in two unequal halves. This tree is often identified by its fragrant smell each spring, when hundreds of sweet-smelling, yellow flowers cover it. Bees swarm these flowers giving this tree its nickname, "bee tree." The pale yellow flowers are transformed into an abundance of small clusters of nut-like seeds attached to a leafy wing which carries them far and wide.

american

River birch *Betula nigra 49-82' (15-25 m) leaf 1-3" (3-8 cm)*
Yellow birch *Betula alleghaniensis 32-72' (10-22 m) leaf 3-4½" (8-11cm)*
Paper birch *Betula papyrifera 60' (18 m) leaf 2-5" (5-13 cm)*

No matter in what part of the Midwest and East you reside, one of the native birch trees will be your neighbor. From the paper birch of the north woods, to the river birch of the great water ways, to the yellow birch of the Northeast, these trees grace our woodlands. Birch trees rarely grow very large, allowing you to reach all the way around their trunks. Birch bark is famous for making baskets. Often, small thin sheets will naturally peel off from these trees. All birch have simple leaves born alternately on the branch. The leaves

river

yellow

paper

have fine teeth encircling the entire leaf and turn a vibrant yellow in autumn. Birch trees are monoecious, meaning they have both male and female flowers on the same tree. Each spring tiny yellow male flowers called **catkins** droop from the ends of the twigs. Greenish female flowers, also called catkins, sprout closer in on the same branch. Later in autumn, after pollination, the female catkin hardens and opens up like a pine cone, releasing many winged seeds. Look for these catkins in winter when they become more obvious. These seeds are often seen covering the ground and are especially noticeable if they are on a blanket of snow.

Black cherry	*Prunus serotina 60' (18 m) leaf 2-6" (5-15 cm)*

Black cherry tends to be a tall, straight tree, about 40 – 60' (12 – 18 m), growing amongst its forest companions. What sets this native tree apart from all the others is its unusual "potato chip" bark. Large, black scales that are similar in shape and size to a potato chip are easily broken off for closer examination. The shiny smooth leaves of the black cherry are long and narrow with many fine teeth lining the edge called the margin. Look on the underside of the leaf to see a row of reddish hairs lining the vein "midrib" that divides the leaf in half. Upon closer examination you can see two glands or bumps where the stem attaches to the leaf. These two points will positively identify this tree. The leaves attach alternately to the main stem. Each spring, clusters of tiny white flowers hang from a single stem. By mid-summer, the nearly black, juicy, edible fruit ripens, much to the delight of berry-eating birds and squirrels and people.

American elm	*Ulmus americana 82-115' (25-35 m) leaves 2-4" (5-10 cm)*
Slippery elm	*Ulmus rubra 49-82' (15-25 m) leaves 3-6" (8-15 cm)*

Because of the way they majestically arch their branches, elms have been selected as the favorite tree for lining roadways in some parts of the country. Unfortunately, this provided an easy way for the beetle carrying the Dutch elm disease to spread. Few trees are as wide-spread as the elms and, just as the

slippery　　*american*

oaks, elms are easy to identify because they all have similar characteristics. In spring each elm tree sets forth both male and female flowers on the same tree that are so tiny, they go unnoticed. These flowers produce small flat disk-like seeds with small wings that float away on the wind from the parent tree. Both the slippery and American elm are elegant trees with large trunks that gently fork into many arching branches, slightly drooping at the ends, forming an overall vase-like shape to the tree. It is not uncommon for these trees to reach 100' (31 m) tall with trunks larger than one can reach around. Leaves are arranged alternately on small twigs with each twig borne alternately from larger branches. Each leaf has a very distinctive, asymmetrical or unequal leaf base. Look for this where the green leaf attaches to the stem. Bark is light gray and tends to be thick and scaly. Stop and feel the leaf of the elm. Notice that the top side is relatively smooth and the bottom lighter side is rough.

Hackberry　　*Celtis occidentalis 90' (28 m) leaf 2-4" (5-10 cm)*

Hackberry is a large native tree obtaining heights of 90' (28 m). The trunk often has a girth too large to reach around and once you have tried, you're not likely forget it. Hackberry has a distinctive bark that is smooth and light gray with many scales or wart-like patches, often running in long ridges. This member of the elm family has similar leaves to the elm tree, so don't be confused. One central vein gives way to many smaller veins. Between each smaller vein, other veins run cross-wise, often giving it the appearance of cracked skin. Each autumn these leaves turn bright yellow. This drought-resistant tree grows fast and sets out flowers at the base of each leaf early in spring. The fruit that develops from the pollination of this flower is another unique feature worth noting. Later in summer, the entire tree can be covered with small, dark purple, one-seeded fruits called drupes. They are so small that they go unnoticed by most people. They are sweet but dry and consist mostly of seeds. Many birds, as well as mammals, relish these fruits.

PLANT SMART

Eastern hop hornbeam *Ostrya virginiana 23-40' (7-12 m) leaf 3-5" (8-13 cm)*

This is a tree with two common names, hop hornbeam and ironwood. Both names refer to something specific about the tree. Ironwood reflects that this tree has extremely hard and strong wood that is used to make handles for tools. Hop hornbeam refers to the fruit clusters of this tree that resemble hops, an ingredient to make beer. No matter what you call this native tree, it is commonly found throughout eastern North America as an understory tree, which means it grows in the shade of other larger trees, such as oaks and maples. Look closely at the trunk. Note that the bark has slightly scaly ridges and the pattern will slowly twist up the trunk. This tree is easy to identify in the winter as it keeps its brown leaves. The trunks will rarely grow larger than a foot (.3 m) in diameter making this tree easy to reach around. Flowers are borne early in spring before the leaves develop. The leaves are dark green on top and pale and silky smooth underneath, and they are oval and double-toothed. Take a minute to feel these leaves. You can always confirm you have found an ironwood tree if the leaves are silky soft. Late in summer, papery, cone-like clusters (which resemble hops) hang from the branches. These contain seeds, called nutlets, which are good food for pheasants, grouse, deer and rabbits.

Sugar maple *Acer saccharum 98' (30 m) leaf 3-8" (8-20 cm)*
Silver maple *Acer saccharinum 98' (30 m) leaf 5-8" (13-20 cm)*
Red maple *Acer rubrum 92' (28 m) leaf 2-6" (5-15 cm)*

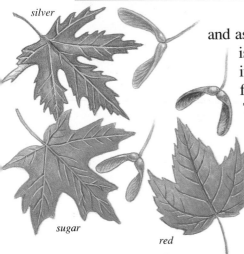
silver
sugar
red

It's fun to approach this tree with a group of people and ask, "What part of this tree is edible?" The answer is slow to come because the sap is not visible and it's hard to think of this beautiful tree as the source for the maple syrup you had on your pancakes. These native trees belong to another group that is easy to identify and are found throughout the Midwest, East and Canada. All maples grow to a handsome stature reaching 60 – 100' (18 – 31 m) tall with trunks too large to reach around. All maples have thin, gray bark that becomes thicker and darker with age. They are often planted in yards and along our city streets because they are rapid growers and provide much needed shade in summer. The basic shape of a maple leaf is the same— only the leaf edge, called a margin, changes. Sugar maple leaves have smooth margins, while the silver and red have ragged teeth. The over-all shape is the same, having three prominent and two minor pointed lobes for a total of five lobes on each leaf. To find these lobes, follow the five large obvious veins to the pointed ends; each end is a lobe. Each leaf has a long stem that attaches opposite (across from each other) to the branch. In spring, small red flowers appear and are often confused with the leaf "buds." Male and female flowers are on different trees. Like most trees, maples are wind-pollinated long before the leaves develop on the tree. Only the female trees will produce the familiar paired-winged seeds that helicopter to the ground each autumn. All maples can be tapped for their sugary sap in the spring when the day time temperatures are above freezing and the nights are still frosty.

Boxelder   *Acer negundo 65' (20 m) leaf 2-5" (5-13 cm)*

Most people consider this hardy and fast growing tree to be of low value, perhaps because it grows just about everywhere and is therefore thought of as weedy. We don't think so. It is a member of the maple family and produces a sugary sap each spring like the rest of the maples. It is a quick growing tree that never attains much height, only about 50' (15 m). Trunks rarely grow too large to reach around. The bark is thin, pale gray and often deeply divided. Often this tree will grow with several trunks that have divided near the ground. Just like other maples, this tree will flower early in the spring and is wind-pollinated. Only the female tree will have the paired, winged seeds like other maples. Unlike other maples, boxelders have a compound leaf with three leaflets making up each leaf. Each leaflet has large teeth and only one vein per leaflet. Leaves are in an opposite arrangement.

White oak	*Quercus alba 115' (35 m) leaves 4-8" (10-22 cm)*
Red oak	*Quercus rubra 59-82' (18-25 m) leaves 4-9" (10-23 cm)*
Bur oak	*Quercus macrocarpa 65-132' (20-40 m) leaves 6-12" (15-30 cm)*

Oaks are some of the most common native trees no matter where you go in North America. Whether it's a red, white, bur or any of over 350 oak species of the world, they all share similar characteristics, making them all easy to identify. Oaks are broken into two groups based upon whether the leaves have *bur* pointed or round lobes (ends). Oaks with pointed lobes are considered to be in the "red" oak group and have bitter acorns that take two years to mature. Oaks that have round lobes are considered to be in the "white" oak group and have sweeter acorns that mature in one year. The red oaks will retain their leaves well into winter making winter identification easy. The bark of red oaks is blackish and in white oaks it is light gray. Like most native trees, the flowers of oaks are wind-pollinated in the spring before the leaves start to develop. Many people mistake these flowers for "buds" each spring. Each oak tree has both male and female flowers endowing all oaks *white* *red* with acorns. Each leaf is attached alternately along the stem. Animals such as deer, turkeys and squirrels rely heavily upon the acorn crop for food each year.

TREES (CONIFERS)

| Eastern red cedar | *Juniperus virginiana 90' (28 m) leaf .6" (1 mm)* |

This is the most common and wide spread native conifer (evergreen) tree in North America. Red cedars are not very tall trees with a trunk only about a foot (.3 m) in diameter. Although it would be small enough to reach around, the trunk is usually covered with branches, making this difficult. The trunk is covered with an aromatic reddish-brown bark that peels off in long thin strips, which many birds and animals use to line their nests. The leaves of the red cedar are not typical evergreen leaves. On close examination, you will see many individual "scales" that are closely overlapping. Each scale has a sharp point that lets you know you have grabbed it in the wrong place. Often plants that have sharp points are plants that animals like to eat and so it is with the red cedar. The sharp leaves help prevent it from being eaten. Like all evergreens, the red cedar has cones instead of flowers. Red cedar cones appear as small (¼", .6 cm) dark blue berries that are enjoyed by many birds. Look closer, they are actually small cones. Each cone has only one or two seeds. Look for an unusual orange jelly blob growing on the branches of the red cedar after summer rains. This odd growth is cedar-apple rust, a fungal disease of many apple trees that doesn't hurt the cedar.

Red *Pinus resinosa 65-100' (20-31 m) leaf 2 per bundle 4-6" (10-15 cm)*
White *Pinus strobus 98-230' (30-70 m) leaf 5 per bundle 3-5" (8-13 cm)*
Jack *Pinus banksiana 32-90' (10-27 m) leaf 2 per bundle .8-1.5" (2-4 cm)*

The name *pine* is a generic term used to describe many different kinds of evergreen trees. Among them are the red pine, white pine and jack pine as well as others not covered in this section such as the Scotch pine, Norway pine and yellow pine. All pines are evergreens but not all evergreens are pines. For example, members of the cedar family retain their leaves all year so they are evergreens, but not pines. Pines have from 2 – 5 needles coming from one papery sheath. Any evergreen that has only one needle (leaf) is not a pine, but probably a spruce or fir. The pines don't actually retain the same needles all the time, but instead are constantly replacing needles, just not all at the same time. Each

white

jack

is replaced about every five years. White and red pines grow so large that you can't reach around the trunk. The jack pine has a much smaller trunk. The bark is highly variable and usually thick and scaly. Often small plates of bark will break off and pile up at the base of the tree. The tiny, yellow, male cones release a huge amount of pollen early each spring, often covering the surface of lakes with a yellow hue. The female cone starts life as a purple structure. It captures pollen and only develops into a full-fledged cone the following year. Each cone contains dozens of winged seeds that helicopter to the ground when released. Squirrels collect unopened cones and strip them apart to feed on the nutritious seeds.

red

VINES

Poison ivy   *Toxicodendron radicans leaf 8-10" (20-25 cm)*

This native plant is a close relative to sumacs and the edible cashew nut. Poison ivy is the master of change. In northern parts of the country it grows as a low vine or shrub with a thick woody stem. Poison ivy that grows in the southern states is just the opposite. It has massive woody vines covered with **aerial roots** (roots growing out all over the stem giving it a hairy appearance) and attaches to trees. Pale white clusters of flowers turn to greenish white berries in autumn. Leaves are compound with three leaflets; remember "leaves of three, let them be." The leaf edge can be smooth or irregularly toothed. Leaves often are glossy dark green but can be dull and pale. In autumn, they always turn bright red. To confirm poison ivy, look for the center leaflet to have a stem twice as long as its flanking two leaflets. All parts of this plant contain the irritating chemical **urushiol** (u-roo´she-ol). The "poison" in poison ivy is a misnomer, because contact with this plant causes an allergic reaction, not a poisoning and it is not an ivy.

Virginia creeper   *Parthenocissus quinquefolia leaf 6-8" (15-20 cm)*

A look-alike to the wild grape vine, Virginia creeper is a fast growing native vine with a smooth woody stem. It also has tendrils, but, unlike the forked tendrils of grapes, has small round "suction cups" on its ends, allowing it to attach to flat surfaces, such as the sides of buildings. In some areas this vine covers entire hedge rows and even trees. Each palmately compound leaf is made up of five individual leaflets. Many confuse Virginia creeper with poison ivy, but Virginia creeper has five leaflets and poison ivy has three leaflets. Autumn turns the leaves of Virginia creeper scarlet red. The poisonous berries look similar to those of grapes. Distinguish the difference by looking at the stem going to the fruit; grapes are clustered without much of the stem being seen. Virginia creeper has individual berries attached directly to a red stem. New plants are started when birds eat creeper berries and eliminate the seeds in their droppings.

Wild grapes · *Vitis spp. leaf 5" (13 cm)*

Creeping and crawling over just about any tree, shrub or even the tallest wall or house, native grape vines are prolific growers. Trees use tall trunks with strong branches to get their leaves up into sunlight; grape vines use a quick growing flexible stem to snake their way out of the shade of other plants and up into the sunlight. Large grape vines have thick woody stems covered with a scaly bark that is often stripped by birds and small animals and used to line nest cavities. Wild grapes have large edible leaves and small forked tendrils (thread-like stems) that secure themselves to other plants. Distinguish wild grapes from other vines by these forked tendrils and tight clusters of small purple grapes. The leaves are large and have a saw tooth edge and attach opposite the tendrils on the stem. Wild grapes are close relatives of grapes used for jelly and wine. Clusters of white flowers give way to tight clusters of grapes with several pear-shaped seeds within each berry. Grapes are enjoyed by birds and people alike.

SHRUBS

Red-osier dogwood *Cornus stolonifera 16' (5 m) leaf 2-4" (5-10 cm)*

Clumps of this red-stemmed shrub are most obvious in winter when the red stems stand out against the white or brown background. Growing near water most of the time, the red-osier also grows in drier upland locations. It has become a popular shrub to plant around homes, with its young, green twigs that turn red in late autumn. The leaves of any dogwood have long veins, parallel to each other, and are arranged in opposite fashion along the branch. Large flat-topped flower heads sprout white flowers that mature into white berries that birds, such as Robins, love to eat. Look near the base of this shrub to see air-borne roots. Check any small branch that is in contact with the ground to see if it has taken root.

| Smooth sumac | *Rhus glabra. 6-20' (2-6 m) leaf 15-20" (38-51 cm)* |
| Staghorn sumac | *Rhus typhina 6-20' (2-6 m) leaf 15-20" (38-51 cm)* |

Depending on your point of view, either you love or hate sumacs. Their tenacious growth maddens some, while their clusters of cheery red berries delight others. Once this woody shrub is established, it is nearly impossible to eradicate. Sumacs reproduce with underground runners that send up new growth every couple of feet. Most clumps of sumac are not an accumulation of many individual plants, but rather a cluster of one individual plant with many offshoots. Sumac can be a large shrub or small tree, going to 20' (6.1 m) tall. Sumac shrubs have female and male flowers on separate plants. It is the female plants and flowers that will have the red clusters of seeds. Tell the difference between the smooth and staghorn sumac by the smooth or fuzzy stems and branches just below the seed clusters. The sumacs have compound leaves with 9 – 21 leaflets per leaf. These leaves are some of the first to turn red each autumn.

staghorn sumac

smooth sumac

| Wild rose | *Rosa spp. .5-5' (.1-2 m) leaf 3-6" (8-15 cm)* |

These native plants are the source for all of the roses found in all of the world's gardens. Different species of roses grow everywhere from open prairies to shady woodlands and river bottoms. Apples, pears, apricots, raspberries and strawberries are just some of the rose's closest relatives. Each rose has five petals, usually pink or red and are usually pollinated by bees. From this flower comes the well known rose hip. Each hip is shaped like an upside down apple that turns red in autumn and contains many seeds. These edible hips are high in vitamin C and are eaten by a wide variety of birds and animals. Rose leaves are made up of 5 – 9 small leaflets that are attached alternately along the thorny branches. All roses have thorns; some have fine, hair-like, prickly thorns, while others have stout, curved thorns. Either way, the thorns protect these plants from the hungry deer and other plant-eating animals.

NON-WOODY

FIELDS AND PRAIRIES

Birdsfoot trefoil — *Lotus corniculatus 6-24" (15-61 cm)*

Driving along any road you are likely to see this showy non-native plant. It grows low to the ground and spills off the curb to brighten the street with its bright yellow flowers. Take a closer look at this pea-like flower with its wide fan-shaped petal called a **standard**. Note how it is striped with fine orange lines to guide insects such as bees to the nectar. Now note the two side petals, called **wings**, that come together to form a cover. The lower two petals are called the **keel** and join to form a shape like the bottom of a boat. Stop and take a minute to watch a bee land on these special flowers. See how the weight of the insect triggers the flower to open and deposit pollen on the bee while it gets a drink of nectar. These flowers are in continuous bloom from spring to autumn. The flowers are not the only thing that resemble a pea. The leaves have three leaflets with two small leaf-like leaves at the base of the leaf stem called **stipules** (stip´oolz). Once these flowers are pollinated, the resulting pods resemble a bird's foot and give this plant its common name.

Black-eyed susan — *Rudbeckia hirta 1-3' (.3-.9 m)*

Poking their bright cheery, flowers out from both woodlands and fields, the native black-eyed susan is a wonderful flower to find. Numerous daisy-like, bright, yellow flowers stand at the end of stiff, hairy stems. Each flower has a dark purplish center containing disk flowers ringed by the yellow or sometimes orange ray flowers. Do a little dissection and you will see that these flowers are an accumulation of many smaller flowers. The leaves are hairy and attach opposite to each other on the stem. Notice how the leaves at the base of the plant, called **basal leaves**, are larger and wider than the leaves up higher, which are referred to as **cauline leaves** (kaw´lin). Look for three veins on each leaf and how the stem of the leaf is an extension of the leaf blade.

Chicory   *Cichorium intybus 2 - 4' (1 m)*

Another member of the sunflower and daisy family, this aggressive flower grows in any place where the soil has been disturbed. This type of growth is common among non-native plants like chicory and dandelion. Many sky blue flowers are scattered along the long stiff stem and are open from spring to autumn. Each flower has a square-tipped, fringed, ray flower and just as many disk flowers and looks very similar to dandelions. The similarity to the dandelion doesn't stop there. The leaves at the base of the plant, called basal leaves, are a similar shape. Further up the stem the leaves are very different. They are small and narrow with the base of each leaf clasping the stem. Only a few flowers open at a time and each flower lasts only a day or so.

Common mullein   *Verbascum thapsus 2-6' (1-2 m)*

This very tall and erect plant towers above all others in open fields and prairies. It is not hard to detect this plant with its woolly leaves and tightly packed spike of yellow flowers. Looking closer at each flower, notice that the individual flowers look very similar to those of a snapdragon. They are closely related to each other. Each flower by itself is small, about ¾" (.2 cm), but hundreds grow together on the spike. At the base of this plant are large basal leaves with smaller oblong leaves without stems ascending up the main stalk. A non-native plant, the common mullein is a **biennial**, which means the first year of growth is just a low group of leaves. The second year it sends up a tall stalk and sprouts flowers. Like many non-native plants, the common mullein grows in areas that have had the original vegetation removed and more aggressive plants take over. Take the time to feel the leaves of the mullein. The thick fuzzy leaves were used to line shoes and socks for comfort and warmth. Give it a try!

Dame's rocket   *Hesperis matronalis 1-3' (.3-.9 m)*

This tall growing member of the mustard family grows to about 3' (.92 m) tall and is not a native plant. It is an ornamental plant that has escaped from gardens and now grows in the wild along roadsides and in open fields. With large clusters of pink, purple or white flowers, dame's rocket looks very similar to the plant called phlox. You can count only four petals on the dame's rocket and five on phlox. The flowers produce long, thin, pointed, seed pods, about 1" (2.5 cm) long, filled with tiny black seeds that taste like pepper. These elongated seed pods indicate this plant is a mustard. Long, pointed leaves connect alternately along the stem. Each leaf is lined with a fine toothed edge while phlox has a smooth edge.

Goldenrod   *Solidago spp. 24-48" (7-15 m) leaf 3-9" (8-23 cm)*

Woodlands and prairies are favorite places for the native goldenrods. No matter where they are, their clusters of bright yellow flowers always announce the goldenrods. Look closer at this cluster. Tiny flowers (¼ – ⅓", .6 – .7 cm) are surrounded by small flower coverings called bracts which are also yellow and add to the overall appearance of the flower. Each autumn, fields glow with the yellow hue of goldenrods. Many people mistakenly blame these highly visible flowers for allergies and hay-fever. In reality though, allergies are usually caused by other plants, such as ragweed. Goldenrods are closely related to sunflowers and daisies and are pollinated by insects visiting each tiny flower for nectar. The leaves are highly variable on each species of plant (125 species of goldenrods in the U.S. and Canada), but they are all attached alternately along the stem of this perennial plant.

Milkweed   *Asclepias syriaca 3-5' (.9-2 m)*

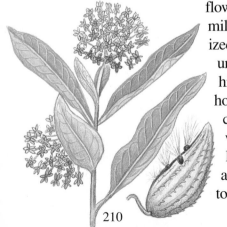

Dotting many open fields and prairies, the milkweed stands proud and tall. There are many different kinds of milkweeds and all share the same kind of flowers, leaves, large seed pods and most importantly, milky juice. A common native plant, they have a specialized and extremely complex pollination process that is unlike any other. Insects that visit the cluster of purple, highly aromatic flowers, inadvertently step into a leg-hold trap and emerge with two attached packets of pollen, called **pollinia**. When an insect visits another milk-weed flower, the same trap accepts the packets and pollination is complete. Sometimes, if the pollen is not ripe and ready to be transferred, the entrapped insect is forced to wait until the pollen packets come loose and the insect can fly away. This is not the only special feature of this plant. If you break a stem or leaf, a very toxic, white, milky juice will flow forth, giving the milkweed its common name. This fluid is so toxic that just a taste will make you feel ill. Many insects, such as the monarch butterfly, have evolved to live solely on this special plant. Feeding upon the plant and absorbing the toxic milk, butterflies make themselves toxic to birds and other predators. Stop and look at the insects on the milkweed to see if they are not the same kind on each.

Mustard   *Brassica spp. 1-2' (.3-.6 m)*

There are many different kinds of mustards. All share similar leaves, flowers and seed pods, making these plants easy to identify. Early each spring, before all the snow has melted, some of the mustards sprout and set forth clusters of bright yellow or white flowers, each with four petals in the shape of a cross. Take a closer look to see that all of the flower parts are in groups of four. After the flowers have been pollinated by visiting insects, thin, pointed seed pods develop and these are divided into two chambers. The chambers are separated by a thin papery sheath and contain a dozen or so seeds. Examine the pods to see these parts. When you are sure that you have a mustard in hand, give the black mature seeds a taste to see that they taste like pepper. The leaves are also unique to the mustard family. The leaves near the base of the plant, called basal leaves, have several small lobes gradually enlarging towards the end of the leaf. Most of the common mustards were introduced to America from Europe and all are related to common garden vegetables like broccoli, cabbage, cauliflower and brussel sprouts.

black mustard

Oxeye daisy   *Chrysanthemum leucanthemum 1-3' (.5-1 m)*

This is the common daisy found growing in fields and roadsides just about anywhere in the eastern U.S. and Canada. This delicate flower is a favorite of many gardeners but is not a native plant. The oxeye daisy was introduced from Europe. The bright white flowers with the yellow centers are actually two different kinds of flowers together in one place. Pull one of the white petals called a ray flower, and look where it was attached to the plant. The base is like a tube which contains female flower parts. The yellow center is a cluster of many small flowers. Each yellow disk flower, if removed, will show both male and female flower parts. These flowers continue to bloom all summer long, producing thousands of seeds. The leaves of the oxeye daisy are dark green with many irregular lobes or finger-like projections.

Queen Anne's lace   *Daucus carota 2-3' (.5-1 m)*

The common name fits this elegant and stately plant perfectly. A tall thin member of the carrot family, Queen Anne's lace has tiny cream-white flowers arranged in large, flat-topped clusters that flower all summer long. Look closer at this cluster to see a reddish brown to purple single flower nestled in the middle of all of the white flowers. At the end of each season the flowers turn brown and curl up into a bird's nest shape. Each fern-like leaf resembles a carrot or parsley leaf and attaches alternately to the main stem. These aggressive, non-native plants take two growing years to reach maturity. They line the roads of many of our cities. Each plant grows from a single long tap root. Though not recommended because of its similarity to poisonous plants, the first year tap root can be unearthed and eaten like a carrot, which is no coincidence. This plant is the ancestor to the garden carrot. It often grows in open fields and becomes a nuisance when it takes over, becoming the only plant to survive.

Red clover   *Trifolium pratense 6-16" (15-41 cm)*

Red clover is probably one of the most common plants anywhere. Look in any open field or along any roadside and you are likely to see this non-native plant. Large, dense, red masses of flowers make this plant easy to identify. These flowers are the center of attention when hundreds of insects visit for a sip of nectar. Red clover flowers bloom from early spring straight through to the first frost. Each plant has groups of three leaflets, each with a white "V" shaped **chevron** to help you identify it. Red clover is so wide spread because it was planted by farmers extensively for hay and pasture crops. Although you can't see it without digging up the plant, the roots have nodules containing bacteria that capture air-borne nitrogen and return the nitrogen to the soil, improving the soil's fertility.

212

| Yellow sweet clover | *Melilotus officinalis 1-6' (.3-2 m)* |
| White sweet clover | *Melilotus alba 2-8' (.6-3 m)* |

yellow clover

The clovers are non-native plants that have found a home in open fields and along roadsides throughout North America. A tall, spindly plant that is topped off with either white or yellow spike-like clusters of flowers, it was planted by farmers as a pasture crop and to enrich soil with its nitrogen converting ability. The leaves are divided into three rounded leaflets, attached oppositely on the stem. Crush a leaf and smell the vanilla-like fragrance. This plant grows from a long, strong tap root and has become a pest in many parks and in the remaining native prairies. Indeed, controlled prairie burns are conducted to get rid of plants like sweet clover. Bees love clover and many bee keepers plant fields of them for the bees to gather nectar.

| Bull thistle | *Cirsium vulgare 2-6' (.6-2 m)* |
| Canada thistle | *Cirsium arvense 1-5' (.3-2 m)* |

This common group of plants are non-natives that have made themselves at home in our fields, along roads and prairies. Originally from Europe, these plants all have large, beautiful purple flowers that develop into dozens of tiny black seeds with a white downy silk attached. The silk acts like a parachute and carries the seeds away on the wind. The seeds are eaten by many birds, while the silky down is used to line the nest of Goldfinches, who wait to nest just to obtain this silk. Be careful when you go to take a closer look at these obvious plants; they are clad in spines and thorns to protect them from being eaten by animals like deer. These plants are biennial, which means they only grow a rosette of leaves the first year and send up a flower stalk the second year.

bull thistle

WOODLANDS

Columbine — *Aquilegia canadensis 1-2' (.5-1 m)*

Columbine is an elegant woodland flower usually standing in the shadow of other woodland trees and shrubs. Orange, red and yellow drooping flowers stand out amongst the other woodland flowers. They have five upside down tubes fused together, with the tops of the tubes tipped with a red spur containing a drop of nectar. These flowers attract insects, such as butterflies, that have long tongues and are able to cling to the flower to reach up into the tube for the nectar. Look for small holes at the tip of the tubes where some insects without long tongues have chewed through to steal the nectar. The leaves have long stalks tipped with 9 – 27 small, light green, three-lobed leaflets.

Common blue violet — *Viola papilionacea 3-8" (8-20 cm)*

Carpeting the floor of just about any forest is the native common blue violet. What this plant lacks in size it makes up for in vivid blue color. Yellow and white violets are also common. No matter which violet you find, each flower will have white and purple veins which guide bees to its nectar treat. Often there are two kinds of flowers on each violet. The small white flowers near the ground don't seem to open. Look closer to notice that each leaf and each flower originates from its own stem. The leaf stem is longer then the flower stem. Violets that don't grow like this are called "stemmed" violets, because the flowers are perched on the end of the same stem as the leaves. The leaves are heart-shaped and remain long after the flowers have finished blooming.

Jack-in-the-pulpit — *Arisaema triphyllum 1-3' (.3-.9 m)*

This native plant wins the award for the most unusual flower of the forest. Its large flower looks like a combination of a leaf wrapped around a spike of flowers. The center spike of the flower looks like a thin erect club called a **spadix** (spa´diks). It contains many separate male and female flowers. Surrounding the spadix is the **spathe** (spath) which looks like a green leaf wrapped around the flowers. The top of the spathe is arched and forms a roof to protect the flowers within. If you use your imagination, this flower looks like a preacher on a pulpit, thus lending the common name, Jack-in-the-pulpit. One or two large three-lobed leaves per plant tower over this unique flower and are often confused with trilliums. Insects visit the flowers, attracted by their smell. The remarkable flower turns into a more remarkable cluster of bright red berries. These berries may look attractive, but they contain a toxic substance made up of calcium oxalate crystals that cause a burning sensation if eaten.

Trillium — *Trillium spp. 1-2' (.3 m-.6 m) leaf 3-9" (8-23 cm)*

Our native trilliums are the darlings of the forest. They grow in abundance in some forests and are non-existent in others. Early each spring these short, erect, non-woody plants shoot up and set flowers long before the trees overhead have had a chance to sprout leaves. About a half a dozen trillium species grace our woodlands. All trilliums have leaves and flowers in three parts. All trilliums are members of the lily family with flowers ranging in color from white and yellow to pink and red. Flowers can be large and drooping or small and erect depending upon the species. Either way, most trilliums will only flower after maturing to six years old. Bright, red berries, technically called its fruit, adorn trilliums each autumn.

Trout lilies — *Erythronium spp. 4-10" (10-26 cm)*

Carpeting the forest floor in the shadow of trilliums, trout lilies are native plants that have small white, yellow or pink flowers. Each spring the trout lilies sprout, carpeting the forest floor with hues of green, white, yellow, and pink. These are truly native plants growing in large colonies. One or two long, pointed, lance-shaped leaves are mottled brown similar to the scales of a fish, giving this plant its common name. Like most lilies, these plants grow and reproduce from underground bulbs, although they take about seven years to produce their first flower. Flowers droop from a single erect stalk

215

inviting flying insects to visit and pollinate these plants. Even though this plant produces seeds, rarely do these seeds result in any new plants.

WETLAND

Bulrush   *Juncus effusus 3-6' (1-2 m)*

Often confused with cattails, the bulrush is a common marsh plant that grows in wetlands as well as damp open ground. The soft, grass-like leaves grow to about 4' (1.2 m) tall and are more cylindrical than flat. From a single stem, a cluster of very small greenish-brown flowers shoot off to one side of the stalk. Take a closer look at the individual flowers and notice that all of the flower parts are in groups of three or six. Once you have seen this plant, you are unlikely to confuse it with the more common cattail.

Cattail   *Typha latifolia 3-9' (1-3 m)*

A true aquatic, native plant, the cattail grows with tall narrow leaves that gently wave in the breeze. Each spring these water plants sprout from points all along an underground rootstock called a **rhizome** (ri´zom). The leaves grow up to 9' (2.7 m) tall and usually are no wider than 1" (2.5 cm). In early summer a flower stalk shoots up, topped with two regions of flowers. The top is yellow and thick with pollen. This pollen is easily shaken off by the wind, falling onto the lower group of green female flowers. It is the female flowers, that after being pollinated, turn into the familiar brown cigar "cattails." Just about every part of the cattail is used by the animals that live in wetlands. Stems are eaten by muskrats, while red-winged blackbirds build their nest supported by the cattail stems. Cattails are an important filtration plant, helping to clean the water and provide shade and shelter to smaller aquatic animals.

Yellow Pond Lily
White Pond Lily

Nuphar variegatum leaf
Nuphar adorata

Scattered across the surface of the ponds are the floating leaves of the yellow and white pond lily. Raised above the leaves are the white or brilliant yellow flowers which attract flying insects for pollination. Heart-shaped leaves, floating on the water, have a V-shaped notch where the stem attaches. The leaves are important resting spots for dragonflies and frogs to sun themselves or to hunt for an afternoon snack. Pond lilies are rooted in the bottom of the pond and only shift slightly when surface winds blow across the water. This plant is also valued by wild animals. Ducks eat the seeds; moose and deer graze on the greens; and muskrats and beavers eat the roots, storing them for winter. Indians and frontiersmen cooked and ate the rootstocks like potatoes or pounded them into flour.

Purple loosestrife

Lythrum salicaria 2-4' (.6-2 m)

Anyone who lives near a lake, stream or pond probably knows this tall showy plant. A non-native plant, that was introduced from Europe as a showy garden flower, it is now taking over most of our waterways and pushing out the native plants, such as cattails. Erect spikes of purple-pink flowers with four to six petals each rise above opposite and whorled leaves. Leaves lower on the stalk tend to be hairy, referred to as **downy**. Each leaf is attached directly to the stalk without a stem. In large groups, these plants are colorful, but other than attracting insects to their flowers, they don't provide the food or habitat for wildlife as cattails do.

Rock Smart

Rocks are important to all animals, including people. We live on a rock, one giant rock circling the sun. The earth is 7,927 miles (12,754 km) in diameter and weighs about 6.6 sextillion tons—and our hats are off to anyone who can comprehend sextillion tons. This rock we call home is about 4.5 billion years old. When you skip a stone across a lake, you're flinging a tiny fragment of our home, a fragment that may be thousands or millions of years old.

We often take rocks for granted. We forget that rocks shelter us, nurture us and even fuel our lives. For example, rocks have been used as building material since ancient times. Even today, granite and marble grace the exteriors of city skyscrapers, adorn the fronts of churches, and dress up the hearths of our fireplaces. We drive on asphalt and cement which contain rocks, and we wear rocks on our fingers and around our necks. We extract uranium and coal from rocks to fuel our electric power plants. Our watches keep accurate time because of a rock called quartz. We cover the space shuttle with a mixture of rocks called ceramics to keep it from burning up when it re-enters our atmosphere. And small rocks (sand) are part of a loose accumulation (soil) that is essential to all terrestrial life.

Geology is the science of earth and its history. Geology is divided into **mineralogy**, the study of minerals, and **petrology**, the study of the composition of rocks. Mineralogy is the study of the distribution, identification and properties of minerals.

Rocks are made up of minerals. A mineral is an inorganic, natural substance found in the earth. Sometimes rocks can occur in a pure form of minerals, but usually they are a combination of several minerals. It might help to think of most rocks as many minerals all glued together. Literally hundreds of different combinations of minerals make up hundreds of different kinds of rocks.

There are three types of rocks: igneous, sedimentary and metamorphic. In the eastern U.S. and Canada we have mostly sedimentary, or layered rock, with only small outcroppings of metamorphic and igneous rocks. Within these three broadly defined categories fall the many distinct forms of rock such as quartz, limestone and gneiss (nice).

The history of the earth is recorded in rocks. In rocks we find the remains of plants and animals, frozen in geologic time as fossils. Fossils are imprints

219

or bones that have become rock over time. Even dinosaur footprints have been fossilized. Fossils of ocean animals that are found high in the mountains or buried in a desert, far from any ocean, indicate that the area was once at the bottom of an ancient sea. Fossils also show scientists how the plants and animals have changed over time.

Why are minerals important?

Minerals not only make up the rocks of the earth but are also important to our health. Minerals are just as important to our health as vitamins. Minerals make our bones strong and they also regulate the function of our hearts and several other major body functions. In fact, we require some in large amounts, such as calcium, magnesium and potassium. That doesn't mean all minerals are helpful. Some minerals are toxic, even in small amounts. These include lead, mercury and cadmium.

Where does soil come from?

The earliest life on earth existed in the sea. Scientists estimate that it took millions of years for the first signs of life to move onto the land and millions more until the first vascular plants evolved. With the help of plants, rocks were broken down and converted into soil. They did this by persistently growing into cracks and crevices. When plants die, they themselves contribute to the accumulation of soil. As the soil accumulates, it supports more plants and more life on land. Conservation of our precious soil should be one of our most important tasks. Reduced or minimal tilling, proper crop rotation and resting of the soil all help to maintain fertility and reduce the massive loss of soil each year.

What kind of rocks make up the earth?

To start, think of the earth as three layers of rock covered by a thin rock skin, or crust. The three layers are the earth's inner core, outer core and mantle. The **inner core** is 3,200 miles (2,900 km) below the earth's surface. It is truly the core or center of the earth and is made up of only two elements: iron and nickel. These elements are in solid form because of the extreme pressure in the center of the earth. The temperature of the inner core is about 13,000° F (7,000° C). Compare this to the boiling point of water of 212° F (99° C) and we can imagine how hot it is. It is estimated that the center of the earth is so hot that it would shine like a star if it were exposed.

The earth's middle layer, called the **outer core**, is about 1,800 miles (2,896 km) below the surface. Like the inner core, it is made up primarily of iron and nickel, but due to decreased pressure, the outer core is liquid. Next is the **mantle**, a thick layer of rock extending from the outer core to just below the crust. This area is also hot, averaging about 4,000° F (2,000° C), still hot enough to keep rock in the liquid form.

Last, the **crust** is the uppermost layer of rock that covers and shields us from the mantle. The crust was formed from magma from the mantle. **Magma** is lava which has not reached the earth's surface. Liquid and molten when part of the mantle, it has come up to the surface through cracks and has cooled to form the crust. The crust of earth is about 5 to 25 miles (8 to 40 km) thick and is made up of many layers of different types of rocks. On top of the crust is the topsoil which varies in depth from inches to many feet. We, of course, live on top of the crust and topsoil.

What is a rock?

Rocks are made of ingredients just as a cake is made of flour, sugar and baking powder. Most rocks are aggregates, or combinations of one or more minerals. There are about 3,000 kinds of minerals, but of these, only 100 are common. Just eight make up more than 98 percent of all the rocks in the world.

The biggest differences among rocks are accounted for by the different amounts of one or more minerals in the rock. For example, basalt contains crystals of feldspar and pyroxene. Some minerals form crystals that are arranged in a very orderly pattern; these result in solid rocks with smooth, flat surfaces. All of our metals come from rocks called ores. Some rocks, such as borax and graphite, have non-metal minerals. Most gems are minerals. Exceptions include amber, coral and pearls, which come from plants and animals. Emeralds come from black limestone, while diamonds come from the rock, kimberlite.

How are rocks formed?

Rocks are formed in three very different ways. They are classified as igneous, metamorphic or sedimentary, depending on the way in which they were formed. The different origins of rock give rocks their varying characteristics.

Igneous rock is derived directly from the mantle of the earth. In the mantle, molten rock called magma is heated to such extreme temperatures that it is in a liquid form. When magma forces its way through cracks in the earth's crust and it reaches the surface, it cools to form rocks like basalt. Sometimes, if the magma cools more slowly beneath the surface, it forms granite. Look for igneous rocks along rivers and natural gorges.

Sedimentary rock is made of sediments composed of tiny particles of sand or carbonates. When these small particles are moved by the action of wind or water, they eventually settle and are deposited in layers. These layers compress over time by their own weight and harden into sedimentary rock.

Good examples of this are sandstone and limestone. Look for sedimentary rocks when a road has been cut through a hillside. Notice the different layers of this type of rock on the exposed hillside. This is the most common type of rock in the eastern half of our continent.

Metamorphic rocks occur when heat and pressure fundamentally change either igneous or sedimentary rocks into a metamorphic state; metamorphic means change. The changes usually result in new minerals and sometimes a coarsening of the texture. Metamorphism occurs when rocks are compressed by mountain building events (regional metamorphism) or when molten magma comes into contact with host rocks (contact metamorphism).

How are fossils formed?

Fossils are rocks that contain the preserved remains of once-living plants or animals. They consist of bones or shells of animals, fish and sea creatures and even leaves or stems of plants. Often fossils are created when a plant or animal dies and becomes buried in the sediment of a lake or stream. Particles of sand and mud sink to the bottom of the lake or river and slowly cover the remains. When the sediment builds up, its weight squashes the future fossil and compresses the sand and mud into rock, trapping the corpse or plant material within. After millions of years of being compressed, the remains of the plant or animal turns to stone and it is called a **fossil**. We find fossils only when we dig into these layers of sedimentary rock. The next time you pass a hillside that has been cut into, look for sedimentary layers that might contain fossils. Keep in mind that a long, long time ago the sediment you're seeing was at the bottom of an ancient river or ocean.

> **If a child is to keep alive his (her) inborn sense of wonder — he needs the companionship of at least one adult who can share it, rediscovering the joy, excitement and mystery of the world we live in.**
>
> RACHEL CARSON

Often these fossilized images are of plants and animals that are now extinct. They reveal the history of life on earth millions of years ago, long before any people lived. Fossils of leaves often show the original detail and texture, allowing scientists to be able to identify the plants. **Amber** is an unusual kind of fossil. It is fossilized tree resin. It occurred when a tree became damaged and yellow-gold resin oozed at the damaged site to seal up the opening and protect the tree. Insects attracted to the sticky resin became entangled. When the drop of resin fell from the tree, it became buried and over time became fossilized. Some amber has preserved insects for million of years in perfect detail.

Wood can also be fossilized when silica replaces the woody material. This often happens when a log is submerged in water and the silica in the water replaces the wood, leaving a quartz fossil called **petrified wood**. This rock-wood is harder than steel and many details of the plant structure are visible.

What are the different shapes of rocks?

Rocks break in different ways leaving different shapes. When rocks break, they usually break in one of three ways: cleavage, fractured and weathered. When a rock breaks, leaving a flat surface, it is called **cleavage**. When a rock breaks without any flat or smooth surfaces it is called **fractured**. The way a rock breaks helps to identify that rock. Some rocks break only at 90 degree angles, for example halite and galena. Geologists use the number of cleavage surfaces and the angle to help identify some rocks.

Lastly, some rocks are smooth and round. Small stones and rocks can be carried by currents in a river. While washing down the river, rocks bump into one another knocking off small pieces. Jagged edges are the first to break off, leaving a smooth rock. This constant wearing of a rock is called **weathering**. The next time you are exploring on the banks of your favorite river or lake, notice how the rocks are smooth and round with few angular edges.

How do rocks break into smaller rocks?

All rocks have started out as hot molten magma deep within the earth. After cooling, the magma solidifies into massive rocks. Over millions of years these rocks break apart into smaller rocks. Eventually they become as small as grains of sand and settle to form sedimentary rock and the process starts over. Small rocks are broken away from the larger mother rocks by several natural events such as water and plants.

Most mother rocks have small pores or holes within. Over time, rainwater has a way of working into these holes. If the water freezes it can expand by about ten percent. The pressure exerted on the rock by the expanded frozen water causes bits and pieces to break off or cracks to form. Over time, rocks can be broken apart due to the repeated freezing and thawing. You can see this process in action in your own driveway or street—pot holes. That's why highway crews must constantly repair cracks in the road.

The same small cracks can collect soil and seeds over time. Once the seeds start to grow, the plant's roots grow deep into the rock, driving a "root wedge" into the crack. This causes more water to enter the rock, causing more expansion cracks from freezing and thawing water. As the roots grow, the rock will break apart, making more room for new plants to grow.

What are the different types of igneous rocks?

Igneous rocks are formed when molten magma cools and solidifies. Two types or kinds of rock are formed during this process, intrusive and extrusive. **Intrusive rocks** like granite have a coarse-grained texture. Large crystals result when molten magma cools slowly underground. Slow cooling allows time for the crystals to grow. Only after the earth's crust has been eroded away by rivers or the uplifting of mountain ranges, are these types of rocks exposed.

Extrusive rocks are formed when molten magma breaks the surface of the earth and becomes a lava flow. Rapid cooling at the surface results in small crystals when magma is quenched by water, with the result being fine-grained obsidian (volcanic glass).

What is a quartz?

Quartz is a very common mineral found in the earth. Quartz was present in the original rocks that cooled and formed the earth's crust about 4.5 billion years ago. Quartz still makes up 10 to 20 percent of all the earth's crust. Over millions of years, quartz has been broken apart or weathered down from stones to pebbles to sand. In its final form it is so small that you would hardly recognize it as quartz. A good example of this is common beach sand which is actually ground-up quartz.

Quartz is formed when molten magma cools slowly far below the earth's surface. Within this intrusive rock, heated water with dissolved silica fill the cracks and pockets. When hot silica water cools, crystals may grow as large as the space permits. Many very large quartz crystals are found in this hard igneous rock. Where only small pin holes are filled with silica water, tiny quartz crystals form. A good example of this is granite. Larger spaces result in geodes.

What is a geode?

In the same way that quartz is formed, geodes are formed when hot silica water flows into a round cavity. Gradually the hot water cools, precipitating crystals. The crystals stop growing before they fill the entire space. These nests of crystals, called **geodes**, can be the size of a baseball up to a basketball. Often they are different colors. The edge or outer portion can be made up of one color of tiny crystals and the inner edge often is large crystals of another color.

What are agates?

Agates are a type of quartz that do not form visible crystals such as geodes. Agates occur when hot silica water fills small, hollow spaces in cooling igneous rocks. Microscopic crystals pack the entire space. You will never see the large showy crystals like the geodes. Any rock formed like this is called a

chalcedony (kal-sed´n-e). Dozens of varieties and forms of chalcedony occur, with agates being just one type. Bands of alternating colors make these gems easy to identify. Chalcedony, with light and dark bands or stripes, is called **onyx**. There are moss agates and leaf agates, to mention just a couple. The colored bands sometimes run around the stone and others form circles or other patterns.

Is coal a rock?

Coal is one of the few rocks of organic origin. Millions of years ago, branches, leaves and even whole trees sometimes fell into marshes or lagoons and were buried under sediments. The weight of these sediments squeezed the water out and compressed the plants into a solid mass. Heat, pressure and a lot of time eventually turned the plants into what we burn as coal. Layers of coal are sandwiched between layers of rock, such as sandstone or clay and are mined by large machines. There are many different types of coal. **Household coal** is hard, brittle and dirty to handle. The highest quality coal is called **anthracite** (an´thre-site). It is hard, shiny and clean to touch. This coal burns hotter with less smoke. Lower grade coals contain sulphur, which when burned, give off sulphuric acid and cause acid rain.

Can I find gold?

Gold and silver are considered precious metals. They were among the first metals discovered and are valued for their beauty and rarity. They have been used for coins and jewelry and for fillings in teeth. Most gold is mined in South Africa but some still comes from the U.S. and Australia. Gold frequently occurs in association with quartz veins. Gold nuggets and flakes occur in some gravel and sand deposits in Rocky Mountain rivers. These areas are panned or dredged to remove the gold.

Amateur rockhounds often mistake either chalcopyrite or pyrite for gold because of its gold color. Often they are called **fool's gold**. Pyrite generally forms a cubic shaped crystal. The name **pyrite** (py´rite) comes from the Greek words *pyrites* and *lithos* which mean "stone that strikes fire." Pyrite will spark when struck by a piece of iron. Pyrite is very hard compared to gold, which is very soft. Chances are if you have found a gold rock with many flat sides you have found pyrite, fools gold. You might not get rich, but you can start a fire with it.

Is a gem a rock?

Gemstones are rocks that occur naturally and are valued for their beauty and rarity. Diamonds, emeralds and rubies are just some of the rocks we call gems. When cut properly, these precious stones often reflect and refract light to create intense colors and give the gem "fire." Gemstones are measured by weight called a **carat**, which is equal to one fifth of a gram and has nothing to do with the vegetable. Diamond comes from the Greek word *adamas*, meaning unconquerable, because it is the hardest of all known minerals. They range in color from yellow and brown to green and blue. Most diamonds used in jewelry are colorless and have high fire. Red diamonds are very rare. South Africa is the leading supplier of diamonds today.

Why can I write with some rocks?

In order to write with any rock it must be made of soft minerals. Minerals, such as talc, are soft and easy to write with. Geologists will write with a rock to help identify it. To find the true color of a rock, you need to scrape the rock across the back side of a unglazed tile. The color of the mineral's mark is called the **streak color**.

How have we incorporated rocks into our lives?

The use of rocks by humankind goes back to the days of primitive people, around two million years ago. Throughout the entire history of human culture, people have used stones for hunting, preparing food and defending themselves. Stone Age hunters 15,000 years ago discovered deposits of glass-like obsidian and chert and were able to break off chunks that they shaped into spear points and knife blades. As time went on, tool-making skills became more refined. The Bronze Age heralded the discovery and use of copper and tin. These metals dominated the tool and weapon scene until the Iron Age. During the Iron Age, which preceded our modern industrialized world by many centuries, iron was fired and shaped into everything from pots to knives.

Today, our industrialized world is built with minerals. Our building materials, fuel sources, communication systems, transportation systems, recreational equipment and more, are all made up of rocks and minerals. In fact, anything that is not living was originally a raw material that came from the earth. For example, our cities are made of cement, which is made from crushed limestone, sand and water. Aluminum is another critical modern metal and is used in everything from soda cans to canoes. It comes from the rock bauxite and it takes a lot of energy to mine. For this reason, and because there is only a finite supply of bauxite, recycling cans is very important.

How have rocks been used for tools?

Early people used stones for weapons and tools. In the beginning these were crude hammers, scrapers and knives. Later they learned how to shape and cut the stone to make light-weight and more effective tools and weapons, such as arrowheads. The stone of choice was flint because it splits in any direction and leaves a very sharp edge. Everything from sickles to axes were crafted from stone. Obsidian, like flint, was used to fashion tools, primitive mirrors and jewelry. Large pieces of obsidian and flint were used for trading with other tribes.

These stones were shaped using several methods. The earliest tools were shaped by striking the flint against another stone to remove large flakes, resulting in a sharp edge. This crude method was good only for making large axes or chopping tools. **Pressure flaking** is a method that refined the shape of many tools. Flint was held in one hand while the other held a deer antler. Small chips were flaked off with downward pressure on the edge of the stone. In the hands of an experienced flint naper, a simple arrowhead could be made in under an hour.

Do any natural dyes come from rocks?

Many early paints and pigments were extracted from rocks. Early people crushed colored rocks and mixed them with water and animal fats to produce a wide range of color dyes and paints. Some rocks are always the same color, providing a constant source of natural dyes. Many shades of white were obtained from chalk. Different colored clays were used to produce red and brown. They were widely available and their fine grains made them easy to grind up. Black came from charcoal. Vibrant reds came from cinnabar (mercuric sulfide). A copper compound was used to create a classic blue. The browns and yellows of limonite are known as ochres.

> **66 Man's heart away from nature becomes hard. A lack of respect for growing, living things soon leads to a lack of respect for humans too. The Lakotas keep their youth close to nature's softening influence. 99**
>
> RACHEL CARSON

How does a rock help my watch keep time?

Quartz has many interesting properties. In the 1880's it was discovered that when quartz was put under pressure, small electrical charges appeared on their edges. When an outside electric current is sent into the crystal, it causes the crystal to vibrate at a constant rate. This accurate vibration or frequency is utilized to measure time. By the 1920's, quartz crystal clocks were accurate to one-thousandth of a second per day. It wasn't until the 1970's that technology advanced to the point that wrist watches became controlled by quartz crystals.

In these watches a tiny quartz crystal is mounted and an electric charge, supplied from a battery, is passed through the rock. The tiny quartz vibrates once per second. The current from the vibrating quartz is passed on to a very small motor that moves the second hand once each vibration. Gears then turn the minute and hour hands.

How can I identify the rock I found?

Some scientists, called **petrographers**, study and identify rocks but it is difficult for the casual nature observer to determine what kinds of minerals make up a rock. However, you can decide if the rock is igneous, sedimentary or metamorphic by noting how they look and where they are found.

Igneous rocks vary in color and texture, but all are solid and crystalline. Most have small but visible crystals. The crystals vary, depending on their composition and cooling rate. Magma that leaks to the earth's surface and cools rapidly forms a rock with tiny, smooth crystals that seem to flow together like smooth, shiny glass. Magma that cools slowly on the surface forms rocks with small individual crystals, resulting in a crustier appearance like basalt. Finally, magma that never reaches the surface cools even more slowly and forms coarse-grained rocks, such as granites and syenites. Igneous rocks usually occur in the eastern half of our continent in volcanic areas or areas with large cracks in the earth's crust.

Sedimentary rocks are some of the most common types of rocks. They are usually flat and layered. They are fine-grained and are usually a uniform color. Fossils occur in sedimentary rocks.

Metamorphic rocks sometimes display characteristic bands and irregularities as a result of their exposure to heat and pressure. Quartzite is metamorphosed sandstone, marble is the changed form of limestone, while mica is a highly changed form of shale. Some metamorphic rocks can easily be split into sheets or slabs.

Where can I find rocks?

Before you go hunting for rocks, you might want to check the library to get information on established places to find rocks in your area. Most science museums will have someone on staff that can help you get started. The best places to look for rocks are cliffs and quarries. A word of caution—these places can be dangerous and you should never go near without permission of the landowner. Helmets are helpful to protect you from falling rocks. Visit these places after hard rains. The water will wash out hidden rocks. Search the bottom of the cliff or quarries, as this is where most rocks can be found and it is the safest.

Rivers and wave-swept beaches are constantly moving rocks around, making them good places to search for rocks. Another good place to look for rocks is along roads that have been cut through a hillside, but traffic is a concern here.

What are the environmental issues concerning rocks and minerals?

Our appetite for mineral resources is intense because minerals have become such an essential part of life. It's hard to imagine a world without coal and crystals, yet humans have lived longer without them than with them.

The danger of our dependence on mineral resources is two-fold. One is that all of the minerals on the earth took billions of years to form and they occur in finite amounts. As the population explodes, we will eventually run out of them. The second danger lies in how we mine or otherwise extract rocks and minerals. Mining can be damaging to our environment. The use of mercury in mining gold, for example, is dangerous since mercury is toxic to plants and animals and highly polluting. We need to take great care to conserve rocks and minerals, and to extract them wisely.

How can I use the Rock Smart identification section?

Rocks are frequently encountered on a nature walk, but identifying the hundreds of different kinds of rocks is not easy. Rather than trying to identify every rock you find, the Rock Smart identification section will guide you in grouping what you have found into more general types of rocks. Rocks are divided into one of three different kinds of rock based upon how they were formed: igneous, sedimentary and metamorphic.

The rocks illustrated here are a representative of each of the three basic types. By making some simple observations you will be able to see if a rock was formed at the bottom of an ocean or cooled underground from magma millions of years ago. Once you start including rock observations in your nature walks, they won't be just something you step on or skip across a lake.

IGNEOUS ROCKS

Granite

Like all igneous rocks, granite starts below the earth's surface as a molten (melted) mixture of minerals, such as quartz, feldspar and mica. These three minerals are easily distinguished from each other by color and give granite a multi-colored (white, gray and black) or speckled appearance. Granite comes in several colors ranging from pink to yellow-brown, depending upon the color of the quartz and feldspar. Granite can be found where the earth has been opened by a river valley or uplifted by a mountain range. Granite is usually coarse-grained, light-colored, extremely hard and semi-smooth to coarse to the touch.

Basalt

In the eastern portion of the continent, most smooth, uniformly dark-colored rocks are basalt. They range in color from black to dark gray or green to light gray, but all are smooth to the touch. Basalt is equally made up of two minerals, feldspar and pyroxene. Look for basalt outcroppings where rivers have cut deep valleys. Molten basalt that cools slowly, deep within the ground has semi-coarse grain or texture. Molten basalt that reaches the earth's surface cools quickly, producing a finer texture.

Quartz

Quartz is a very common rock. It ranges in color from clear and white to rose and violet. Quartz has several flat sides, indicating the growth pattern of the particular quartz. Most quartz rocks are semi-transparent and smooth or glass-like to touch. Look for quartz on beaches, gravel pits and as veins along excavated roadsides and natural cliffs. This popular crystal is used in jewelry and is considered to be a semi-precious gemstone.

R O C K   S M A R T

Agate

An agate is essentially a quartz stone that has different bands or stripes of color, instead of one solid color. The different colors are a result of different microscopic crystals. Agate bands may be of different colors and thickness as well as straight or wavy. Agates are formed within cavities of basalt rock, so areas of the country that have exposed basalt will have agates. Look for agates along lake shores and eroded slopes that have many exposed rocks. This is a popular rock to polish and is commonly found for sale in rock shops or in novelty shops where it is often made into jewelry. It is the state rock of several states.

SEDIMENTARY ROCK

Sandstone

Most sandstones were formed on the beaches of ancient oceans, along riverbanks or where wind has piled up sand. The settling created smooth layers of uniformly colored and textured rock. To consolidate the rock, the sand grains were "glued" together by silica. Other "glues" produce different degrees of hardness ranging from soft to hard. Sandstone can be white to gray or red to brown. Iron oxide tints sandstone brown, resulting in the sandstone that is used for brownstone buildings. Look for sandstone where roads have been cut through hillsides and along large rivers. Sandstone rocks are a common place to find fossils.

Limestone

Limestone is a highly variable rock that can be smooth and uniform like sandstone or a rough conglomerate of smaller rocks and shells. It ranges in color from white to green. If you find this ancient rock, you are holding evidence that millions of years ago you would likely be standing in a sea. Composed mostly of calcite (calcium carbonate), these rocks were created from the remains of ancient plants and animals, such as coral and algae. Limestone cliffs are soft and are easily eroded by wind and rain.

Look for limestone around waterfalls, in streams and rivers and where roads have been cut through hillsides. Many fossils are found in this type of rock.

METAMORPHIC ROCK

Gneiss

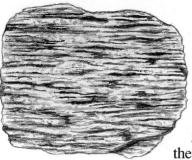

Gneiss, pronounced "nice," is a simple metamorphic rock which was formerly granite. There are several kinds of gneiss such as granite gneiss, hornblende gneiss and muscovite gneiss. In general, gneiss is a coarse-grained rock with parallel lines or bands. Gneiss has a wide range of colors. Many look similar to the original light-colored granite. Other gneiss contain a lot of feldspar or mica, which give these rocks a dark appearance.

Schist

This rock, pronounced "shist", is a highly-changed (metamorphosed) form of shale or quartz. It is coarse with a large content of mica or other minerals. It fractures in wavy, uneven faces, a property called **schistosity**. Each type of rock is named for the most common mineral it contains, such as chlorite or quartz schist. The rock ranges in color from green to gray-black and white. Some schists contain small garnets, making them a special find.

Star Smart

It doesn't matter if it's a warm summer evening or the end of a bitter, windy, winter day—each can be followed by a night filled with thousands of stars to dazzle and amaze us. The night sky is a visual playground we can all enjoy. From our own small vantage point, we can observe multitudes of stars, planets and a moon. We feel something deeply soothing and yet powerfully awesome when we watch them. Humans have always looked into the night sky and wondered what's out there. Is there life on other planets? Can we find the answers to our origins in the star-studded dark? Past and present civilizations have divided the night sky into regions and named them after mythological characters which we now call constellations. We spend millions of dollars sending spacecrafts, telescopes and satellites into space, yet most of us earthbound humans know little about this celestial frontier.

We have to stretch our imaginations just to grasp the most basic concepts of space. Who among us can fathom how far away our neighboring planets are? We measure distances on Earth in miles (kilometers) and time in hours. But our universe is so perversely large that measuring space distances in miles would be grossly inadequate.

In space, we measure distances in light-years. Nothing travels faster than light; it flashes along at 186,000 miles (299,274 km) per second—yes, per second. A **light-year** is the distance light would travel in one Earth year, or approximately 6 trillion miles. The star nearest to us, our sun, is only 93 million miles (149,637,000 km) away. Light travels from the sun to Earth in only eight minutes and 20 seconds; it's about .00001 of a light-year away. Most stars that are visible from Earth are about 20 light-years away. That means that when we are viewing the night sky, we are seeing light left by the stars many years ago. For example, if a star is six light-years away, it could explode today, but we wouldn't see the burst of light for six more years! On the next starlit night, try lying on your back and gazing up at the stars. Imagine what the sky would look like if we were able to see the light as it was being emitted to us. Would there be areas of new stars or voids of stars? Would the Big Dipper retain its current configuration or the North Star point the way to the pole?

Our current knowledge indicates the universe is limitless. Even with our most powerful telescopes, we are unable to detect the ends of it, nor do we have the ability to travel in space with any regularity or to any great distance to see for ourselves. To date, travel beyond our own galaxy, the Milky Way, is physically impossible because the trip would take so long that we wouldn't live long enough to make it.

The study of the universe is called **cosmology**. Scientists can trace galaxies back about 12 to 20 billion years, compared to the Earth's existence of 4.5 billion years. In space, an uneven pattern of stars, planets and interstellar dust spreads in all directions away from a central point. Scientists believe it is expanding in all directions and started from one central explosion. According to these scientists, this **big bang** marked the beginning of time.

> **❝If we can change our priorities, achieve balance and understanding in our roles as human beings in a complex world, the coming era can well be that of a richer civilization, not its end.❞**
>
> SIGURD OLSON

Just as light travels forever in space, astronomers have identified sound waves from this event traveling in space, which supports the big bang theory. To picture the beginning of our universe, think of a balloon being blown up with air. Inside the uninflated balloon is all the matter of the universe (the parts to make up planets and suns). The first puff of air into the balloon represents the explosion that sent all of this space matter flying in all directions. With the second breath the balloon starts to take shape. Millions of planets and stars come together and start to form. Some are attracted together and form galaxies while other renegades are off on their own. With each breath, the balloon "universe" continues to expand, just as our universe is expanding. As the balloon "universe" inflates larger and larger, what is it displacing or covering over? Just like a real balloon would displace what is around it as it inflates, so must the universe. Try to imagine what the edge of the expanding universe looks like. Does it just drop off? Or does it move into another universe? These are the questions that keep curious star-gazers awake at night. Our vast universe is something to marvel about and to behold and not to take for granted. To do this, all you have to do is go outside and look up.

How many planets and stars are there?

The utter vastness of our universe is beyond most imaginations. Even the most powerful telescopes don't penetrate deep enough into space to give a clue as to its size. The best we can do to determine how many planets and stars there are, is to use mathematics. Although there are only nine planets that revolve around our sun, it is estimated that there are 100 million planets and stars in our own Milky Way galaxy. Furthermore, it is estimated that there are

100 million galaxies, some bigger and some smaller than our own, within our universe. And that's only a guess based upon what can be seen. Who knows what's beyond what we can't see?

What is a constellation?

A **constellation** is merely a region of the sky in which the arrangement of the stars resembles a mythical person or creature. When some ancient societies looked skyward, they visualized groups of stars that resembled characters in their mythology or made up stories that fit a perceived shape. Each civilization did this with its own mythological figures and legends. Many of the names applied to the constellations today, such as Orion the great hunter, came from the ancient Greeks.

The International Astronomical Union agreed in 1930 to divide the entire sky into 88 constellations. Each star in the night sky belongs to only one constellation. You can learn the major constellations best in an urban environment. The bright lights of the city wash out many of the minor constellations and highlight the major ones. Once you've located the major constellations, take your family or group to a rural area and try to locate them from there. They'll be harder to find since many more stars are visible when you get away from the glare of a city. These additional stars might be confusing, but of course, you can always just sit back and soak up the starry display.

Why are stars different colors?

Stars are basically one of three colors: blue-white, red or yellow. Most are yellow. It might seem at first glance that all stars are the same color, but if you take a few minutes to allow your eyes to become accustomed to the night sky, you will notice a difference in color. The color of a star reveals what temperature it is. **Blue-white stars** have the hottest temperatures. **Red stars** are relatively cool. **Yellow stars** such as our sun, have moderate temperatures. You might want to see who can spot the most red or blue stars in two minutes.

Why do stars twinkle, but planets don't?

All stars twinkle to some degree, but the twinkling we see has nothing to do with the star itself. The light from these distant stars travels a long distance to reach us. On its trip to Earth, the light passes through clouds of celestial dust and other space debris. These obstacles shift or bend the pathway of the light. Then, before the light reaches us, it must pass through our atmosphere, which bends the light even more. With each bend and shift of the light, it is interrupted for a split second and it appears to twinkle. The next time you find yourself looking at a star twinkling, think about how many layers of space dust, debris and atmosphere its light has passed through before reaching your eyes.

If stars twinkle because their light passes through dust and the Earth's atmosphere, then why doesn't the light from planets twinkle? The planets that we can see are closer than the stars and therefore brighter. They have enough light power to punch through the Earth's atmosphere without too much interruption. A stronger light appears steady. You can tell the difference between a star and a planet just by noting whether the light is twinkling like a star or steady like a planet.

What planets can I see in the night sky?

We are most likely to see the planets that are either nearest to us or ones that are very large. Of the nine planets in our solar system, the nearest are Mercury, Venus and Mars while Saturn and Jupiter are the largest. Each planet is on its own elliptical orbit around the sun, so the times of night and times of year we can see them, varies for each.

Astronomers can calculate long into the future when the planets will be visible. A current star chart can be very useful when you want to know where and when to look for a particular planet. But you can see several planets, including Jupiter and Venus, without a star chart.

If you see a bright object in the western sky just after sunset, or in the eastern sky just before sunrise (and if it doesn't have landing gear), you probably have located Venus. Venus is on a nine month cycle, which means that for nine months it is visible in the evening sky and then for nine months it is visible only in the morning sky. Sightings of Venus account for about 90 percent of all reported UFO's in the northern hemisphere. This is probably because Venus is the brightest object in the night sky, except for the moon. Venus orbits between the Earth and the sun, following the sun closely. When Venus is visible as the sun sets, it is referred to as the **evening star** and it is called the **morning star** at sunrise.

Jupiter is the largest of the nine planets, which helps us spot it. It is 11 times the size of Earth. Its orbit around the sun is outside that of Earth, which makes it visible in the middle of the night at most times of the year. It appears as a bright, shiny planet in the southern half of the sky. By using binoculars, you can see four of Jupiter's moons: Io, Callisto, Ganymede and Europa. Careful observers might be able to see a red spot on the surface of Jupiter. This giant red spot is a large, circulating storm that has been raging for hundreds of years. The storm alone is larger than Earth.

What are the planets in our solar system?

There are nine planets, including Earth, that revolve around the sun in our solar system. To remember the nine planets just remember this sentence: My Very Educated Mother Just Sent Us Nine Pizzas. The first letters of each word represent Mercury, Venus, Earth, Mars, Jupiter, Saturn, Uranus, Neptune and Pluto. Mercury is closest to the sun and Pluto is farthest away. The farther away from the sun the planet is, the more "earth years" it takes to revolve around the sun. If you would like to be older, move to Venus or Mercury. Those planets go around the sun more times in one of our years, so a Venus or Mercury year goes faster than an Earth year.

How many stars are there in the Big Dipper?

You might be tempted to answer quickly and say seven, but stop and take a closer look. The Big Dipper is made up of eight stars, not seven. Most casual observers miss a double star in the handle; the second star in the handle is a double star. At one time this question was used to test visual acuity. Try looking for this double—it is right where the handle bends. If you can't see it, use a pair of binoculars. Asking your family to count the Big Dipper's stars is a great Nature Smart question. Be sure you have a pair of binoculars with you to prove that you are correct.

Is the Big Dipper always visible?

In the northern hemisphere, the Big Dipper is visible all year long and is easy to locate. The Big Dipper is bright enough to be seen from the city and can be picked out from the millions of stars visible out in the country. The Big Dipper is considered a **circumpolar group**, which means it revolves closely around Polaris, the North Star. At different times of year the Big Dipper will be either right side up or upside down. From January through June, the cup tilts upside down, spilling out its imaginary contents and then returns upright for the remainder of the year.

Is the Big Dipper a constellation?

Some people refer to the Big and Little Dippers as the constellations **Ursa Major** and **Ursa Minor**, but that's incorrect. The term Ursa means "bear" in Latin while major and minor means "big" and "little," respectively. Ursa Major and Ursa Minor refer to two different constellations in the shape of a big and little bear. Ursa Major is the larger of the two—the big bear. The Big Dipper is the tail and hind quarters of the big bear, not the whole bear. The Little Dipper is only the tail and body of Ursa Minor, the small bear. The dippers are considered **asterisms** (as´te-riz-em); that is, they are smaller shapes within larger shapes. They are only a small part of the larger constellations. Very often it is easier to see an asterism than the actual constellation.

Can I tell which way is north from the North Star?

Yes, you can, and fortunately, finding the **North Star** is as easy as finding the Big Dipper. First locate the Big Dipper, then look for the two stars that make up the outermost portion of the cup. They are referred to as the pointers because they will point you to the North Star. Imagine a line passing through these two stars from the bottom of the cup to the top, then continuing up. Imagine this line extending about three widths of your clenched fist when held at an arm's length. The first bright star at this point is the North Star, also known as Polaris. The North Star is very close to **celestial North**, the point in the sky that is directly over the North Pole—about one degree away. That's about half the width of your thumb when held at arm's length. All stars in the night sky revolve around this point in the sky—the North Star.

When you have located the North Star, draw an imaginary line straight down to the horizon. You have located the direction north. This never changes and can be relied upon all year long. That's because the North Star is stationary in the night sky; all other stars revolve around it.

How do I find the Little Dipper?

The **Little Dipper** is easy to find once you have located the North Star. The North Star doubles as the end of the handle of the Little Dipper. Anchored by the end of the handle, the Little Dipper spins around the North Star. To see the Little Dipper, look for a group of stars similar to the Big Dipper, but with the handle bent in the opposite direction.

The Little Dipper is not as bright as the North Star or the Big Dipper. It is also only about half the size of the Big Dipper, so you might have to wait for a moonless night or move away from bright city lights to see it. It is well worth some effort to see this little beauty with its guiding star.

What do we know about our sun?

Our sun is one of an estimated 50 billion stars within our universe. When you gaze into the night sky, only about 6,000 of these stars are visible. The estimated number is a mathematical calculation based on the expected size of our universe. Our sun, a yellow star, is approximately 93 millions miles (150 million km) away from Earth. The next closest star, Alpha Centauri, is about 250,000 times further away. Yellow stars are considered stable. Our sun has been shining for billions of years, and it is expected to continue for several billion more.

The temperature of the sun's core is extremely hot—an estimated 15 million degrees Celsius. Fahrenheit is not used in scientific measurement as it does not have the range to measure such extremes. By the time the internally produced energy reaches the sun's surface, it has cooled to 6,000 degrees Celsius.

Here on Earth, we receive about one two-billionths of the sun's total energy output. This tiny amount of solar energy warms our planet, and fuels the marvelous process called photosynthesis. It is the sun that powers the growth of plants, which in turn feeds all creatures on Earth. Plants also produce the air we breathe. Compared to other stars, our sun is small and rather unimpressive. But life on Earth is dependent on it; even a few days without the sun would result in the death of our planet.

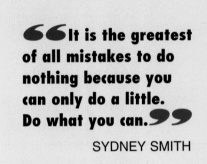

❝It is the greatest of all mistakes to do nothing because you can only do a little. Do what you can.❞

SYDNEY SMITH

What are northern lights?

The story of northern lights begins with the sun. The surface of the sun occasionally has dark blemishes called **sunspots**. They are huge, relatively cool regions compared to the rest of the sun, which typically average more than five times the diameter of the Earth. Sunspots are not understood, but are known to be regions of strong magnetic fields. These magnetic fields send off **solar winds** of electrically charged particles called **ions** and **electrons** that travel through space.

When solar winds approach the Earth, they arrive at an estimated 250 miles per second (400 km). As they collide with the magnetic field in the Earth's upper atmosphere, they disturb it. The ions and electrons collide with opposite charged air molecules and transfer their energy. When the energy is transferred, the air molecules become excited and the energy jumps to a higher energy level. When the molecules settle down, they release energy as radiation. If the energy released is in a wavelength that is in the visible range, we see glowing green, red and blue light—called the **northern lights**, also known as the **aurora borealis**. Other colors such as purple and violet are also sometimes visible.

Why are the northern lights different colors?

Our atmosphere is made up of several different gases. The most common of these atmospheric gases is **atomic oxygen**. It is abundant in our atmosphere at heights of 62 to 93 miles (100 to 150 km) When one of the electrons from the solar winds hits atomic oxygen, the oxygen takes on some of the energy of the electron and is able to store that energy. If the newly charged oxygen molecule doesn't bump into another oxygen molecule and lose the energy, it will radiate off a tiny burst of green light. Multiply that by thousands and millions of oxygen atoms, all giving off a tiny green light, and you have the northern lights. Now take the same incoming electrons from the solar winds and allow them to penetrate deeper into our atmosphere to where **molecular nitrogen** is abundant. Because nitrogen molecules glow red when charged, they give off a pinkish to red color.

If you are fortunate enough to see the aurora borealis, you will notice that it appears to move like a giant current in a gentle wind. That's because the waves of solar winds contact our atmosphere at different levels and intensities. The base of the aurora is rarely under 50 miles (80 km) and averages 100 miles (63 km) above the Earth's surface.

How old is the "old man in the moon?"

Our moon was formed about the same time as the Earth, about 4.5 billion years ago. It is a small moon and has no atmosphere. Since it has no air, rain, or wind, it also has no erosion to affect its surface. Instead, what you see on the surface of the moon reflects the result of large meteors impacting its surface. These large meteors are rare, so the moon's surface doesn't change much. Historical maps of the moon show it exactly as it appears today.

When you look at a full moon, you might notice what appears to be a face, which is commonly referred to as "the old man in the moon." His features are made up of a catacomb of craters, cracks and ridges formed by meteor impacts and ancient lava flows over millions of years. If you want a better view of these features, an ordinary pair of binoculars will reveal many details unseen by the naked eye. The moon can provide your family with hours of nighttime observations. You might even want to try your hand at sketching the moon's surface on a piece of paper.

What are the phases of the moon?

The moon has four phases, each being about a week long. The four phases together take 29⅓ days. That's how long it takes for the moon to complete one full orbit around Earth. As the moon circles Earth, it changes its relationship to the sun. The first phase, called the new moon, is when the moon is positioned between the sun and Earth, reflecting light away from Earth so that we can't see it at night. During this phase the moon is often seen during the daytime. One week later, the moon is a quarter of the way into its orbit, and we see the first quarter moon phase because the moon is quarter lit. Two weeks into the orbit, the moon is halfway around, when Earth is between it and the sun. We see the moon's full reflection then, so we call this the full moon phase. Three weeks into the orbit, the **third quarter moon phase** occurs and again only a quarter is lit. At the fourth week it returns to the new moon phase. To view this in a different way, consider the moon to be full at all times. That is, the sun is always shining on the surface of the moon, but we here on Earth are seeing the illuminated moon at different angles. When we view the moon from the side or from an angle, we see it half lit and half dark. Each new angle gives us a new look at the moon.

What is a crescent or gibbous moon?

The four phases describe the different appearances of the moon at one week intervals, but how do we refer to the moon phases that fall between? Anytime the moon is less than half lit, it is called a **crescent moon**. When the moon is more than half-lit, but not yet full, it is called a **gibbous moon**.

What does waxing and waning moon mean?

These terms are used to describe the moon as it heads toward a full moon or moves away from a full moon. **Waxing** indicates the moon is becoming fuller and moving towards the full moon. **Waning** describes the moon as it grows less full, becoming a new moon.

What is the terminator?

Tell your friends you are watching the moon to observe the terminator and they might think you've been watching too many movies. Actually, the **terminator** is the line that divides the dark (or night) and the light (or day) sides of the moon. Picture a thin, crescent-shaped moon. The terminator is the curved line between the light and dark side of the moon. A quarter of the way through the moon's orbit, the terminator is straight up and down. As the moon moves toward the full moon phase, the terminator bends the opposite way until a full moon is achieved.

Is moonlight like sunlight, only dimmer?

No, the moon has no light or energy source of its own. The light we see from the moon as moonlight is really reflected sunlight. The moon acts like a mirror, bouncing sunlight back to Earth. Our moon is Earth's constant companion. It illuminates our night while it pushes and pulls at our oceans. The moon orbits around Earth in a fixed fashion. We always see the same side of the moon because Earth's gravity has drawn it into a close orbit, a hold so tight that the moon doesn't rotate. Moonlight affects animal behavior because they can see better at night, but despite the werewolf stories, the moon does not create amazing transformations.

Plan a night for your family to walk and explore when the moon is full. A star chart or calendar will tell you when to expect a full moon. Excursions under a full moon can be some of your families' most memorable outings. Many animals become more active at night and you will notice that with the reduced visibility your other senses, such as smell and hearing, become more acute. You may need to calm younger night travelers by telling them there is nothing that will hurt them and the animals are more afraid of people than we are of them. We are only afraid of the things we don't know or understand.

Why can we sometimes see the moon during the day?

If you can see the moon during the day, the moon is in the new moon phase, which means it is not out during the night and visible during the day. We can see the moon during the day because the light from the sun is reflected off the surface of Earth and illuminates the moon. This is an example of **earthshine**. Earthshine is also responsible for why we can sometimes see all of the moon at night when only part of it is lit.

What is a meteor shower?

What most people call shooting or falling stars are really meteors. Meteors are the nighttime equivalent to rainbows and sundogs. In a split second, a beam of light races across the sky, often resulting in "ooh's" and "ahh's" and fingers pointed skyward by humble observers on Earth.

Meteors are not falling stars in the sense of a star actually falling from the sky to Earth. As you recall, stars are suns just like ours but much farther away. Imagine the sun falling on Earth and you can realize how unlikely it would be to have a star fall. Meteors are caused by **comets**, which are large accumulations of ice and rock traveling through space. Comets orbit the sun, just as Earth does. However, comets leave a trail of cosmic debris behind them, much like a garbage truck with debris flying out of the back. Whenever Earth passes through these bands of debris, they interact with Earth's atmosphere. Upon contact with our atmosphere, bits of the debris begin to fall. The friction caused as they accelerate produces heat—heat of such intense temperatures that the bits of debris begin to glow. These bits, or particles are **meteors**.

Most meteors are very small, about the size of a grain of sand, but meteors can weigh up to several tons. Large meteorites have struck Earth, leaving large craters like those on the moon. The results of meteorites that have impacted Earth can still be seen in the American Southwest. Extremely large meteors would glow so brightly they would light up the entire night sky and have catastrophic affects upon Earth. It is theorized that a large meteorite colliding with Earth is the reason for the extinction of the dinosaurs. It's extremely unlikely that a giant meteorite would hit Earth during our lifetimes but tiny meteors are in nearly constant contact with Earth. In fact, they add about 4 million tons (3.6 million t.) of dust to our planet each year. That is about 100 tons (90 t.) of meteorite dust each day.

Can I see a meteor shower?

A meteor shower is just several meteors at the same time. At certain times of the year, you can see meteors speeding earthward. Sometimes observers of the night sky can enjoy a show of cosmic proportions. Meteor showers are easy for astronomers to predict. One of the most common is the meteor shower **Perseid**. Like all meteors, it is named after the constellation near which it appears. The reference to the constellation is just a convenient way to help locate the region of sky where the meteors can be seen and has nothing to do with where the meteors originated.

Perseid is visible for nearly a week, but the best time to see this spectacular display is on or near August 11th. The best time to view any meteor show is after midnight, because at that time Earth tilts directly into the path of the orbiting cosmic dust. A good meteor shower will have two or three shooting stars per minute. Even if you look for meteors when a meteor shower is not taking place, you should still be able to see a renegade meteor every ten minutes or so.

How fast do meteors fall?

The speed at which meteors fall varies. A casual observer will be able to see the difference between fast and slow meteors. Understanding the difference is as simple as understanding the direction in which the meteors impact our atmosphere. Earth spins in a counter-clockwise direction around the sun at $18\frac{1}{2}$ miles (29.8 km) per second. Meteor particles travel at a faster rate of 25 miles (40.2 km) per second and don't follow the counter-clockwise rule. **Slow meteors** are meteors that impact Earth's atmosphere traveling in the opposite direction as the rotating Earth. Thus they impact our atmosphere at a reduced speed of $6\frac{1}{2}$ miles (10.5 km) per second (25 minus $18\frac{1}{2} = 6\frac{1}{2}$). They have faint, luminous tails, or trains. **Fast meteors** appear as quick, bright streaks and impact our atmosphere in the same direction that the Earth is rotating. Their speed plus the speed at which Earth is turning away from them equals $43\frac{1}{2}$ miles (70 km) per second ($25 + 18\frac{1}{2} = 43\frac{1}{2}$).

How can I use the identification section of Star Smart?

Exploration into the dark night sky is more of a journey with your eyes and mind rather than your body. However, a working knowledge of the stars is a good way to round out your Nature Smart skills. Traversing the stars with your eyes can make you feel a part of a much bigger picture. It puts into perspective our place in the vastness of the universe and the fact that we have only one Earth.

Because our view of the night sky is constantly changing, we have not attempted to help you identify everything you might see on a particular night. The celestial objects we have identified are best viewed at 9:00 p.m. in the winter and 10:00 p.m. in the summer.

When preparing to spend some time star watching, consider comfort. A chair or blanket will make star gazing more comfortable. Give yourself some time for your eyes to adjust to the darkness. A regular pair of binoculars will bring the stars a little closer. Wait to look directly at the moon using your binoculars until the end of the night. The extreme brightness will constrict your pupils and make it hard to see any other stars. Don't forget bug spray if you are out in the summer. A pad of paper and pencil are useful for making notes or sketching patterns to investigate later. A flashlight with some red clear plastic over the beam will give you enough light to draw or look something up in a book without disturbing your night vision. Having fun is the most important part of any excursion into the night sky. Start with identifying the basic star clusters and then move on to constellations.

Star hopping

To know and understand the vastness of the entire night sky would take several lifetimes of study. Here we'll only present four basic summer and four basic winter constellations. With this information you will be able to orient yourself to the night sky. This orientation will be very helpful when an exciting event is predicted such as a meteor shower or a planet becoming visible in your area.

To establish this orientation, we recommend using a simple "road map" to the stars called **star hopping**. Star hopping is one of the most useful techniques for beginners to quickly find several major stars, asterisms (part of constellations) or constellations. Using this process you first locate a common obvious star group and utilize this home-base to point the way to "hop" to the next star group. For example, in summer simply find the Big Dipper (a group of stars within the constellation Ursa Major). Using two or more stars within the Big Dipper, simply draw an imaginary line across these stars to point the way to hop to the next star group (see North Star question).

Don't be surprised if you cannot see the mythical people or animals that the constellations are named for in the night sky. It is almost always easier to see asterisms than the full fledged constellations. To see a constellation often takes quite a bit of imagination.

To help you put all of this into perspective, asterisms and constellations are only in the shape they are in when viewed from Earth. The stars that make up any star group are only a human interpretation and really don't have any significant meaning. If you were able to view the Big Dipper from any vantage point other than Earth it would not look the same. These stars are so distant from each other that they don't have any relationship to each other than from our view from Earth. Please note that the stars we are calling "summer" are actually visible year-round because they are circumpolar stars. They are always near the star that points north. We are just simplifying this introduction to star hopping.

SUMMER

Star hopping through the summer night sky is an enjoyable way to spend an evening with friends and family. Start by looking for the most obvious summer star group, the Big Dipper. This large asterism, not a constellation, will be your key to star hopping and will open the secrets of the night sky.

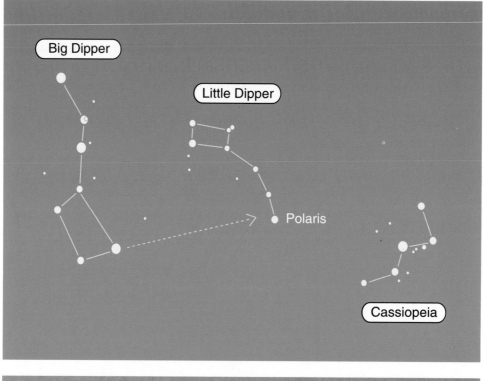

The Big Dipper

There are eight stars that make this asterism. The Big Dipper is only part of the constellation Ursa Major, the great bear. The bear myth comes from the Greeks, who tell of Zeus, their king of gods who, according to one version of the story, changed a woman he loved into a bear to protect her from the jealousy of his wife. Later on he also changed his son into a bear to protect him and then threw both of them into the sky by holding onto their tails. This would explain why their tails (the handles of the dippers) are so long. The Big Dipper forms the tail and hind quarters of the great bear and are visible all year long. This famous constellation revolves in a large, arching circle around Polaris, the North Star. Take a closer look at the second star or curve in the handle. This star may look brighter than the others because it is actually two stars close together, called Mizar (brighter) and Alcor (dimmer). Use a pair of binoculars to see this for yourself.

Polaris, the North Star

Standing as the Star of the North, Polaris remains stationary in the night sky. It is visible all year long while all other stars revolve around this central point in the sky. It doesn't move because it is directly over the North Pole, the point around which the Earth revolves. To find this star, return to the Big Dipper and draw an imaginary line through the outer two stars, the pointers, in the cup. (These two stars are called Merak and Dobhe). Traveling up and out of the opening or top of the cup, the first bright star will be Polaris. This star can be used to find the direction north. Simply follow a line directly down from the North Star to the horizon and you have found the direction north.

Little Dipper

When you find the North Star, you'll soon find another popular asterism in the summer sky. The North Star is the end of the handle of the Little Dipper. Seven stars make up the Little Dipper. It is about half as bright and half the size of the Big Dipper. The handle is attached at the lower side of the cup, unlike the Big Dipper which attaches at the top. The Little Dipper is the tail and body of Ursa Minor, the little bear, and might be hard to see if there is any interference from city lights.

Cassiopeia

According to mythology, Cassiopeia (meaning cassia juice and pronounced kass-ee-o-pee´a) was a beautiful queen of Ethiopia married to Cepheus, the gardener. She was a boastful queen who thought that she was more beautiful than the sea nymphs who punished her by having a whale, Cetus, destroy the kingdom. To find this mythological figure, follow the same line you did to find Polaris, but go beyond the North Star to find the queen of the sky, Cassiopeia. You know you have found her by the five bright stars forming a "W" shape in summer and an "M" shape in winter. Once you have located Cassiopeia, you may use a telescope to see several **nebulae** (clouds of gas and dust) near this star group.

WINTER SKY

Cold winter nights might not seem a very good time to explore the stars, but nothing could be farther from the truth. Cold, clear, winter air masses tend to be free from dust and haze that is more common in summer, making it easier to see many more stars. However, thousands of additional visible stars might make it harder to find what you are looking for. Use Orion as your key to star hop to other well-known groups in the winter sky.

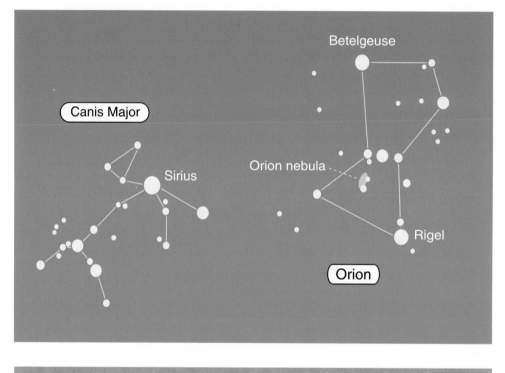

Orion

Clearly visible in the southern sky on winter evenings, Orion, the mighty hunter, is one of the brightest groups of stars in the winter sky. According to Greek mythology, the sun-god Apollo didn't want Orion to get together with his sister Artemis, goddess of the hunt. Apollo tricked his sister into shooting and killing Orion, who had leapt into the sea after a planned attack by the scorpion Scorpious. Artemis then placed him in the heavens where Scorpious still pursues him. In the sky he is poised with shield and club, ready to fight Taurus the bull. By his sides are his two faithful dogs. Orion is in the opposite sky from the Big Dipper—look for three very bright stars appearing in a straight line. This is the belt of the great hunter, Orion. Above the belt and representing the shoulder is a red star called Betelgeuse, pronounced "beetle-juice." It is a cool super-giant star, one of the largest stars known. About the same distance to the other side and representing the other shoulder, is a blue star known as Rigel. It is a very hot star. The actual constellation of a man holding a club and shield is very large and spreads across the sky and may be hard to discriminate.

Orion Nebula

Located within the boundaries of Orion are several nebula, each about 1,500 light-years away. Use binoculars to scan the sky below Orion's belt to locate the faint, red and blue glowing mass, the Orion Nebula, which is a hotbed for producing stars like our sun. It will appear like a faint hazy region. It might help to think of it as a colored cloud, floating in space. The Orion Nebula is considered the most spectacular deep-sky object in the night sky. Within this nebula, large clumps of space material are compressed and fused together with extremely hot temperatures to create new stars. This is one of the most prolific star nurseries in our galaxy.

Sirius, the Dog Star

After you have located Orion's belt, you can star hop to the brightest star in the sky, **Sirius**. Draw an imaginary line through the three stars in Orion's belt. Extend this line to the east or to your right (the belt slants down and to the left) to find Sirius. The Dog Star is another common name for Sirius because it is located within the constellation Canis Major (one of Orion's hunting dogs, the big dog). The exact origin of the word Sirius is not known, but one theory is that it comes from the Greek word *seirios*, which means scorching and applies to any bright star.

Canis Major, the Big Dog

In mythical stories, Canis Major, the Big Dog, is identified as Orion's hunting companion. It is next to Orion and contains the star Sirius, located at the dog's shoulder. Its long tail stretches out and away form Orion. The big dog is positioned in the sky to pounce upon Lepus, the rabbit.

Weather Smart

A cool, gusty wind arises from the west. Purplish black clouds billow on the prairie's horizon, foretelling yet another summer afternoon storm. Rain falls gently at first and then pours from the sky. Lightning blazes and thunder cracks. This deluge may seem threatening, but it nurtures prairie flowers and grasses. It's an aspect of nature we can never take for granted—weather. Weather is the general atmospheric condition at any particular time and place. Much of the time, we isolate ourselves from the effects of weather in comfortably heated and cooled houses and cars, but a keen awareness of weather enhances our experience in the natural world. Whether you are in a prairie, woodland, or wetland, weather will affect the way you feel and behave in these special places. Who doesn't feel energetic on a warm, sunny morning or lazy on a cold, drizzly afternoon? Weather influences all of nature's inhabitants in subtle and not so subtle ways.

Rain, for example, is the atmosphere's gentle way of cleaning house. Thunderstorms, which are the result of intense sun energy heating up the land, are more dramatic. Blizzards, tornadoes and hurricanes are weather in extreme forms. They happen infrequently, but they are attention-getters. Nonetheless, the mild intervals we experience most often are still considered weather. Weather is a constant. It never goes away. Its mood is always changing, but it is always present.

The science of weather is called **meteorology**. The term dates back to the Greek philosopher Aristotle, who wrote a book in 340 B.C. entitled *Meteorolgica*. In those days, anything that fell from the sky or was seen in the air was called a meteor—hence the term *meteorology*. We no longer use this definition for weather, but the name persists.

Modern meteorology involves tracking storms and weather patterns via satellite, radar and computer programs. Professional meteorologists claim that their short-range forecasts (a day or two ahead) are 95 percent accurate. (You'll learn tips to forecast weather in this chapter, so you can make short-range predictions with some degree of accuracy, too.) Predictions three to four days ahead are less certain. Ninety-day forecasts are based on what the weather has done in similar situations in the past. But at any given time, one of the many elements that create weather can shift, changing the overall weather pattern and the weather that results. Since weather is dynamic and ever-changing, long-range forecasts are the least accurate. These changing elements really put the wild in weather and weather forecasting. Also much can happen to alter the environment which affects the weather.

Weather patterns are greatly affected by environmental degradation. For example, reduced rainfall and acid rain are weather problems brought on by deforestation and pollution. When rainforests are cut down, the amount of moisture returned to the atmosphere is reduced, which has the overall effect of reducing rainfall. Acid rain occurs when pollutants are pumped into the air and are then picked up by rain and deposited in surface waters. This creates unlivable habitats for plants, insects and fish, sometimes killing entire aquatic ecosystems. Ozone depletion and the greenhouse effect are also weather-related problems. Understanding weather clarifies your perception of the natural world and your place in it. Learning more about weather, you can learn to help conserve the natural resources of that world, as well.

Scientists are looking toward the weather as an answer to our energy shortages. Knowing more about wind patterns and sunlight will help them to harness both solar and wind power as forms of renewable energy and help to keep pollution and shortages down.

What makes weather?

The components of weather are heat, circulation, pressure and moisture. The earth first needs to be warmed to make weather. Warmth is created by the sun's energy heating land surfaces. Even though the sun is, on average, 93 million miles (149,637,000 km) away from the earth, it bathes our planet with 126 trillion horsepower of energy every second. (For comparison, most car engines have under 200 horsepower of energy.) Sun-warmed land, in turn, heats the air above it. Conversely, air moving over frozen tundra is cooled. In the same way, air becomes moist or dry when passing over oceans or deserts.

When air is heated, it becomes lighter and rises. When air is cooled, it sinks. The rising and sinking of great masses of air, a kind of mixing, is called **circulation**. It is circulation that creates air pressure. **Air pressure** is the total weight of air above any given point on the earth. When air sinks, its downward movement pushes heavily against the earth's surface and creates a condition called **high-pressure**. Clear skies and dry weather are associated with high-pressure systems. **Low-pressure** occurs when air rises, thus easing the weight of air pushing against the earth. When air rises, it cools and loses its ability to hold moisture. So, rain is often associated with low-pressure systems.

What makes wind?

Wind is the movement of air from high-pressure to low-pressure systems. Under high-pressure conditions, air is settling to earth. When it collides with the earth's surface, it has no place to go but out, away from the center of the highest pressure. To demonstrate this, lean forward and blow on the surface of a table. The air you blow travels straight down until it comes in contact with the tabletop. Then it diverges, or moves outward, from that point. Winds blow outward from what is called a **cell**. Due to the rotation of the earth from west to east, wind created by a high-pressure system spins clockwise north of the equator.

Low-pressure occurs where cells of air rise, easing the weight of the air pushing against the earth's surface. Air converges, or rushes inward, toward the center of the cell and is forced upward. This air spins counter-clockwise in the northern hemisphere, again due to the spinning of the planet. The rising and falling of air creates winds racing around the earth in clockwise and counter-clockwise directions.

Why does the wind change in intensity?

Wind is directly related to air pressure. The closer you are to the center of a high-pressure or low-pressure system, the less the winds will blow. The strongest winds occur at the overlapping edge of the two systems. Often winds are the strongest just before a storm hits. These winds are on the leading edge of the low-pressure system that is bringing the storm. At the same time, the storm is being fed by wind rushing in from the adjacent high-pressure system. Wind direction is always identified by the direction the wind is coming from. If the wind is blowing from the north, it is called a north wind.

How can I predict the weather?

The first step in short-range weather prediction is to visualize high-and low-pressure systems, since they bring wet or dry weather with them. To do so, stretch out your right arm, palm up, and bend it at the elbow. Now rotate your forearm in a clockwise circle, imitating the spinning of a high-pressure cell. Then do the same thing with your left arm, rotating your left forearm in a counter-clockwise circle to represent a low-pressure cell.

Keep in mind that typical weather systems in North America come from the west. Now you're ready to predict which system, and its associated weather, is approaching.

Go outside and stand with your back to the wind. Then turn slightly to your right (about 30 degrees) to compensate for changes in the surface winds. A high-pressure cell is now on your right, turning clockwise and blowing winds at your back. A low-pressure cell is on your left.

Next, consider which direction you are facing. If you are facing south, the high pressure cell to your right is in the west. You can expect it to come your way, since most weather comes from the west. The high-pressure cell will bring fair weather. If you are facing north, the cell in the west is a low-pressure cell; you can expect clouds and possible rain. Winds from the south will be warmer, but they can often bring clouds and moisture.

How important is water in affecting weather?

Water covers two-thirds of the earth's surface, so it is no surprise that it has a great influence on our weather. Fresh water lakes and oceans are reservoirs from which water is evaporated into the atmosphere, helping to create weather. Moisture is found in the atmosphere in three ways: as liquid rain, as invisible gas (or water vapor) and as the condensed vapor called clouds. Obviously, the type of water in the atmosphere contributes to the kind of weather we experience.

But water also contributes to weather in another way. Water has the ability to store heat energy, called **latent heat**. Latent heat is released when condensed vapor changes into clouds or liquid and it starts to rain. Every time it rains, the latent heat released adds to the atmospheric energy, producing dramatic weather, such as thunderstorms and lightning, snow and tornadoes. This effect of water on weather is more noticeable when the air is warm. Summer storms are more violent than cold winter storms. Warm air has a greater ability to hold water than cold air. Thus, it holds not only more moisture, but also more latent heat and more dramatic weather.

How do clouds affect weather?

Clouds are made up of condensed water vapor. They help to cool the earth during the day by shading it, and they help to keep it warm during the night by trapping heat like a gigantic blanket. Warm air near the equator contains a lot of moisture, producing many clouds. A narrow band around the earth at the equator produces so many clouds that nearly all of our major weather events originate there. The huge amount of latent energy in equatorial clouds contributes to equatorial storms, which spin off the equator, moving up into the higher latitudes of North America. They cool as they move northward, losing the ability to hold moisture and give off their latent heat. This results in storms and rain.

What is atmosphere?

The atmosphere is all of the air that surrounds the earth. The word **atmosphere** comes from the Greek word *Atmo*, or vapor, and *sphere*, which means around or circle. The earth's atmosphere has evolved over billions of years from one composed mostly of hydrogen and helium (which are simple compounds) into one rich in nitrogen and oxygen (which are complex compounds). Our oxygen-rich atmosphere is a result of plants, which give off oxygen.

The atmosphere can be considered the thermostat that controls the earth's heating and cooling. It protects us from too much solar radiation by screening out the dangerous part of sunlight, ultraviolet light rays. At the same time, the atmosphere traps heat at night, like clouds, acting as an insulating blanket. Without its protective layer of atmosphere, the earth would be boiling hot during the day and freezing cold at night.

The atmosphere can also be thought of as an ocean of air. We live at the bottom of this ocean, with 1,000 miles (1,609 km) of atmosphere above us. There is no definite end to the earth's atmosphere. Rather, it becomes thinner and thinner, eventually merging with empty space. Life exists only in a narrow band of compressed air, about 18 miles (29 km) thick, next to the earth. Our weather occurs in the bottom 3½ miles (5.6 km).

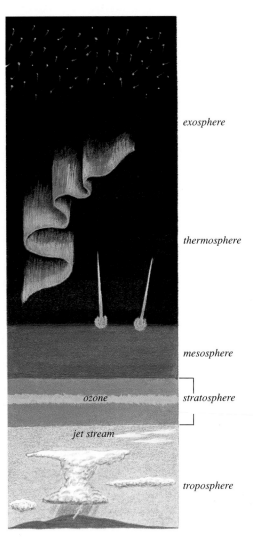

exosphere

thermosphere

mesosphere

ozone

stratosphere

jet stream

troposphere

What are the different layers of atmosphere and what do they do?

Our atmosphere consists of five layers. The top layer is the **exosphere**, which begins about 310 miles (500 km) above the earth and extends 500 to 1,000 miles (804 to 1,609 km). The atmosphere is extremely thin in this region and represents the upper limits, where atoms and molecules shoot off into space.

The next layer is the **thermosphere**. It begins about 58 miles (85 km) above the earth and is the widest layer of our atmosphere. This is where northern lights and shooting stars occur. The word thermosphere comes from the Greek word *therme*, which refers to heat or temperature. A temperature inversion, which is a flip-flop of normal temperature, occurs here. Normally, air is warmer closer to earth and cooler higher up. But in the thermosphere, the temperature is cooler on the bottom and warmer above.

Average temperatures in the middle of the thermosphere range from 1,300° F (700° C) to 3,200° F (1,700° C). That's pretty hot! However, this is a bit misleading, because if you were in the thermosphere, you would feel profoundly cold. The disparity exists because traditional methods of measuring temperature don't work in this region, where so few atoms exist. It is the activity of atoms that causes heat. The faster an atom moves, the higher the temperature; the slower it moves, the colder. When we measure temperature near earth, we are measuring the motion of a lot of atoms. In the far reaches of our atmosphere there are very few atoms, but they are moving as fast as if they were very warm. Where only a few atoms are whizzing around to produce heat, the atmosphere will always feel cold.

The **mesosphere** is the portion of the atmosphere that starts about 32 miles (48 km) above the surface of the earth. Unlike the thermosphere, the mesosphere has temperatures along a normal gradient; temperature increases closer to earth. Temperatures in the mesosphere range from -130 to 50° F (-101 to 10° C). In this region the air is extremely thin, and although the sun is shining brightly, the sky is black, making it difficult to see.

The **stratosphere** begins about seven miles (11.2 km) above the earth's surface. Although it contains about 97 percent of all the ozone in the atmosphere, this layer is surprisingly thin. If all of the ozone was brought down to earth's surface and compressed, the layer would be only as thick as a dime. Nonetheless, life on earth relies on this layer for protection from harmful amounts of ultraviolet radiation from the sun.

Nearest the earth is the troposphere. The **troposphere** is a thin layer that extends from earth's surface to about seven miles (11 km) above earth. The temperature in the troposphere is warmest near the earth and cools higher up, dropping to minus 71° F (-57° C) at its top.

The troposphere takes its name from the Greek word *tropein*, meaning to turn or change. And change it does. It is here that our weather wheels around in ever-changing patterns. All weather occurs in the troposphere. Clouds are restricted to this layer of atmosphere, as are lightning, hail, tornados and other forms of weather.

Near the top of the troposphere, about 7 miles (11.2 km) above earth, constant strong winds blow. These winds, known as the **jet stream**, generally blow from west to east across North America. As the jet stream travels eastward, it propels systems of high-pressure, which generally bring clear weather, and systems of low-pressure, which in turn usually bring stormy weather. For that reason, the jet stream is the driving force for most weather on our continent.

What is ozone?

Ozone is a simple, blue, gaseous form of oxygen; it is three molecules of oxygen bonded together, O_3. It is formed naturally when atomic oxygen (O) and molecular oxygen (O_2) are exposed to ultraviolet radiation and combine. If ozone existed on the surface of the earth, it would be a poisonous gas with powerful bleaching properties. Despite what sounds like a bad gas, ozone acts like the glass of a greenhouse. Short-wave sunlight passes through the ozone and is absorbed by the earth. The earth, in turn, releases long-wave heat energy back to the atmosphere. This energy is then trapped by the stratosphere, thus maintaining a delicate balance of heat. Without the ozone found in the stratosphere, our days would be boiling hot, and our nights would be freezing cold.

While ozone is continually made and destroyed naturally in the stratosphere, it is also being destroyed by human-made chemicals. Because the natural process that produces ozone can't keep up with this added destruction, the ozone layer is being depleted. One of the most dangerous chemicals posing a threat our thin ozone layer is nitrous oxide. Nitrous oxide is emitted by nitrogen fertilizers and drifts into the stratosphere. Chloroflurocarbon (CFC) used in aerosol spray cans, refrigerators and air-conditioners is another ozone depleting chemical. Each CFC releases a chlorine atom, and when the chlorine reaches the stratosphere, it reacts with the ozone, resulting in the destruction of the ozone. In a final reaction, the chlorine is released again, freeing it to destroy more ozone. Each chlorine atom in the stratosphere remains active for five to ten years.

When was the thinning of the ozone detected?

Scientists first discovered the thinning of the ozone in the early 1970's, when the U.S. was debating whether it should build a supersonic jet transport system. The jets would have flown in the stratosphere just below the ozone. The emissions of the jets contained the chemical nitric oxide, that some people feared would mix with the ozone and deplete this important covering. For that reason, Congress decided to halt the development of the jets.

Scientists are just starting to understand the destruction of the ozone layer and its effects. The loss of our protective ozone layer could result in increased cases of skin cancer. It could also raise the overall temperature of the earth, causing agricultural changes. At this time, no one can project the ultimate cost of ozone destruction. We do know that ozone depletion is not a local, but worldwide, problem and needs serious study and action.

Why are the clouds white?

The key player in this answer is sunlight. Sunlight is made up of many bands, or waves, of differently colored light. These waves appear white when

blended together, which is the reason bright sunlight looks white. When sunlight strikes an object, the object absorbs certain light waves and reflects others. We see only the reflected waves. For example, a green leaf absorbs most light waves, but reflects green waves so that we see it as green. Clouds, on the other hand, don't absorb any light waves. Instead, they scatter all wavelengths of light equally. Just as we see the combined bands of sunlight as white, the scattered light coming from a cloud also looks white.

Why is the sky blue?

The atmosphere is made up of many individual air molecules. Most are nitrogen and oxygen molecules. Nitrogen and oxygen molecules tend to reflect blue, violet and green bands of sunlight, while letting other bands pass through. When we view the sky, we see only the scattered bands of blue, violet and green, which combine to appear as varying shades of blue.

Any planet with an atmosphere will have a sky color corresponding to the specific air molecules in that atmosphere. For example, the atmosphere of Venus has an excess of carbon dioxide, which makes the sky there appear yellow. On Mars, dust in the air turns the sky red and purple.

How are rainbows made?

Rainbows are colorful spectacles of nature, that are formed by a surprisingly simple process. A rainbow demonstrates the ability of water to bend sunlight. When sunlight enters raindrops, it disperses into its spectrum of color, or wavelengths of light, just as it does in a prism. This spectrum, including red, orange, yellow green, blue, indigo and violet, is reflected off the back of the raindrop and out into the sky as distinct bands of color. It is because of the rain drop being the shape that it is, that the rainbow appears as an arch.

> **"If facts are the seeds that later produce knowledge and wisdom, then the emotions and the impressions of the senses are the fertile soil in which the seeds must grow. The years of early childhood are the time to prepare the soil."**
>
> RACHEL CARSON

How can I see a rainbow?

The only way you can see a rainbow is to face the sky where it's raining while the sun is at your back. Only then will sunlight be hitting the rain at the particular angle necessary for a rainbow. In the morning, when the sun is in the east, you'll see rainbows in the west. In the evening, they appear in the eastern sky. Since rainstorms tend to travel from west to east in North America, a rainbow in the morning suggests rain coming toward you from the west. A rainbow in the evening indicates a storm in the east, moving away from you.

How many raindrops does it take to make a rainbow?

It takes millions of raindrops to produce a single rainbow. Incredibly, only a single color from each drop comes back to your eye at any moment. Each time you move, even slightly, a new angle is created. A different ray of light from the raindrop enters your eye, and you see a new rainbow. Because of this, the rainbow you see is not exactly the same rainbow that the person standing next to you is seeing. In a sense, every rainbow is a personal rainbow shining just for you.

Is there such a thing as a double rainbow?

Double rainbows are not uncommon. They occur only with intense sunlight. The stronger the sunlight, the more likely you are to see a double bow. The lower rainbow is always brighter and is considered the main bow. The secondary bow is produced when sunlight enters the raindrops in the main rainbow at an angle that makes two internal reflections in each drop. While the colors of the main bow go from indigo on the bottom to red on the top, the secondary bow will have the colors in the reverse order. The additional reflection weakens the intensity of the light and creates a dimmer, secondary rainbow. Your rainbow is still a personal one—only doubled.

Why are sunsets red and orange?

At midday, when the sun is directly overhead, the incoming sunlight passes through less atmosphere than at any other time of day. At sunrise and sunset, because of the altered angle of the sun, the sun's light must travel a greater distance through the atmosphere. When the sun is just above the horizon, either east or west, its light passes through the most atmosphere—up to 12 times as much as at midday. Since air molecules scatter light, the more atmosphere that light passes through, the more scattering takes place. By the time the sunlight has punched its way through the thicker atmosphere, most of the sunlight has been scattered. The only waves of color that make it through are the yellows, oranges and reds of a brilliant sunrise or sunset. Any clouds will increase the effects of scattering and intensify the color of the sunset or sunrise.

Red sky at night, sailors' delight — truth or fiction?

"Red sky at morning, sailors take warning; red sky at night, sailors' delight." This old adage is reliable, because most storms pass from west to the east in the northern hemisphere. A red eastern sky in the morning indicates that clouds have advanced from the west but not far enough to block the sunrise. Soon the sky will be completely overcast, and it may rain. A red western sky at night indicates the clouds are breaking up or passing over.

Why does sky color vary from city to city and day to day?

You can expect to see a wide range of color in the sky when the atmosphere is laden with smoke, dust, or pollutants. It can even contain ash from a volcano. Some large cities have an orange cast to their skies during hot summer days because of pollutants produced by factories and automobiles. This localized air pollution will remain to color the sky until winds break it up and pass it on to the next city downwind.

Where do clouds come from?

Clouds form in four ways: through convection, topographic uplift, convergence and lifting along fronts. In each case, warm air rises, cools and condenses into clouds. The difference lies in how the warm air rises. In the process of **convection**, air rises due to heating by the sun. In **topographic uplift**, air rises due to mountains or other topography. **Convergence** occurs when two air masses push against each other and force each other up. **Lifting** along a front means that warm air will rise up and over a cold mass of air. In each of these cases, the rising of warm air produces clouds.

To understand how clouds are formed, we'll discuss air/water relationships. Warm air can hold more water in the form of vapor (invisible gas) than cool air can. That's why hot summer days are humid and cold winter days are dry. Warm, moist air that breaks away in a large bubble will rise. As it rises, the mass of air cools (temperatures naturally decrease higher up) and loses its ability to hold water vapor. The escaping water vapor condenses to form clouds, and the process of convection is complete. On a warm summer day you may notice that the puffy fair weather clouds, called **cumulus clouds**, all have flat bottoms. This flat bottom is the point at which rising air is condensing. Below the flat bottom, the air is still holding water vapor. Above that point, the water has condensed.

The tops of cumulus clouds are often puffy, like a kernel of popped corn. These bulges show the height to which the warm air has risen. When the cloud has formed, it shades the ground and slows the process of heating and rising air. Once the cloud drifts away, the sun again heats the ground and the process starts over. Cumulus clouds usually have even spaces of blue sky between them and dot the summer sky. They indicate fair weather, rarely produce rain and evaporate by nightfall.

The same bubble of warm air also can be pushed about on the earth's surface by winds. If it is pushed up a mountainside, the air will cool as it rises. This is **topographic uplift**. The bubble condenses into clouds as it cools. Usually before the air reaches the top of the mountain, most of its moisture is squeezed out as rain and snow. On the other side, the dry side of the mountain, the bubble of air rewarms as it moves downhill, increasing its ability to hold water. The dry side of the mountain is referred to as being in the **rain shadow**.

Clouds are also formed by **convergence** when two large air masses come together and push against one another, causing each air mass to be displaced. This usually occurs between two storms (low-pressure systems) and produces many clouds. The air has two directions in which to move—up and down. Since the earth blocks the air from going down, it rises and condenses into clouds.

Warm air also can lift along a cold front. When traveling warm air meets a cold, stationary mass of air, the warm air travels up and over the cold air. Once again, the warm air will cool and condense into clouds.

How does it rain and snow?

Not all clouds produce precipitation, but all precipitation comes from clouds. The particular form of precipitation (rain, snow, hail or sleet) is determined by the temperature at which each is formed and what it falls through before reaching the ground. Much of the rain from thunderstorms begins high up as snow. After a cloud has formed, a condition of high humidity, **supersaturated air**, is needed to start the growth of a raindrop or snowflake. Clouds without high humidity only produce gray, overcast skies without rain or snow.

All raindrops or snowflakes begin as tiny droplets about the size of a grain of dust. At first they are so small that the winds within a cloud are enough to keep them aloft. They grow by the process of **coalescence**. About one million cloud droplets must combine to make an average-sized raindrop. Coalescence within the supersaturated cloud continues until the droplets become large enough to succumb to gravity. Then they tumble from the cloud as rain or snow, depending upon the air temperature.

Does it ever rain in the air but not on the ground?

Sometimes on hot sunny days, raindrops pour from a cloud but never hit the ground. This occurs when the air humidity below the cloud is so low and the temperature so warm that the rain evaporates quickly and completely. This condition is called **verga**. You can see this phenomenon beneath a single cloud on a sunny day. Gray streaks appear to hang from the bottom of a cloud, like curtains blowing in the breeze.

Is rain pure?

Not all rain is clear and pure. Brown rain can be common during dry summers. Strong winds carry dust and dirt up into the clouds, where the grit mingles with the raindrops causing them to appear brown when they return to earth. Dust and dirt can also hang in the air below a cloud. In a strong downpour, pelting raindrops drive the suspended dust and dirt particles out of the air, leaving the sky exceptionally clear and blue.

Are all snowflakes created equal?

Snow is created by chain reaction. Small ice crystals grow when combined with other crystals in the same way rain is produced by coalescence. Giant snowflakes are really many snowflakes clumped together. They occur when ordinary-sized snowflakes fall through moist, warm air (just above freezing). The edges of the flakes then melt slightly, and a thin layer of water develops. The water causes the snowflakes to stick together, and they refreeze as over-sized versions of themselves.

Sometimes snow doesn't fall as flakes but as pellets. **Pellets** start out as tiny flakes and fall through super-cooled clouds (clouds whose moisture is just below freezing). Instead of colliding together and becoming full-sized snowflakes, the tiny flakes collide with super-cooled water droplets and freeze into spherical balls of ice. The white, opaque pellets are about an eighth to quarter of an inch (3–6 mm) across. They fall to the ground in small quantities, bouncing when they hit. **Sleet** also starts out as flakes that turn into ice. However, the ice in this case is transparent. Also, the icy flecks of sleet are smaller than pellets. Contrary to the idea you may get from news media weather reports, sleet is not a mixture of rain and snow.

What is hail — snow or rain?

Hail is the enemy of auto insurance companies, home owners, gardeners and farmers. It can break windows, dent cars and shred plants. On rare occasions, severe hail can even cause death. Some weather experts estimate that hail causes approximately 700 million dollars in damage each year.

What, precisely, is this phenomenon that wreaks such havoc? Hailstones are pieces of ice similar to pellets and sleet. But to be considered hail, the stones must be larger than ice pellets (that is, larger than a eighth of an inch, 3 mm). Hailstones are often marble-sized, but they can be as big as a golfball or even larger. Hail is usually a summertime event, while sleet and pellets are mostly winter occurrences.

Hail starts out as frozen raindrops within large thunderclouds called **cumulonimbus clouds**. It takes about 10,000 raindrops to form one golfball-sized hailstone. Hailstones grow very large by surging up and down on strong air currents within a cloud. During each cycle down, a hailstone thaws slightly and merges with other partially thawed hailstones. This produces large irregular, shaped stones. On the cycle up, the clumped hailstones re-freeze as a larger hailstone. The stronger the air currents are, the longer a hailstone is carried through this cycle, and the bigger it grows. When the hailstone becomes too heavy for the air currents to carry it, it falls from the cloud.

Large irregular-shaped hailstones are not as common as simple round hailstones. Round stones are formed in the same way as larger stones, but they don't combine with other individual stones. If you cut a regular round hailstone in half, you'll see concentric layers of clear ice and milky ice. These layers were built during the hailstone's repeated trips up and down within the cloud. As each stone is carried up through super-cooled air, its accumulated moisture freezes quickly, trapping air bubbles. The air bubbles frozen in this layer give it a milky appearance. When the hailstone descends through warmer air (but still near freezing), the accumulated moisture freezes slowly, allowing air to escape. This frozen layer is clear ice. The clear ice cubes you buy in the store are made this way; they are frozen slowly. Each trip a hailstone makes up and down creates a new layer of either milky or clear ice. During the next hail storm, collect a few large stones and break them in half. Count the rings and see for yourself how many trips the stone made within the cloud.

Why is it so quiet after a snowfall?

The muffling effect of a fresh snowfall contributes to the enchantment of a wintertime walk. Dry, fluffy snow traps air and absorbs sound. The more it snows, the more air is trapped and the quieter it gets. After snow settles, however, it compacts and loses its ability to trap sound. So, hurry outside during the next fluffy snowfall and listen to the quiet!

Why does snow squeak when you walk on it?

While dry, fluffy snow is quiet underfoot, another kind of snow makes noise; it squeaks. Squeaky snow occurs only when temperatures are below 14° F (-10° C). When you walk on snow above 14° F, your weight causes the snow to melt a little and slide silently under your boot. Below 14° F, snow underfoot no longer melts. Instead, its ice crystals are crushed together, and they squeak as they collide. The next time you are out for a winter walk, listen to your footsteps in the snow, and try to determine if the temperature is above or below 14° F (-10° C).

What is wind-chill?

In colder northern regions of the country, it is just as important to know the **wind-chill** as the actual air temperature. The wind-chill has everything to do with your skin and nothing to do with objects like your car. The metal on your car will never get below the outside air temperature no matter how hard the wind blows. When you are outside, your body is making heat to keep you warm. This internal heat is transferred to your skin producing a thin layer of warm air next to your skin. When the wind blows, it robs you of this heat. The faster the wind blows, the greater the heat loss and the colder you feel; also, the harder your body works to keep you warm.

The wind-chill factor correlates with how cold you actually feel when you're outside. All wind-chills are calculated on a chart that aligns outside temperature with the speed of the wind. Very cold temperatures along with very strong winds will produce a very low wind chill factor. To combat wind-chill, cover any exposed skin. This will trap warm air next to your skin and make it harder for the wind to take it away. Extreme wind-chills can remove heat so quickly, that exposed skin can freeze within seconds. Areas like your nose, ears and fingers are most susceptible to freezing from low wind-chills.

How does dew form?

Dew-covered lawns are a sure sign of clear summer nights and cool temperatures. On nights with calm winds and no clouds, the area near the ground cools rapidly. (Clouds often trap the earth's heat; without this blanket, heat is quickly lost to space.) Often the grass and other plants cool to temperatures below that of the surrounding air. When this happens, any air that comes in contact with these extra-cooled plants, loses its ability to hold any moisture. Water vapor, held in the air, condenses onto the nearest available surface, forming tiny water droplets called **dew**. Because the cold air sinks and it is nearest the ground, dew will most likely form on grass rather than on taller shrubs or trees.

Dew is a valuable source of moisture for many plants, animals and insects. Dew deposits about ½ to 2 inches (12-55 mm) of moisture on lawns, fields and prairies each year. It can be an important source of water for insects and small critters in times of drought, when clear skies prevail.

How does lightning form?

Few of nature's spectacles are as awesome as thunder and lightning. Each year approximately 10,000 fires are started by lightning, and about 100 people in the U.S. and Canada are killed by it. It's surprising that these numbers aren't greater, since hundreds of millions of bolts of lightning strike the ground around the world each year. How is it that clouds, as seemingly harmless collections of condensed water, produce such powerful and deadly force?

Clouds alone are difficult to understand; lightning is even more complicated. Scientists don't fully understand it. We do know that lightning is a massive discharge of electricity from a cloud to the ground, from cloud to cloud, from a cloud into the air, or within a single cloud. Dry air acts as an electrical insulator and inhibits lightning. As moisture is added to air, the air's electrical potential builds, reducing its insulating effect.

Lightning comes to life within negatively and positively charged regions within a single cloud. These charged regions are not clearly understood, and many theories exist as to how they are formed. However, it is known that the negatively charged bottom of a cloud causes the ground beneath it to become positively charged. The positively charged region below a cloud travels along the ground, following the cloud. Since opposite charges attract, the negative charge in the cloud is soon attracted to the positive charge on the ground, and lightning strikes. The tops of tall objects, such as buildings and trees, accumulate positive charges when they are underneath a negative cloud, the same way your hair stands on end if you are caught in an electrical storm. Since these objects bring the positive charges closer to the cloud, they act like a magnet and attract lightning.

Lightning rods work in a similar way. They also accumulate positive charges and attract lightning. After lightning strikes a lightning rod, an insulated conducting wire passes the electrical energy to a solid metal rod buried in the ground, carrying it safely away from the building to which the rod is attached.

What causes thunder?

Whether we hear it or not, lightning always produces thunder. Thunder is the sound of lightning. When a lightning bolt occurs, it heats the air around it suddenly, to temperatures over 54,000° F (30,000° C). That's over 15 times hotter than the temperature of boiling lead. The extreme heat causes the surrounding air to expand rapidly, pushing it away from the bolt in air shock waves. When these shock waves reach our ears, we hear thunder.

Can I tell how far away a storm is from the sound of thunder?

We hear thunder as **rumbling**, **cracking** and **clapping**, but the shock waves of thunder are always the same. They seem to make different sounds only because we hear them at different distances from the storm. These differences provide clues as to how far away a storm is. When lightning strikes

nearby, you hear the shock wave from the top and bottom of the lightning bolt; it sounds like a sharp clap or crack. When lightning strikes at a greater distance, you hear the shock from the bottom of the bolt, which is closer to you, before you hear the top, which is farther away. This produces a rumbling sound. If hills or buildings intervene, the rumbling will be extended over a longer period of time. Another way to estimate the distance of a storm combines sound and sight.

We see the light from lightning nearly instantaneously, but the sound travels more slowly. Because light travels faster than sound, you will always see lightning before you hear it. The sound of thunder travels at only 1,100 ft.

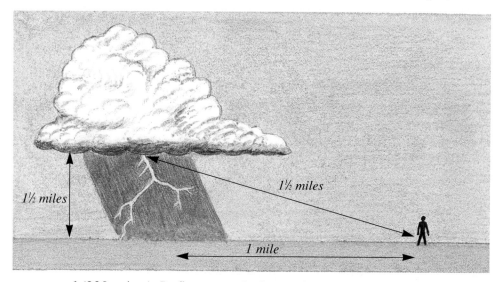

1½ miles

1½ miles

1 mile

per second (330 m/sec). In five seconds, it travels almost a mile (1.6 km). The difference between the time you see lightning and the time you hear it indicates how far away you are from the lightning. You can determine the distance by counting the seconds between the two occurrences. Start counting when you see the strike, and stop when you hear the thunder. If you see a strike and count to five, it is one mile (1.6 km) away. Ten seconds equals two miles (3.2 km), and 15 seconds is three miles (4.8 km). Also, you can tell if a storm is coming closer or moving farther away by noting whether the intervals between lightning and thunder grow shorter or longer.

What is heat lightning?

When we see **heat lightning** on warm summer nights, we don't hear thunder. Nonetheless, heat lightning comes from a lightning storm complete with thunder. The storm is close enough for us to see its lightning, but too far away for us to hear its thunder. People standing closer do hear it!

What are the effects of the environment on weather?

Many potential weather-related threats to the environment can be attributed to human-made conditions, including acid rain, global warming, ozone depletion and ground-level ozone. One of the more common environmental concerns is **acid rain**. Through a complex chemical reaction involving sunlight, the condensed vapor in clouds combines with sulfur dioxide (which is emitted by factories and automobiles) or nitrous oxide and this results in highly corrosive chemicals. These acids are deposited in lakes and streams when it rains. It has been proven that both acids can be harmful to the plants and animals that live in these waters and on land. The problem is not confined to urban areas, since pollution in the atmosphere can travel thousands of miles before being deposited.

Global warming refers to an increase in the average temperature over many years. An especially hot summer doesn't indicate that the globe is warming, but an increase in average temperatures over many years does. For example, during the last ice age, the average temperature in North America was only five degrees lower than it is now. A rise of just two to four degrees above our current average temperatures would cause extreme changes in the earth's weather. Actual weather changes are still speculative, but any change could result in a major upset in the growing season for important food crops.

Global warming is caused by a buildup of heat-trapping gases in our atmosphere. The burning of coal, oil and natural gas and the production of synthetic chemicals is turning our planet into a hothouse. Emissions, such as carbon dioxide from cars, and methane from the break down of plants, build up in the upper limits of the atmosphere and trap heat. These gasses are normally absorbed by vegetation like trees, but due to the rapid deforestation of North America and the rain forests of the world, the effectiveness of this natural cleansing process has been reduced. Also, while great strides have been made in the reduction of auto emissions, more cars are on the roads now than ever. Undoubtedly, global warming is an issue we will have to deal with in the future.

Ozone depletion is a reduction in the protective layer in the upper atmosphere. Ozone normally reduces the amount of ultraviolet radiation from the sun. Over the past 20 years, scientists have noticed that certain areas of this protective blanket are wearing thin. As a result, more harmful sunlight reaches the earth, causing excessive heating, increased chances of skin cancer and a detrimental effect on plants and animals. It has been determined that increased ultra-violet light has caused frog and toad eggs to die before hatching. It is also predicted that over the next several decades, people will suffer from skin cancer at an unprecedented rate. Although the specific, long-term effects of ozone depletion is still being studied, common sense dictates a cautious approach to this potentially serious threat.

Ground level ozone is created by exhaust from cars and factories reacting with sunlight. While ozone in the upper atmosphere serves a positive function as a filter for ultraviolet radiation from the sun, ground level ozone causes eye irritation, respiratory difficulty and severe damage to trees, crops and animals.

How can I use the Weather Smart identification section?

Weather may not be the first thing that comes to mind when you think of nature observation, but weather sets the stage for all of nature's players. Birds fly south and some animals hibernate because of winter. Hawks soar on the wind and plants grow with nourishing rains. The Weather Smart identification section introduces you to some basic cloud types and the weather that accompanies them, as well as other weather phenomenon.

Cloud observation will help you predict weather and enhance your understanding and enjoyment of the world of nature. The two-part Latin names of clouds are simply descriptive words chosen to reflect their height and appearance. The first part of a cloud's name indicates its height category: high, medium, low and towering (vertical/single clouds that are taller than they are wide).

Cirrus means curl of hair, stratus means layer, cumulus means heap and nimbus means rain.The second part of a cloud's name suggests how it was formed or if it is a rain cloud. When you put these two parts together (height and appearance) you will be able to describe any of the ten basic cloud formations. Sometimes the first and second names are switched around but they still mean the same.

Here are the four cloud groups and their cloud types.

1. HIGH CLOUDS 16,000–45,000'

cirrus	thin, wispy, clouds blown by high winds
cirrostratus	thin sheet of high clouds covering the entire sky
cirrocumulus	small, round, individual white puffs

2. MIDDLE CLOUDS 6,500–16,000'

altostratus	gray clouds covering the entire sky
altocumulus	gray, puffy masses often rolled out in parallel waves or bands

3. LOW CLOUDS Surface–6,500'

stratus	uniform, gray cloud covering the entire sky
stratocumulus	low, lumpy clouds with patches of blue sky between
nimbostratus	dark gray cloud layer with continuous rain fall

4. VERTICAL CLOUDS Growing upright

cumulus	the familiar white, puffy clouds in many shapes
cumulonimbus	all, giant clouds associated with thunderstorms

There are types of clouds other than those mentioned here, but these are the most common and easiest to identify. Like most things in nature, clouds may not appear as a single type but several kinds can be mixed together. Take a minute each day to note the cloud type and see if your predictions match the evening weather forecast.

HIGH CLOUDS

Cirrus

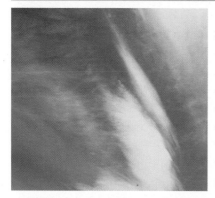

These thin, very high, wispy clouds are never substantial enough to block out the sun and usually indicate a storm is on the horizon. Known as **Mares' tails**, cirrus clouds often are a result of very high winds blowing off the top of storms. As a rule, they stretch out like feathers moving across the sky from west to east following the prevailing wind; they often indicate generally fair weather for a day or two before stormy weather.

Cirrocumulus

Not as common as the cirrus, but just as high, these tiny, puffy clouds scatter evenly across portions of the sky. The characteristic fish scale pattern of cirrocumulus is often called a **mackerel sky**. Cirrocumulus are responsible for spectacular sunsets, when they reflect red and orange sunlight.

Cirrostratus

Although cirrostratus clouds cover the entire sky, they are so thin and high, they often go unnoticed. During the day, these clouds give the sky a glaring white appearance with a distinct ring around the sun. At night they often create a halo around the moon. Either way, cirrostratus clouds frequently form in advance of a storm and may signal a change in weather within 12 to 24 hours.

MIDDLE CLOUDS

Altocumulus

Middle level clouds, altocumulus, often blanket the sky in gray puffy masses. Slight even breaks between clouds and sunlight give these clouds an appearance of being different shades of color. Because they can form from moist, rising air on early summer mornings, they are good indicators of afternoon thunderstorms. Often these clouds dissipate at night.

Altostratus

Another middle level cloud, altostratus, often covers the entire sky. The dimly-visible sun, struggling to shine through, is referred to as a **watery sun**. The sky appears gray and halos don't form because the clouds are too thick. Don't look for your shadow on these days. Altostratus clouds spell foul weather with widespread rain or snow.

LOW CLOUDS

Nimbostratus

A uniformly gray sky and nimbostratus clouds foretell rain. Small, ragged, renegade clouds that form just below the cloud layer are called **scud**. These clouds produce light, continuous rain or snow. Fog is also common with this cloud formation. Rarely can you see the sun or moon shining through nimbostratus, so sit back and enjoy the rain; it will be around for awhile.

Stratocumulus

Stratocumulus clouds often form near sundown. They take shape as a thick layer of dark gray clouds broken here and there with patches of blue sky. The cloud deck stretches to the horizon, becoming thicker and grayer in the distance. These clouds rarely produce rain or snow and indicate fair weather for the coming day.

Stratus

Stratus is often a very low, thick layer of gray clouds covering the entire sky. It is not uncommon for these clouds to be so low that they touch the ground. A light mist or drizzle often accompanies stratus, but rarely does it rain very hard. This is a common cloud formation near the ocean.

VERTICAL CLOUDS

Cumulus

These are the common, bright, fluffy, cottony clouds of warm summer afternoons. It is these clouds that entertain people as they lay on their backs, imagining different shapes of people and animals floating in the sky. Cumulus often have flat bottoms and popcorn tops. They are not as tall as they are wide. If these clouds don't grow in size, they foretell fair weather.

Cumulonimbus

If a cumulus cloud grows vertically, it will develop into huge cumulonimbus clouds. These clouds are the giants of the sky, with a single cloud tower as high as 40,000' (12,000 m). These clouds often form singularly and are capable of releasing a huge amount of rain and lightning. Winds within these clouds contort the shape into billowing masses that are often blown off the main cloud to shape the characteristic **anvil head**.

OTHER WEATHER PHENOMENA

Sundogs

Often flanking the late afternoon sun, **sundogs** are the jewels of the winter sky. They look like mini-rainbows, but sundogs are a **refraction** (bending) of sunlight through ice crystals. The ice crystals are usually part of a thin layer of winter clouds (cirrus) that spread thinly across a late afternoon sun. Look for sundogs on either or both sides of the sun. They always appear in a position 22 degrees lateral to the sun. This is because the plate-like ice crystals orient themselves horizontally to the ground and act like small prisms, refracting sunlight out to the side. You can find the 22 degree mark by holding up an outstretched arm with fingers spread. The distance from the tip of the thumb to the tip of the little finger is about 22 degrees. Often, a pair of polarizing sunglasses help to see these "winter rainbows."

Sun pillar

Shooting forth like a beam of light from a larger-than-life flashlight, sun pillars are seen at sunrise or sunset. Vertical shafts of light beam from the sun like a "pillar" extending up into the sky. Tiny ice crystals that are falling in still air reflect (turn back) sunlight causing a bright area of light in the sky above the sun. These sun pillars can be orange, yellow and sometimes red. They are associated with cirrus clouds and can indicate an incoming storm.

Halo

Seen as a giant white ring around the sun or moon, a halo is a grand visual spectacle of nature. It is caused by refracted light as it passes through tiny ice crystals in high cirrus clouds. The light emerges from the crystals at an angle that forms a perfect ring. It is seen as a bright,

white ring, usually observed at mid-day, or mid-night when a thin blanket of very high cirrus clouds cover the sky. This ring is always the same distance from the sun, 22 degrees. Halos foretell of a coming storm.

274

Where to See Migrating and Other Birds

The Bird Smart chapter introduced you to some of the birds you are likely to encounter in your area but many migrating birds may pass through your state, stopping to rest and eat. You may wish to visit places where you can see some of the birds not native to your region, birds you wouldn't otherwise have an opportunity to see. Each year thousands of people grab their binoculars, pack a lunch and head out to witness the annual migration of millions of water birds or birds of prey. You and your family may want to join the fun. Here is a small sampling of either refuge areas or preserves in your state that are good places to watch birds. You may see large numbers of birds congregate during migration or even some rare and unusual birds. You will likely see many native species as well.

Although there are many areas in every state to see birds, we have chosen only two or three as suggestions to visit. Many of these areas are State and County Parks or are within National Parks or National Wildlife Refuges. Please follow all park rules. Be sure to check in at the visitor center when you arrive. They can give you detailed information concerning the types of birds present and where to see them. The phone number of the state tourism board or office or local Audubon Chapter is provided to help you plan any birdwatching trips you may want to take. Also included are the bird "hotlines" for each state. Use these numbers to report and find out about any rare bird sightings. The times of year and types of birds listed here are only general guidelines. Be sure to call ahead or check with your local Audubon office for more details.

Birding Sites

ALABAMA

Jacksonville
Boozer's Pond
Visiting time: March and September, October
What to see: water birds
Location: 2 miles west to Boozer's pond

Birmingham
Lake Purdy
Visiting time: all seasons
What to see: water birds
Location: Southeast of Birmingham on US 280

Department of Tourism
Bureau of Tourism & Travel
P.O. Box 4297
Montgomery, AL 36103
(800) ALABAMA

Birding Hotline: (205) 987–2730

ARKANSAS

Manila
Big Lake National Wildlife Refuge
Visiting time: winter
What to see: water birds, birds of prey
Location: 2 miles east of Manila off of Hwy. 18

275

Turrell
Wapanocca National Wildlife Refuge
Visiting time: winter
What to see: water birds, birds of prey
Location: 16 miles north of West Memphis off of Hwy. 42

Department of Tourism
Dept of Parks & Tourism
1 Capitol Mall
Little Rock, AR 72201
(501) 371–7777, (800) NATURAL

Birding Hotline: (501) 753–5853

CONNECTICUT

Bridgeport
Seaside park
Visiting time: November to April
What to see: water birds
Location: Sound View Drive in Bridgeport (Marine Blvd.)

Stonington
Barn Island Wildlife Management Area
Visiting time: April to October
What to see: water birds
Location: 1 mile east of Stonington off of state Hwy. 1

Hartford
Connecticut River at South Windsor
Visiting time: spring and fall
What to see: backyard birds
Location: 6 miles north of Hartford off of I 84

Department of Tourism
Connecticut Tourism Division
865 Brook St.
Rocky Hill, CT 06067
(800) 282–6863, (203) 258–4355

Birding Hotline: (203) 254–3665

DELAWARE

Smyrna
Bombay Hook National Wildlife Refuge
Visiting time: all year
What to see: water birds, birds of prey
Location: just south of Smyrna off of US 85

Delaware City
Thousand Acre Marsh
Visiting time: August
What to see: water birds
Location: just off Dutch Neck Road in Delaware City

Department of Tourism
Delaware Tourism Office
P.O. Box 1401
99 Kings Highway

Dover, DE 19903
(800) 441–8846

Birding Hotline: (215) 567–2473

FLORIDA

St. George Island Hawk Lookout
Visiting time: fall
What to see: birds of prey
Location: east of Apalachicola off of US 98

Immokalee
Corkscrew Swamp Sanctuary
Visiting time: any season
What to see: birds of prey, backyard birds
Location: 16 miles west of Immokalee in Big Cypress Swamp

Department of Tourism
Division of Tourism
126 W. Van Buren St.
Tallahassee, FL 32399
(904) 487–1462

Birding Hotline: (813) 657–4442

GEORGIA

Brunswick
Jekyll Island State Park
Visiting time: spring
What to see: water birds
Location: southeast of Brunswick off of State 50

Atlanta
Chattahoochee River Bottomlands
Visiting time: April–May and September–October
What to see: backyard birds
Location: west of Atlanta off of US 78

Department of Tourism
P.O. Box 1776
Atlanta, GA 30301
(404) 656–3590, (800) VISITGA

Birding Hotline: (404) 493–8862

ILLINOIS

Danville
Forest Glen County Preserve
Visiting time: all seasons
What to see: backyard birds, birds of prey
Location: south of Danville off of I 74

Hamilton
Montebello Conservation Park
Visiting time: winter
What to see: Bald Eagles
Location: just north of Hamilton off State 96

Olive Branch
Horseshoe Lake Conservation Area and
Nature Preserve
Visiting time: October – March
What to see: water birds, Bald Eagles
Location: 1 mile southeast of Olive Branch
on State 3

Department of Tourism
Illinois Department of Tourism
James R. Thompson Center
100 W. Randolph, Suite 3–400
Chicago, IL 60601
(800) 223–0121

Birding Hotline:
Chicago (708) 671–1522
Central (217) 785–1083
Northwestern (815) 965–3095

INDIANA

Bloomington
Lake Lemon
Visiting time: March–April and
October–November
What to see: water birds
Location: east of Bloomington off State 45

Medaryville
Jasper–Pulaski State Fish and Wildlife Area
Visiting time: March and April
What to see: water birds
Location: 3 miles north of Medaryville off
of State 421

Department of Tourism
Division of Tourism
1 N. Capitol Ave., Suite 700
Indianapolis, IN 46204
(317) 232–8860, (800) 289–6646

Birding Hotline:(317) 259–0911

IOWA

Missouri Valley
Desoto National Wildlife Refuge
Visiting time: October and November
What to see: water birds
Location: 5 miles west of Missouri Valley
off of US 30

Wapello
Louisa National Wildlife Refuge
Visiting time: October and November
What to see: water birds, birds of prey
Location: 6 miles east of Wapello off Co Rd
X–61

Department of Tourism
Division of Tourism
200 E. Grand Ave.

Des Moines, IA 50309
(515) 242–4705, (800) 345–IOWA

Birding Hotline
(319) 319–9881

KANSAS

Hartford
Flint Hills National Wildlife Refuge
Visiting time: spring and fall
What to see: water birds, birds of prey
Location: southeast of Emporia off
of Hwy. 130

Stafford
Quivira National Wildlife Refuge
Visiting time: spring and fall
What to see: water birds and birds of prey
Location: northeast of Stafford off of Hwy. 50

Department of Tourism
Kansas Travel & Tourism Dept
700 SW Harrison Suite 1300
Topeka, KS 66603
(913) 296–2009, (800) 2–KANSAS

Birding Hotline: (913) 372–5499

KENTUCKY

Cadiz
Land Between The Lakes Recreation Area
Visiting time: winter
What to see: water birds, birds of prey
Location: west of Cadiz on State 80

Bowling Green
Chaney Lake/McElroy Lake
Visiting time: April and May
What to see: water birds
Location: 7 miles south of Bowling Green
on US 31W

Department of Tourism
Kentucky Tourism
Capitol Plaza Tower, Suite 2200
Frankfort, KY 40601
(502) 564–4930, (800) 225–TRIP

Birding Hotline: (502) 894–9538

LOUISIANA

Rhinehart
Catahoula National Wildlife Refuge
Visiting time: all seasons
What to see: water birds, birds of prey
Location: 28 miles east of Alexandria off of
Hwy. 84

Hackberry
Sabine National Wildlife Refuge
Visiting time: winter

What to see: water birds
Location: 30 miles south of Sulphur off of Hwy. 27

Department of Tourism
Louisiana Office of Tourism
P.O. Box 94291
Baton Rouge, LA 70804
(800) 33–GUMBO

Birding Hotline:
Baton Rouge (504) 768–9874
New Orleans (504) 246–2473

MAINE

Bangor
Bangor Bog
Visiting time: late May through early July
What to see: water birds and backyard birds
Location: north of Bangor, off of state Hwy. 15

Portland
Back Cove
Visiting time: October to April
What to see: water birds
Location: within the city limits,
US 1 (Baxter Boulevard) around the bay to the shore

Evergreen Cemetery/Baxter's Woods
Visiting time: May
What to see: backyard birds
Location: west on State 25 from Portland, right on Stevens Avenue. On left is Evergreen Cemetery, on the right is Baxter's Woods.

Department of Tourism
Publicity Bureau
97 Winthrop St.
Hallowell, ME 04347
(207) 289–2423, (800) 533–9595

Birding Hotline: (207) 781–2332

MARYLAND

Annapolis
Sandy Point State Park
Visiting time: May to October
What to see: water birds (spring) and birds of prey (fall)
Location: seven miles northeast of Annapolis on US 50

Frederick
Washington Monument State Park
Visiting time: September and October
What to see: birds of prey
Location: west of Fredrick off of US 40A

St. Mary's City
Point Lookout State Park
Visiting time: fall, winter and spring
What to see: water birds
Location: 13 miles south of St Mary's City at the end of State 5

Department of Tourism
Office of Tourist Development
217 E. Redwood St.
Baltimore, MD 21202
(301) 269–3517, (800) 543–1036

Birding Hotline: (301) 652–1088

MASSACHUSETTS

Concord
Great Meadows National Wildlife Refuge
Visiting time: summer
What to see: water birds, backyard birds
Location: Refuge headquarters, east of Concord about one mile on Sudbury Road

Gloucester
Halibut point/Andrews Point
Visiting time: October to April
What to see: water birds
Location: northeast of Gloucester off of Hwy. 127

Holyoke
Mt. Tom State Reservation
Goat Peak Tower
Visiting time: fall
What to see: birds of prey
Location: 4 miles north of Holyoke, on US Hwy. 5

Northampton
Arcadia Wildlife Sanctuary
Visiting time: All seasons
What to see: backyard birds, birds of prey
Location: 3 miles south of Northampton off of State Hwy. 10

Sharon
Moose Hill Sanctuary
Visiting time: all seasons
What to see: backyard birds, birds of prey
Location: 18 miles south of Boston, Massachusetts, Audubon Society's oldest sanctuary

Department of Tourism
Office of Travel & Tourism
100 Cambridge St. 13th Floor
Boston, MA 02202
(800) 447–MASS

Birding Hotline: (617) 259–8805

MICHIGAN

Battle Creek
W.K. Kellogg Bird Sanctuary
Visiting time: March–April and
October–November
What to see: water birds
Location: 12 miles northwest of Battle
Creek off County 184

Mackinaw City
Straits of Mackinac
Visiting time: spring
What to see: birds of prey
Location: West of Mackinaw City along
Wilderness Drive

Department of Tourism
Michigan Travel Bureau
P.O. Box 30226
Lansing, MI 48909
(517) 373–1195, (800) 5432–YES

Birding Hotline: (616) 471–4919

MINNESOTA

Duluth
Hawk Ridge Nature Reserve
Visiting time: September
What to see: birds of prey
Location: North of Duluth off Skyline Drive

Wabasha
Eagle Park
Visiting time: winter
What to see: Bald Eagles
Location: Downtown Wabasha park

Department of Tourism
Minnesota Office of Tourism
375 Jackson St.
250 Skyway Level
St.Paul, MN 55101
(612) 296–5029, (800) 657–3700

Birding Hotline: (612) 827–3161

MISSISSIPPI

Clarksdale
Moon Lake
Visiting time: all seasons
What to see: water birds
Location: 17 miles North of Clarksdale off
of US 61

Greenville
Yazoo National Wildlife Refuge
Visiting time: winter
What to see: water birds
Location: off state Highway 436

Department of Tourism
Mississippi Division of Tourism
P.O. Box 22825
Jackson, MS 39205
(601) 359–3297, (800) 647–2290

Birding Hotline: (601) 982–2850

NEBRASKA

Scottsbluff
North Platte National Wildlife Refuge
Visiting time: spring and autumn
What to see: water birds, birds of prey
Location: north of Scottsbluff off of Hwy 71

Kearney
Visiting time: March
What to see: sandhill cranes
Location: any bridge crossing the Platte
river between Grand Island and Lexington
especially near Kearney
Bellevue

Fontenelle Forest Nature Center
Visiting time: spring and autumn
What to see: backyard birds, birds of prey
Location: off of North Bellevue Blvd

Department of Tourism
P.O. Box 94666
Lincoln, NE 68509
(800) 742–7595, (800) 228–4307

Birding Hotline: (402) 292–5325

NEW HAMPSHIRE

Durham
Great Bay
Visiting time: October to April
What to see: water birds
Location: east of Durham or Portsmouth.
On Hwy. 108 between Durham and
Portsmouth, take any side road to the bay.

Concord
Great Turkey Pond/Turee March
Visiting time: May and June
What to see: backyard birds, water birds
Location: just west of Concord, off I–89, at
Bow
Headquarters of the State Audubon Society

Department of Tourism
Office of Travel and Tourism
P.O. Box 856
Concord, NH 03302–0856
(603) 271–2666

Birding Hotline: (603) 224–9900

NEW YORK

Irving
Cattaraugus Creek
Visiting time: March to May
What to see: backyard birds, birds of prey
Location: off of I 90 and State 5

Seneca Falls
Montezuma National Wildlife Refuge
Visiting time: April and October
What to see: water birds
Location: headquarters, on US 20, 5 miles
northeast of Seneca Falls

Pulaski
Sandy Pond Area
Visiting time: May
What to see: water birds
Location: 3 miles west of Pulaski off of
state Hwy. 13 and State Hwy. 3

Oswego
Mouth of the Oswego River
Visiting time: winter
What to see: water birds
Location: south of Oswego, along the river
and at the mouth

Ithaca
Sapsucker Woods Sanctuary
Visiting time: all year
What to see: water birds, backyard birds
Location: north of Ithaca, off of State 13

Department of Tourism
Division of Tourism
1 Commerce Plaza
Albany, NY 12245
(518) 474–4116, (800) CALL–NYS

Birding Hotline:
Albany (518) 439–8080
Buffalo (716) 896–1271
Ithaca (607) 254–2429
Lower Hudson Valley (914) 666–6614
New York (212) 979–3070
Rochester (716) 425–4630
Syracuse (315) 668–8000

NEW JERSEY

Caldwell
Troy Meadows
Visiting time: March and April
What to see: water birds
Location: south of Caldwell

Cape May
The Rips
Visiting time: August, September, October
What to see: birds of prey, backyard birds,
water birds
Location: 2 miles west of Cape May off of
Sunset Boulevard

Montclair
Montclair Hawk Lookout Sanctuary
Visiting time: September and October
What to see: birds of prey
Location: within the city limits of
Montclair, off of Edgecliffe Road

Department of Tourism
Division of Travel and Tourism
Cn–826
Trenton, NJ 08625
(800) JERSEY–7 (609) 292–2470

Birding Hotline: (908) 766–2661

NORTH CAROLINA

Ansonville
Lockhart Gaddy's Wild Goose Refuge
Visiting time: October to March
What to see: water birds
Location: 2 miles south of Ansonville off of
US 52

Washington
Mattamuskeet National Wildlife Refuge
Visiting time: October to March
What to see: water birds
Location: east of Washington at New
Holland off of US 264

Department of Tourism
North Carolina Travel, Tourism
430 N. Salibury St.
Raleigh, NC 27603
(800) VISITNC, (919) 733–4171

Birding Hotline: (704) 332–2473

NORTH DAKOTA

Edmunds
Arrowood National Wildlife Refuge
Visiting time: spring and fall
What to see: water birds, birds of prey
Location: just north of Edmunds on Rts.
281/52

Department of Tourism
North Dakota Parks and Tourism
604 E. Blvd.
Bismarck, ND 58505
Birding Hotline: None

OHIO

Put–in–Bay
South Bass Island
Visiting time: April and May
What to see: birds of prey
Location: one of 21 islands on the west end
of Lake Erie

St Mary's
Grand Lake St. Mary's
Visiting time: all seasons
What to see: water birds
Location: west of St. Mary's and situated
between State Hwy. 703, State 364 and
State 219

Toledo
Ottawa National Wildlife Refuge
Visiting time: fall, spring
What to see: water birds
Location: 18 miles east of Toledo off of State 2

Department of Tourism
Ohio Div. of Travel and Tourism
P.O. Box 1001
Columbus, OH 43266
(800) BUCKEYE

Birding Hotline:
Cincinnati (513) 521–2847
Cleveland (216) 321–7245
Columbus (614) 221–9736
Blendon Woods Park (614) 895–6222
SW Ohio (513) 277–6446
NW Ohio (419) 875–6889
Youngstown (216) 742–6661

OKLAHOMA

Jet
Salt Plains National Wildlife Refuge
Visiting time: spring and fall
What to see: water birds
Location: 14 miles north of Jet off State
Hwy. 38

Vian
Sequoyah National Wildlife Refuge
Visiting time: spring, fall and winter
What to see: water birds
Location: 3 miles south of I 40 at Vian exit

PENNSYLVANIA

Hamburg
Hawk Mountain Sanctuary
Visiting time: September and October
What to see: birds of prey
Location: north of Hamburg off of State 61

Allentown
Bake Oven Knob
Visiting time: September and October
What to see: birds of prey
Location: 20 miles north of Allentown off
of State 309

Moraine State Park
Visiting time: March and April
What to see: water birds
Location: 40 miles north of Pittsburgh near
Butler off of I–79

Department of Tourism
Bureau of Travel Development
416 Forum Bldg
Harrisburg, PA 17120
(717) 787–5453, (800) VISITPA

Birding Hotline:
Allentown (610) 252–3455
Philadelphia (215) 657–2473
Western PA (412) 963–0560
Wilkes–Barre (717) 825–2473
SE/SC PA (215) 383–8840

RHODE ISLAND

Charlestown
Kimball Bird Sanctuary
Visiting time: October to December, spring
What to see: water birds, backyard birds
Location: 2 miles west of Charlestown off
of US Hwy. 1

Tiverton
Sakonnet Point/Warren Point/Brigg's Marsh
Visiting time: year–round
What to see: water birds
Location: south of Tiverton on State Hwy. 77

Department of Tourism
Division of Tourism
7 Jackson Walkway
Providence, RI 02903
(401) 277–2601, (800) 556–2484

Birding Hotline: (401) 949–3870

SOUTH CAROLINA

Hardeeville
Savannah National Wildlife Refuge
Visiting time: all year
What to see: water birds
Location: South of Hardeeville off of US 17

Charleston
Cape Romain National Wildlife Refuge
Visiting time: all year
What to see: water birds and backyard birds
Location: North of Charleston off US 17

Department of Tourism
South Carolina Division of Tourism
P.O. Box 71
Columbia, SC 29202–0071
(803) 734–0235

Birding Hotline: (704) 332–2473

SOUTH DAKOTA

Pickstown
Fort Randall Dam
Visiting time: November through March
What to see: birds of prey

Location: south of Pickstown to Fort Randall Dam

Department of Tourism
South Dakota Tourism
Capitol Lake Plaza
Pierre, SD 57501
Birding Hotline: None

Department of Tourism
Tourism and Recreation Dept.
215 NE 28th
Oklahoma City, OK 73105
(405) 521–2409, (800) 652–6552

Birding Hotline:
Statewide (918) 669–6646
Okla. City (405) 373–4531

TENNESSEE

Chattanooga
Chickamauga Lake
Visiting time: spring and fall
What to see: water birds
Location: Chattanooga

Nashville
Radnor Lake Natural Area
Visiting time: fall
What to see: water birds
Location: 8 miles south of Nashsville off of US 31

Department of Tourism
Tourist Development
P.O. Box 23170
Nashville, TN 37202
(615) 741–2158

Birding Hotline: (615) 356–7636

VERMONT

Swanton
Missisquio National Wildlife Refuge
Visiting time: spring and fall
What to see: water birds
Location: 2.5 miles northwest of Swanton on State Hwy. 78

Vergennes
Dead Creek Waterfowl Area
Visiting time: July to October
What to see: water birds, backyard birds
Location: 6 miles south of Vergennes off State Hwy. 22A

Waterbury
Camel's Hump, Bamforth Ridge Trail
Visiting time: September
What to see: birds of prey
Location: west of Waterbury on US 2 to Jonesville, 2.5 miles outside of Jonesville

Department of Tourism
Vermont Dept of Travel & Tourism
134 State St.
Montpelier, VT 05602
(802) 828–3236

Birding Hotline: (802) 457–4861

VIRGINIA

Richmond
Byrd Park
Visiting time: October to April
What to see: water birds
Location: on the west side of Richmond off of State 161

Charlottesville
Observatory Hill
Visiting time: April and May
What to see: backyard birds
Location: on University grounds off of McCormick Road

Humpback Rocks
Visiting time: September and October
What to see: birds of prey
Location: 6 miles west of Charlottesville off of Blue Ridge Parkway

Department of Tourism
Virginia Division of Tourism
1021 East Cary Street, 14th Floor
Richmond, VA 23219
(804) 786–4484, (800) VISIT–VA

Birding Hotline: (804) 238–2713

WEST VIRGINIA

Petersburg
Dolly Dods Area
Visiting time: September and October
What to see: water birds and birds of prey
Location: 5 miles west of Petersburg off of State 28

Morgantown
Cheat Lake
Visiting time: spring and fall
What to see: water birds, backyard birds
Location: 7 miles east of Morgantown on State 73

Department of Tourism
Travel West Virginia
Capitol Complex
Charleston, WV 25305
(800) CALL–WVA

Birding Hotline: (304) 736–3086

WISCONSIN

Grantsburg
Crex Meadows Wildlife Area
Visiting time: spring
What to see: water birds
Location: one mile north of Grantsburg off of County F

Milwaukee
Schlitz Audubon Center
Visiting time: fall
What to see: backyard birds, water birds
Location: north of Milwaukee off of US 141

Department of Tourism
Wisconsin Division of Tourism
P.O. Box 7606
Madison, WI 53707
(800) 372–2737, (800) 432–TRIP

Birding Hotline: (414) 352–3857

MANITOBA

Stonewall
Oak Hammock March Wildlife Area
Visiting time: spring and fall
What to see: water birds
Location: 16 k (10 miles) east of Stonewall off Hwy. 67

Portage la Prairie
Delta Marsh Waterfowl Research Station
Visiting time: spring and fall
What to see: water birds
Location: 16 k (10 miles) north of Trans–Canada Hwy.

ONTARIO

Amherstburg
Detroit River
Visiting time: fall
What to see: birds of prey
Location: west of Amherstburg on point of land projecting into the Detroit river opposite the south end of Grosse

Grimsby
Visiting time: spring
What to see: birds of prey
Location: half way between Hamilton and St. Catharines

Port Stanley
Hawk Cliff
Visiting time: fall
What to see: birds of prey
Location: 8 miles (13 kilo) south of St. Thomas off of Route 22 to cliffs overlooking Lake Erie

Windsor
Holiday Beach Provincial Park
Visiting time: fall
What to see: birds of prey
Location: parking lot farthest from the park entrance overlooking the water

New Brunswick
St. Andrews research station and tidal inlet
Visiting time: spring
What to see: water birds, birds of prey
Location: St. Andrews tidal inlet

Tourism Board/Office
Ontario Travel
Hearst Block, 900 Bay St.
Toronto, ON M7A 1W3

Birding Hotline:
Provincewide (519) 586–3959
Ottawa (613) 761–1967
Sault Ste Marie (705) 256–2790
Toronto (416) 350–3000 x2293
Windsor/Pt. Pelee (5190 252–2473
Hamilton (416) 648–9537
Long Point BO (519) 586–3959
Durham (905) 668–3070

QUEBEC

Morgan Arboretum
Visiting time: spring and fall
What to see: birds of prey
Location: 32 Kilo (20 miles) west of Montreal off of Hwy. 40

Valleyfield
Visiting time: spring and fall
What to see: birds of prey
Location: west end of bridge just west of Valleyfield at the east end of Lake St. Francis

Tourism Board/Office
Tourisme Quebec
C.P. 20,000
Quebec, PQ G1K7X2
(800) 363–7777, (418) 873–2015
Eastern Quebec: (418) 660–9089
Sagueny/Lac St. Jeans: (418) 696–1868
Bas St. Laurent: (418) 725–5118 (French)
Western Quebec: (819) 778–0737 (French)

Great Lakes States

Illinois, Indiana, Kentucky, Michigan, Minnesota, Ohio, Wisconsin
National Audubon Society
692 N High St. Suite 208
Columbus, OH 43215
(614) 224–3303
(614) 224–3305 Fax

Mid Atlantic States

Washington, D.C., Delaware, Maryland, New Jersey, Pennsylvania, Virginia,
West Virginia
National Audubon Society
1104 Wood Ave. Suite 300
Camp Hill, PA 17011
(717) 763–4985
(717) 763–4981 Fax

Northeast

Connecticut, Massachusetts, Maine, New Hampshire, New York, Rhode
Island, Vermont
National Audubon Society
1789 West Ave
Albany, NY 12203
(518) 869–8731
(518) 869–0737 Fax

West Central

Arkansas, Iowa, Kansas, Missouri, North Dakota, Nebraska, Oklahoma,
South Dakota
National Audubon Society
200 Southwind Place Suite 205
Manhattan, KS 66502
(913) 537–4385
(913) 537–4389 Fax

Southeast

Alaska, Florida, Georgia, Mississippi, North Carolina, South Carolina
National Audubon Society
102 N. 4th Street
Tallahassee, FL 32303
(904) 222–2473

Environmental Organizations for Kids

Kids are forming one of the fastest growing membership groups in the country and the world today - the environmental youth movement. It is no longer enough to educate kids about the environment. Kids want to get out into their communities and do something about pollution and other environmental problems. The following are just some of the groups that will help kids become active in helping the Earth.

Children's Alliance for Protection of the Environment (CAPE)

P.O. Box 307
Austin, TX 78767
(512) 476-2273

This is an international, non-profit organization that offers programs for kids, schools, clubs, and scouts to develop conservation, preservation and restoration projects. Their newsletter, "Many Hands," shares information between kids in more than 35 countries.

Earth Force

1501 Wilshire, Blvd. 12th Floor
Arlington, VA 22207
(703) 243-7400

This is a national organization inspired by, and shaped by, young people for the purpose of environmental education, action and public citizenship. Run by a youth advisory board, they carry out national campaigns and work closely with Nickelodeon Studios to broadcast their message.

Earth Kids Organization

P.O. Box 3847
Salem, OR 97302
(503) 363-1896

This is a non-profit organization for children in grades K-12 that links young people worldwide via computer telecommunications.

Kids For a Clean Environment (FACE)

P.O. Box 158254
Nashville, TN 37215
(615) 331-7381

This is a non-profit organization that is sponsored by Walmart. They concentrate on conservation and anti-pollution issues. They have a newsletter that encourages kids to participate in caring for Kids in Nature's Defense Clubs (KIND)

67 Salem Road
East Haddam, CT 06423-0362
(203) 434-8666

This group is affiliated with the National Animal Humane Society. One of their focuses is a concern for animals - both wild and domestic. They produce a newsletter encouraging earth-friendly activities.

Kids S.T.O.P. (Kids Save The Planet)

P.O. Box 471
Forest Hills, NY 11375
(718) 997-7387

This is a learn and do environmental education/action program for school-aged kids. The thousands of children that already belong acquire a scientific, factual foundation upon which they build their opinions and set goals to achieve success.

The Natural Guard

2631 Durham Rd.
Guilford, CT 06437
(203) 457-1320

This is a free program offering children in grades K-12 the information, tools and mentorship needed to assess their local community's environmental needs and assist in creating service projects that address those needs.

Tree Musketeers

136 Main Street
El Segundo, CA 90245
(800) 473-0263

Tree Musketeers is a youth environmental organization with a mission to bring about environmental improvement through action. It encourages other kids to tackle local environmental problems.

There are so many environmental organizations that have wonderful mission statements to protect our naturally wild areas. These are some of them. We have included a brief description about each. No one can join them all, but pick a favorite one or two and become as active as you are able. The world and you will be all the better for it.

Canadian Wildlife Federation (CWF)
2740 Queensview Drive
Ottawa, Canada K2B1A2

The CWF is Canada's largest non-governmental organization with approximately 600,000 members and supporters. Founded in 1962, the CWF is dedicated to promoting an awareness of wildlife conservation and ensuring protection of Canada's abundant wildlife species for the use and enjoyment of today's and future generations.

The Izaac Walton League of America, Inc.
1401 Wilson Blvd, Level B
Arlington, VA 22209
(703) 528-1818

This wildlife conservation group focuses on U.S. issues of proper conservation practices.

Friends of the Earth
701-251 Laurier Arch
Ottawa, ON Canada K1P5J6

National Audubon Society
700 Broadway
New York, NY 10003-9501
(212) 797-3000

Membership includes a monthly subscription to a beautifully done magazine. The group lobbies for policies which protect our natural resources as well as specific habitat areas for birds and other animals.

National Park Service
(U.S. Department of Interior)
P.O. Box 37127
Washington, DC 20013-7127
(202) 208-6843

This is the federal agency that administers our national parks, monuments and coordinates the Wild and Scenic Rivers Systems and the National Trail System.

National Wildlife Federation
1400 16th Street N.W.
Washington, DC 20036-2266
(202) 797-6800

This group produces award-winning, educational materials for young people including magazines, "Your Big Backyard" and "Ranger Rick". Focused on wildlife conservation issues, it now funds a new Earth Savers program for young conservationists.

The Nature Conservancy
1815 North Lynn Street
Arlington, VA 22209
(703) 841-5300

This non-profit membership group works to survey, and protect our most precious wild areas that haven't been developed. Membership includes a subscription to a wonderful seasonal magazine full of photographs of the places that have been preserved.

North American Association for Environmental Education
1255 23rd Street NW, Suite 400
Washington, DC 20037
(202) 467-8754

The focus of these environmental educators is to promote the most effective type of education possible by assisting groups with research and service.

Sierra Club
730 Polk Street
San Francisco, CA 94109
(415) 776-2211

This group protects the Earth's special places by publishing a magazine, processing litigation and sponsoring wilderness trips and conferences.

The Wilderness Society
900 17th Street NW
Washington, DC 20006-2596
(202) 833-2300

This is a non-profit membership group dedicated to preserving the wilderness and wildlife by promoting a land ethic for America.

World Wildlife Fund
1250 24th Street NW
Washington, DC 200037
(202) 293-4800

A U.S. based group that works all over the world to protect endangered wildlife by creating natural parks and preserves, monitoring international wildlife trade and funds scientific investigations.

Bibliography

Ahrens, Donald C. Meteorology Today. West Publishing Co. 1988.

Audubon Society Field Guide to North American Birds, Eastern Region. New York: Alfred A. Knopf, Inc. 1977.

Audubon Society Field Guide to North American Butterflies. New York: Alfred A. Knopf, Inc., 1985.

Audubon Society Field Guide to North American Wildflowers Eastern Region. New York: Alfred A. Knopf, Inc. 1979.

Blocksma, Mary. Naming Nature. New York: Penguin Books, 1992.

Borrer, Donald J. and White, Richard E. Peterson Field Guide Insects. Boston: Houghton Mifflin Co., 1970.

Burton, Dr. Phillip. Spotter's Guide to Birds of North America. New York: Mayflower Books, Inc., 1979.

Camazine, Scott. The Naturalist's Year. New York: John Wiley and Sons, Inc., 1987.

Carroll, David M. The Year of the Turtle. Vermont: Camden House Publishing, Inc., 1991.

Complete Field Guide to North American Wildlife Eastern Region. New York: Harper & Row, 1981

Cooper, Elizabeth K. Insects and Plants. New York: Harcourt, Brace World, Inc., 1963.

Dickinson, Terence. Exploring the Night Sky. Camden House, 1987.

Ehrlich, Paul R., David S. Dobkin, and Darryl Wheye. The Birder's Handbook. New York: Simon & Schuster, Inc. 1988.

Gill, Frank B. Ornithology. New York: W.H. Freeman and Company, 1990.

Gleason, Henry A. and Arthur Cronquist, Manual Of Vascular Plants of Northeastern U.S. and Canada. New York: The New York Botanical Garden, 1991.

Grzimek, H.C. Bernhard. Grzimek's Animal Life Encyclopedia. New York: Van Nostrand Reinhold Company, 1968.

Heintzelman, Donald S. A Guide to Hawk Watching in North America. Pennsylvania: Pennsylvania State University Press, 1982.

Jones, John Oliver. Where the Birds Are. New York: William Morrow and Company, Inc., 1990.

Lawrence, Gale. Field Guide to the Familiar. New Jersey: Prentice–Hall, Inc. 1984.

Leahy, Christopher. Peterson First Guides, Insects. Boston: Houghton Mifflin Co., 1987.

Mammana, Dennis L. The Night Sky An Observer's Guide. New York: Mallard Press, 1993.

Marchand, Peter J. Life in the Cold. University Press of New England, 1987.

Marteka, Vincent. Mushrooms, Wild and Edible. New York: W.W. Norton & Co., 1985.

Martin, Laura C. The Folklore of Birds. Connecticut: The Globe Pequot Press, 1993.

Martin, Laura C. The Folklore of Trees and Shrubs. Connecticut: The Globe Pequot Press, 1992.

Matre, Steven Van and Bill Weiler. The Earth Speaks. Illinois: The Institute for Earth Education, 1983.

Mehrtens, John M. Living Snakes of the World. New York: Sterling Publishing Co. Inc., 1987.

Milne, Lorus and Margery. The Audubon Society Field Guide to North American Insects and Spiders. New York: Alfred A. Knopf, Inc., 1980.

Mitchell, Alan American Nature Guides TREES. New York: Gallery Books, 1990.

Mohlenbrock, Robert and John W. Thieret. Trees A Quick Reference Guide to Trees of North America. Collier Books New York: Macmillan Publishing Company, 1987.

Montgomery, Sy. Nature's Everyday Mysteries. Vermont: Chapters Publishing, 1993.

Pasachoff, Jay M. Peterson First Guides, Astronomy. Boston: Houghton Mifflin Co., 1988.

Patent, Dorothy. Hinshaw, How Insects Communicate. New York: Holiday House, 1975.

Peterson, Roger Tory. A Field Guide to the Birds East of the Rockies Boston: Houghton Mifflin Co., 1980.

Pettingill, Olin Sewall Jr. A Guide to Bird Finding, East of the Mississippi. Boston: Houghton Mifflin Co., 1980

Phillips, Roger. Mushrooms of North America. Boston: Little, Brown and Company, 1991.

Pough, Frederick H. Field Guide to Rocks and Minerals. Boston: Houghton Mifflin Co., 1976.

Preston, Richard J. Jr. North American Trees. Iowa: Iowa State University Press, 1989.

Reader's Digest. North American Wildlife. New York, 1982.

Savage, Candace. Aurora, California: Sierra Club Books, 1994.

Seymour, Jacqueline. Trees. New York: Crown Publishers, Inc. 1978.

Shipman, Wanda. Animal Architects Pennsylvania: Stackpole Books, 1994.

Smith, Hobart M Amphibians of North America. New York: Golden Press, 1978.

Stannard, Russell. Our Universe, A Guide to What's Out There. New York: Kingfisher, 1995.

Stokes, Donald W. A Guide to Observing Insect Lives. Boston: Little, Brown and Company, 1983.

Tyning, Thomas F. Stokes Guide to Amphibians and Reptiles. Boston: Little, Brown and Company, 1990.

Van der Mer, Ron and Atie. Amazing Animal Sense. Little Brown & Company, 1990.

Zim, Herbert S. and Paul R. Shaffer. Rocks and Minerals. New York: Golden Press, 1957.

Zim, Herbert S. Rocks and Minerals. New York: Golden Press, 1962.

Zim Herbert S. and Clarance Cottam. Insects A Guide To Familiar American Insects. New York: Simon and Schuster, 1956.

Biographies

Stan Tekiela

Stan is an environmental educator specializing in interpreting our natural world using plants and animals. He writes a weekly syndicated newspaper column on the natural world. He holds a Bachelor's degree in Natural History from the University of Minnesota. He is a member of the Minnesota Naturalist Association, Vice President of Minnesota Mycological Society, member of the National Association of Environmental Interpretation, and a board member of Staring Lake Outdoor Center of Eden Prairie, MN.

Karen Shanberg

Karen is a naturalist and director of the Wood Lake Nature Center in Richfield, MN. She has a Bachelor's degree in elementary education and a Master's degree in outdoor education from the University of Minnesota. She has written natural history articles for magazines like New Age Journal, led eco–tours to the rainforests of Costa Rica and has been a guest speaker on rainforest issues. She is a leader in the activities of Minnesota Earth Day Network and is active in the National environmental youth movement.

Both Stan and Karen are winners of the National Association for Environmental Interpretation: "Excellence in Interpretation" award for their book, Plantworks. They also are co–authors of the book Start Mushrooming which won an award presented by the Midwest Independent Publisher's Association. They regularly speak to national and local organizations about nature and environmental concerns.

Nature Smart's
Certificate of Recognition

After reading and using Nature Smart
in the outdoors...

_____

(name/s)

is (are) certifiably and undeniably Nature Smart with all of
its privileges and obligations to continue learning about, caring
about and taking care of our natural world.

Congratulations!

Stan Tekiela

Karen Shanberg